Hermann Schildknecht
Zone Melting

Hermann Schildknecht

Zone Melting

Translated by
Express Translation Service, London

1966

Verlag Chemie · GmbH · Weinheim/Bergstr.
Academic Press · New York and London

With 220 figures and 29 tables

Title of the German original: Zonenschmelzen

Library of Congress Catalog Card Number: 65—27746

PREFACE

Zone melting is a modern, convenient method of obtaining high-melting materials in an extremely pure state without waste. This procedure, which uses a moving liquid zone, can however also be applied to the fractionation of low-melting substances. Even if only a few milligrams of a liquid which solidifies in crystalline form are available, it is possible to separate this, without loss, into pure and impure fractions, or to isolate from it traces of an unknown compound, using micro-zone melting techniques. Thus separations which were formerly achievable by only a few talented experimenters can now be effected by a greatly simplified technique.

Therefore, I have laid particular stress on the aspects of the theory, apparatus, and procedures which are important to the laboratory worker.

Thanks are due above all to my former co-workers, and particularly to Dr. U. Schübel and Dr. H. Vetter of the Institut für Organische Chemie, Erlangen University, for their cooperation.

I should also like to thank Prof. Dr. G. Hesse, the Bundesministerium für Wissenschaftliche Forschung, the Deutsche Forschungsgemeinschaft, the Fonds der Chemischen Industrie, Farbenfabriken Bayer (Leverkusen), and Badische Anilin- & Soda-Fabrik (Ludwigshafen), for financial and other support, without which my own zone melting experiments would not have been possible.

I am grateful to my assistants Dr. K. Maas, Dr. D. Kraus, and G. Hatzmann for expert help in writing the monograph and in the proof-reading. I should also like to thank the publishers for their cooperation.

Finally, I am very grateful to my wife Helga for her generous understanding and for her indispensable assistance in writing the manuscript.

Heidelberg, Autumn 1965   *Hermann Schildknecht*

CONTENTS

Equipment

Special Section

GENERAL

1. Introduction

It was already known to the alchemists that pure substances often separate initially in the crystallization of liquid mixtures. Purification of metals by melting and solidification is still a common process in modern metallurgy. The organic chemist, on the other hand, prefers recrystallization from solution, and above all distillation, and in the course of time distillation became increasingly refined and extended. Little fundamental progress was made with regard to an economical procedure for recrystallization from the melt [1], until 13 years ago Pfann [2] developed a new process for the preparation of very pure metals. This was zone melting, a technique of fractional crystallization.

2. The Solidification of a Melt

If a relatively large quantity of a molten metal is allowed to solidify in a crucible, it crystallizes in a random manner, crystallization sometimes beginning simultaneously at a number of points. The melt which still surrounds the separated crystallizate will also distribute itself in a random manner, carrying all the impurities; they will migrate at random before the crystal front, according to local temperature gradients and crystallization nuclei, and will finally be partly occluded on solidification. A particularly high concentration of impurities is therefore found in the crystal boundaries.

A complex process of this type can never yield very pure compounds, even if it is repeated a number of times. This object can be attained only by controlled freezing.

2.1 Normal Freezing

The distribution of matter in the melt/crystal system at equilibrium changes if the solid mixed phase [A, B] *) is allowed to encroach upon the liquid phase (A, B) *) by crystallization of the latter (Fig. 1). Suppose neither pure [A] nor pure [B] separates out, but a mixture of the two, for example a solid solution. If A is preferentially built into the crystal lattice, the concentration of B in the melt increases slightly at first. As a result, the crystal/melt equilibrium is disturbed, and

---

*) Brackets denote a solid mixture and parentheses a liquid mixture.

the freezing point is depressed. After a time, equilibrium is re-established, but since solid-state diffusion of the components is slow, this equilibration of concentrations would take a very long time. If instead of waiting for equilibrium to be restored the crystals are allowed to continue to grow, the concentration of B in the solid phase also increases.

Fig. 1. Schematic representation of the normal freezing of a "liquid rod".

In practice, normal freezing (or progressive freezing) as this controlled freezing of a melt is termed, takes place slowly, but not so slowly that the crystals which have separated have time to restore frozen-in substances to the melt. Once a new crystal front has been deposited in front of the old, equilibration of concentration with the melt is no longer possible, so that normal freezing of a column of liquid (Fig. 1) ultimately leads to the separation of substances if this process proceeds slowly and from one end towards the other.

The composition of the melt and the crystallizate and the efficiency of the separation depend not only on the similarity of the components present in the mixture, but also on the conditions of growth of the crystals, i. e. above all on convection and diffusion in the melt.

Favorable conditions are created if the residual melt is stirred. Nevertheless, the desired separation will not always be achieved by a single freezing cycle. It is often necessary to remelt the solidified rod, having previously removed both ends, and to allow the mixture to solidify again; this process must be repeated several times. Consequently, in the case of mixtures which are difficult to separate, and particularly in mixed-crystal systems and in the preparation of very pure substances, this method of separation is uneconomical and time-consuming.

2.2 Zone Melting

Further progress is possible with the aid of three new fundamental ideas due to Pfann, which ultimately lead to zone melting:

1) the impure material is arranged in the form of a long ingot;
2) the melt is divided into many successive short zones, separated by solid regions;
3) the molten zones are made to pass along the ingot with the aid of moving furnaces; alternatively the ingot is drawn through the furnaces (cf. Fig. 2).

In this procedure, there is no recombination of the impure melt with material which has already been purified, and recrystallization is repeated many times, giving a purification effect which always proceeds in the same direction. There is no loss of material, provided that no decomposition takes place on fusion.

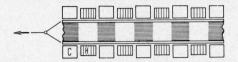

Fig. 2. Scheme of a zone melting arrangement. The ingot is drawn through the cooling and heating units, and is divided into 5 solid and 4 liquid zones.

C = coolers   H = heaters

This process was used by Kapitza[3] as early as 1928, and later by Andrade and Roscoe[4], not for purification, but for growing single crystals. It is illustrated in a greatly simplified form in Fig. 3.

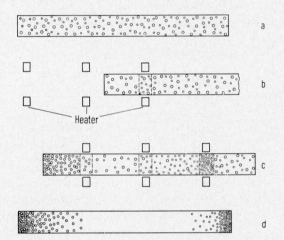

Fig. 3. Distribution of two different impurities (o and ○) in an ingot before (*a*), during (*b* and *c*), and after the passage of a number of molten zones (*d*).

The substance to be purified is initially in the form of a rod-shaped, crystalline ingot, in which all the impurities are more or less uniformly distributed (Fig. 3a). The ingot passes through a furnace, whereupon a molten zone is formed which is very short in comparison with the overall length of the ingot. The molten zone moves from left to right (Fig. 3b and c) at a rate equal to that with which the rod passes through the furnace (from right to left in Fig. 3). If, on partial solidification, the impurities tend to concentrate in the melt, then after the ingot has passed through the first furnace, the still unmelted solid will contain a higher concentration of impurities than the part which has already been zone-refined (Fig. 3b). The molten zone then becomes a carrier for the substances which fit only with difficulty or not at all in the newly formed crystal lattice. It transports part of the impurities to the end of the ingot which solidifies last and occasionally leaves other impurities behind. Thus the ingot is divided into three regions which merge into one another. The part which solidifies first, the left-hand part in Fig. 3d, contains impurities which raise the melting point of the principal substance and generally form mixed crystals with the latter. The middle part of the ingot contains the purified principal substance, whilst the part which solidifies last contains impurities which depress the melting point. This portion generally consists of a eutectic mixture.

3. The Solid-Liquid Phase Equilibrium

Zone melting is a separation process which is subject to the laws governing *phase equilibria* of mixtures as well as to *kinetic laws*.

Binary systems will be dealt with first, distinction being made between *systems with and without mixed-crystal formation*[5]. This will be followed by a discussion of systems of three or more components.

3.1 Binary Systems

3.1.1   Binary Systems without Mixed-Crystal Formation

If no mixed crystals or solid solutions are formed, only the pure components, e. g. A or B, occur in equilibrium with the homogeneous molten mixture or solution. If the equilibrium compositions of the melt are plotted against the equilibrium temperatures, the result is the phase or equilibrium diagram — in this case the melting point diagram — from which the characteristics of the system can be read.

3.1.1.1   A and B Form a Eutectic (Fig. 4)

T_A and T_B are the melting points of pure A and B. The curve $T_A E$ gives all the melt compositions and the corresponding temperatures at which pure A exists in equilibrium with the molten mixture. The same relationship holds for curve $T_B E$ and substance B. The intersection E of the two curves is known as the eutectic point. At this point the entire melt solidifies at a constant temperature and with a uniform composition.

If a liquid mixture corresponding to some concentration c_1 is cooled to a temperature slightly below the intersection of the perpendicular through c_1 with $T_A E$, this melt is no longer stable, and solid A separates out until the melt has reached the equilibrium composition at the temperature in question. If the cooling is continued further, the composition of the melt follows the curve T_AE, with further separation of solid A, until the eutectic point E is reached. Since at this point substances A and B exist together in equilibrium with the melt, further withdrawal of heat leads to the separation of A and B as a microcrystalline mixture. The melting and crystallization behavior of this eutectic mixture is similar to that of a pure substance.

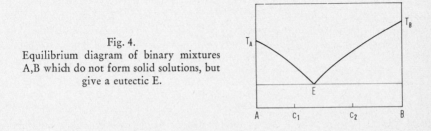

Fig. 4.
Equilibrium diagram of binary mixtures
A,B which do not form solid solutions, but
give a eutectic E.

An entirely similar situation is observed when a melt of composition c_2 is caused to crystallize; solid B crystallizes out until the residual melt again reaches the eutectic composition, where it solidifies at a constant temperature. Thus, if the separation of such a system is carried out in a suitable manner, making use of the phase equilibria, the pure substance A or B (depending on the initial composition) is obtained first, followed by the eutectic. This is true in particular for normal freezing.

3.1.1.2   A and B Form a Compound with a Congruent Melting Point

The general form of the equilibrium diagram for systems of this type is shown in Fig. 5.

Since the compound A_xB_y can exist in equilibrium with a melt of the same composition, the phase diagram of the system is made up of two parts each of exactly

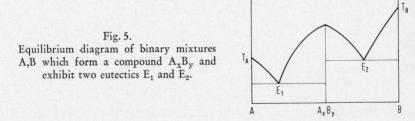

Fig. 5.
Equilibrium diagram of binary mixtures
A,B which form a compound A_xB_y and
exhibit two eutectics E_1 and E_2.

the type discussed in the previous section. It is again possible to predict from the equilibrium curves what happens when a melt of any composition is cooled.

3.1.1.3   *A and B Form a Compound with an Incongruent Melting Point*

According to Fig. 6, a compound A_xB_y may be formed, which does not exist in equilibrium with a melt of the same composition. This compound does not have a congruent melting point at the maximum of the broken curve, but decomposes below this temperature to form melt and solid phase B. The incongruent melting point occurs at P, and is known as the peritectic point. If a melt having a composition between A_xB_y and B is cooled, solid B begins to separate when the equilibrium curve T_BP is reached. As the temperature is lowered, B continues to separate and the composition of the melt follows the curve T_BP towards P. At this point the melt

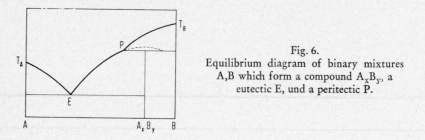

Fig. 6.
Equilibrium diagram of binary mixtures A,B which form a compound A_xB_y, a eutectic E, und a peritectic P.

reacts at constant temperature with the B which has already crystallized, to form the compound A_xB_y, until all the melt has been consumed. The final product is pure B together with a quantity of A_xB_y which depends on the initial composition.

If the initial composition of the melt lies between P and A_xB_y, then on cooling, pure B again separates at first, until the melt reaches the composition corresponding to the peritectic point P. The melt then reacts with the B which has separated out, forming the compound A_xB_y. When all the B has been consumed, further cooling leads to crystallization of the compound, and the composition of the melt follows PE until it reaches E. At this point, a eutectic containing the compound A_xB_y together with A is formed, again at a constant temperature.

Finally, the crystallization of a melt of composition between P and E represents a very simple case: In equilibrium the compound A_xB_y crystallizes out until the composition of the melt reaches the eutectic point, whereupon the eutectic E again solidifies.

3.1.2   *Systems with Mixed-Crystal Formation*

In contrast to the melting equilibria discussed in Section 3.1.1, in which crystallization of the molten mixture yields the pure components, some systems form solid solutions, on crystallization, i.e. mixed crystals. Thus the two components separate from the melt simultaneously, although in a ratio which differs from that in the melt. In the simplest case the temperature-concentration diagram consists of two continuous curves joining the melting points of the pure components. The upper or *liquidus curve* gives the composition of the melt which exists in equilibrium with mixed crystals at any given temperature. The composition of these mixed crystals is shown by the lower or *solidus curve*. The behavior of mixtures of two substances on melting and crystallization can again be easily read from this diagram.

Roozeboom has deduced the existence of five types of mixed crystal systems[6]. If the substances form a continuous and crystallographically uniform series of solid solutions, the system is of type I, II, or III; if the range of solid solutions is broken, the systems is of type IV or V. A common feature of all these types is that the concentration of the component whose addition lowers the freezing point is always higher in the melt than in the mixed crystals.

3.1.2.1 *Roozeboom's Type I — A and B Form a Continuous Series of Mixed Crystals (Fig. 7)*

The freezing points of all mixtures lie between the melting points T_A and T_B of the pure components. Any isothermal tie-line lying between T_A and T_B intersects the two curves at points corresponding to the compositions of the melt and mixed crystals which exist together in equilibrium at this temperature. Only liquid mixtures

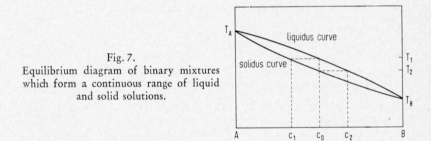

Fig. 7.
Equilibrium diagram of binary mixtures which form a continuous range of liquid and solid solutions.

exist at temperatures above the liquidus curve; the region below the solidus curve gives all compositions of mixed crystals which are stable at these temperatures. The area between the solidus and liquidus curves represents the region of isothermal separation into two phases.

Consider a melt of composition c_0 which is cooled to the temperature T_1. On further cooling to a temperature very slightly below this level, mixed crystals of composition c_1 separate out until equilibrium is established. At the same time, the melt becomes poorer in A, since the mixed crystals formed are richer in A than the starting melt c_0. On cooling still further, this process continues, and if the solid solution of composition c_1 which separated out initially can change its composition in contact with the melt (in accordance with the temperature-dependent equilibrium conditions) then at the temperature T_2, the last remaining melt of composition c_2 will exist in equilibrium with mixed crystals of composition c_0.

The condition that the required equilibrium between the melt and the mixed crystals be established after each temperature decrease can only be satisfied however if diffusion takes place in the crystals and if the crystals are in contact with the melt, since a mixed crystal of composition c_1 is stable by itself at all temperatures below T_1. Only when it is in contact with the melt can its composition change below T_1, provided that diffusion in the solid is possible. However, the diffusion coefficient in the solid is extremely small, and the continuous adjustment of equilibrium is therefore very greatly hindered. This factor is extremely important to the explanation of the separation effect which occurs in zone melting and in freezing methods in general. If on the other hand a homogeneous solid solution of composition c_0 is heated, and its temperature just exceeds T_2, a small quantity of melt of composition c_2 begins to form. On further heating, the composition of the mixed crystals, which are steadily decreasing in quantity, follows the solidus curve; the composition of the melt, which is steadily increasing in quantity, follows the liquidus curve, until at the temperature T_1 the last remaining mixed crystals of composition c_1 dissolve in the melt of composition c_0. Thus the point on the liquidus curve corresponding to a given concentration marks the temperature at which the melt begins to solidify or at which the last crystal dissolves, whilst the point on the solidus curve gives the temperature at which freezing is complete or at which melting begins. Mixed crystals of such a binary system are therefore characterized in that the various compositions exhibit characteristic melting ranges which correspond to the vertical distance between the solidus and liquidus curves.

The result of fractional crystallization carried out on systems of this type is easily predicted with the aid of the equilibrium diagram. For example, if a starting mixture with a composition between c_0 and c_1 is allowed to reach equilibrium at the temperature T_1, the result will be roughly equal quantities of a solid solution c_1 and a melt c_0. If the two phases are now separated and the separation is repeated in the same manner for each fraction at the appropriate temperatures, the final composition of mixed crystals obtained from the melt with the concentration c_1 tends towards pure A, while that obtained from the melt c_0 tends towards pure B. In this way it is possible, by systematic fractionation, to obtain pure substance A and pure substance B. Theoretically, however, it is not possible to obtain the components in the extreme state of purity.

Consider, for example, the binary system naphthalene/β-naphthol. The mixed crystals separating from such a melt are always richer in β-naphthol than the melt, since the melting point of β-naphthol (123° C) is higher than that of naphthalene (80.4° C). The systems azobenzene/stilbene and tolan/stilbene also form a continuous range of solid solutions[7].

Examples from inorganic chemistry include[8] the alloys of Ag/Au, Ag/Pd, Au/Pd, Au/Pt, Co/Pt, Co/Ni, Cu/Ni, Cu/Pd, Cu/Pt, Ir/Pt, Pd/Pt, Pd/Rh, Pt/Rh, Mo/Li, Cd/Mg, As/Bi, Bi/Sb, and Se/Te.

3.1.2.2 Roozeboom's Type II — A and B Form a Continuous Series of Mixed Crystals with a Melting-Point Maximum (Fig. 8)

A remarkable point about systems of this type is that the melting point of each component is raised by addition of the other.

Since the solidus and liquidus curves touch at the maximum, melt and mixed crystals of the same composition exist in equilibrium at this concentration and

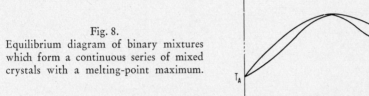

Fig. 8.
Equilibrium diagram of binary mixtures which form a continuous series of mixed crystals with a melting-point maximum.

temperature, and the processes of freezing and melting take place without change in temperature. The melting behavior of the mixture of this composition is therefore similar to that of a pure substance.

The equilibrium relationships of other mixtures are immediately obvious from the discussion in Section 3.1.2.1. Fractional crystallization leads to either pure A and the maximum mixture or pure B and the maximum mixture, according to the initial composition.

Examples of continuous series of mixed crystals exhibiting a melting point maximum are very rare, the best known being the system D-carvoxime/L-carvoxime[9].

3.1.2.3 Roozeboom's Type III — A and B Form a Continuous Series of Mixed Crystals with a Melting-Point Minimum (Fig. 9)

In this case the solidus and liquidus curves meet in a minimum, at which the phases existing in equilibrium have the same composition.

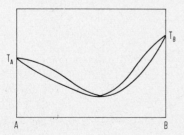

Fig. 9.
Equilibrium diagram of binary mixtures with a melting-point minimum.

This behavior is to be expected mainly when the melting points of the components of the mixture are very similar or equal, as in the case of optical isomers. Continued fractional crystallization, e.g. in zone melting, will lead to the mixture corresponding to the minimum together with either pure A or B, depending on the composition of the starting material.

Diagrams similar to Fig. 9 are frequently obtained[8] with alloys, e.g. Au/Cu, Au/Ni, Co/Fe, Fe/Ni, Fe/Pd, Fe/Pt, Ni/Pd, Ni/Pt, Cr/Fe, Cr/Mo, Fe/V, K/Rb, K/Cs, As/Sb.

3.1.2.4   *Roozeboom's Type IV — A and B Form a Series of Mixed Crystals Interrupted by a Peritectic (Fig. 10)*

There is a miscibility gap in the solid state, and the freezing curve exhibits a transition point P. Roughly speaking, this case corresponds to type I, except that at the transition point P one type of mixed crystal β passes over discontinuously

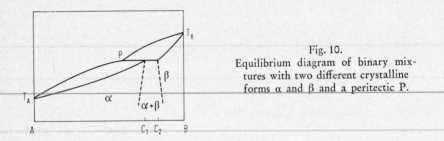

Fig. 10.
Equilibrium diagram of binary mixtures with two different crystalline forms α and β and a peritectic P.

into another type α. According to the equilibrium diagram, at the peritectic point P the melt exists in equilibrium with two solid phases having compositions c_1 and c_2. Following the transition, further decreases in temperature result in crystallization of only phase α. Fractional crystallization of a mixture of substances A and B yields pure A and pure B, similarly to type I. The peritectic has no effect on the result of the separation.

This peritectic type includes[8] the systems Ag/Pt, Au/Fe, Fe/Mn, and In/Tl.

3.1.2.5   *Roozeboom's Type V — A and B Form a Series of Mixed Crystals Interrupted by a Eutectic (Fig. 11)*

Type V is the second principal type of system with a discontinuous series of mixed crystals. The situation is fundamentally the same as that in types II and III, but the solid phase is now no longer homogeneous at the minimum. Instead, a eutectic mixture, consisting of mixed crystals α of composition c_1 and mixed crystals β of composition c_2, is formed. This is stable in equilibrium with the melt of composition E, and melts and solidifies at constant temperature.

If a melt having a composition between c_1 and E is cooled, mixed crystals α of the appropriate composition separate out first. When the composition of the melt reaches E and that of the crystals reaches c_1, further withdrawal of heat results in solidification of the remaining melt at a constant temperature to form the eutectic

Fig. 11.
Equilibrium diagram of binary mixtures forming a discontinuous series of mixed crystals (α and β).

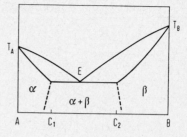

mixture. Fractional crystallization of a system of this type leads to the eutectic mixture, and to either pure A or pure B, according to the initial composition.

3.1.2.6 *Phase Separation in Mixed-Crystal Systems Below the Freezing Point*

In contrast to the cases described above, in which the mixed crystals were stable once they had separated out, it is also possible for the crystals to break down on further cooling into two coexistent solid phases.

Fig. 12.
T-c diagram for a mixed-crystal system which undergoes a transition from the α-phase to the β-phase at lower temperatures.

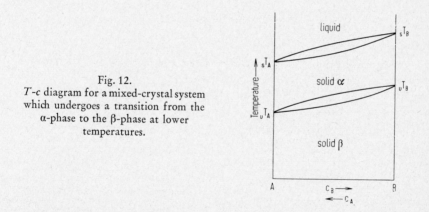

The T-c diagram for a simple case is shown in Fig. 12. Once again, as in type I, the freezing points of all mixtures lie between those of the pure components A and B. However, in this case both A and B have transition points $_uT_A$ and $_uT_B$. Like the freezing process, the transition will take place over a range of temperatures, i.e. the compositions of the α and β mixed crystals existing in equilibrium at a given temperature are not the same. The transition curve need not necessarily be continuous, and may exhibit a maximum or a minimum, like those of types II and III.

Since the freezing curves of types I to V can each be combined with a transition curve analogous to these forms, there are altogether ten possible types of transition. However, the present discussion will be confined to the cases described above, since all the available possibilities can be derived from these.

3.2 Ternary Systems

Ternary melting equilibria are plotted in a three-dimensional temperature-concentration diagram (Fig. 13).

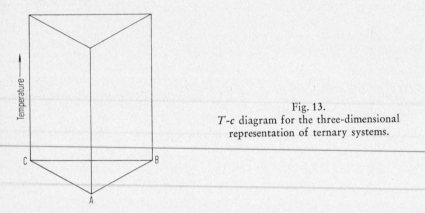

Fig. 13.
T-c diagram for the three-dimensional
representation of ternary systems.

The base of the prism is an equilateral triangle, and represents the concentrations of the components A, B, and C. The planes lying parallel to this base are isotherms; these are sufficient to show the concentration at a given temperature (Fig. 14). The

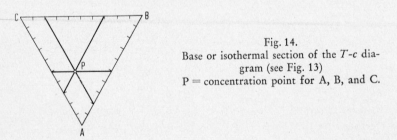

Fig. 14.
Base or isothermal section of the T-c diagram (see Fig. 13)
P = concentration point for A, B, and C.

apices A, B, and C represent the pure components; the composition of any mixture of the three components is defined by the point P. P is the projection of a point inside the prism onto the base ABC. The proportion of component A is found by drawing a straight line through P parallel to side BC and reading off the percentage from the intersection of this line with side AB or AC. The quantity of B and C are determined in exactly the same manner: the proportion of B from the parallel to AC through P and its intersection with AB or CB, and the proportion of C from the parallel to AB through P and its intersection with AC or BC. In the example of Fig. 14, P refers to a mixture consisting of 50% of A, 20% of B, and 30% of C. The compositions of binary mixtures are plotted on the side joining the two components in question.

As can be seen from the following examples, the three vertical faces of the prism show the equilibrium diagrams of the binary systems AB, AC, and BC as discussed above. The equilibrium behavior of the ternary mixtures is represented by surfaces within the prism, and their curves and points of intersection.

3.2.1 Ternary Systems without Mixed-Crystal Formation

The only solid phases in this case are the pure components, although these often occur together.

3.2.1.1 A, B, and C Form Eutectic Systems with One Another (Fig. 15)

The melting points of the pure components are denoted by T_A, T_B, and T_C, and the binary eutectics between A and B by e_1, between B and C by e_2, and between C and A by e_3. The surface $T_A e_1 E e_3$ gives all ternary compositions of the melt which can exist in equilibrium with pure solid A at any given temperature.

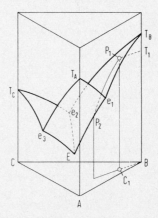

Fig. 15.
Equilibrium diagram of ternary mixtures with three binary eutectics (e_1, e_2, e_3) and a ternary eutectic (E).

The same holds for the surface $T_B e_2 E e_1$ regarding B, and for $T_C e_3 E e_2$ regarding C. The line of intersection $e_1 E$ of the two first mentioned surfaces shows the temperatures and concentrations at which a ternary melt exists in equilibrium with a mixture of solid A and solid B. Similarly the eutectic curves $e_2 E$ and $e_3 E$ give the corresponding equilibrium values for ternary melts which exist in equilibrium with mixtures of solid B and C and of solid A and C, respectively. At the point E, where all three surfaces intersect, the three components form a solid ternary eutectic in equilibrium with a melt of the same composition.

Consider the cooling of a melt with composition c_1. At temperature T_1, corresponding to the point P_1 where the vertical through c_1 intersects the surface $T_B e_2 E e_1$, pure B begins to separate. As this process continues, the composition of the melt follows the curve $P_1 P_2$, which lies in the surface $T_B e_2 E e_1$. The ratio of A to C in the melt remains constant, so that the projection of $P_1 P_2$ on the base is simply the continuation of the line BC_1. After P_2, solid A crystallizes out together with B; consequently on further cooling the composition of the melt follows the eutectic line $e_1 E$ until it reaches the ternary eutectic composition at E. At this point, the remainder of the melt solidifies at constant temperature to form the ternary eutectic mixture.

Exactly the same behavior is shown by mixtures of other concentrations. Provided that none of the mixtures has a composition corresponding to a point on the eutectic curves or to the eutectic E, six different separation sequences are possible:

1. pure A — mixture of B and A — eutectic E
2. pure A — mixture of C and A — eutectic E
3. pure B — mixture of A and B — eutectic E
4. pure B — mixture of C and B — eutectic E
5. pure C — mixture of A and C — eutectic E
6. pure C — mixture of B and C — eutectic E

If the compositions of the starting mixtures already correspond to the eutectic curves, then only mixtures of A and B, B and C, or A and C can crystallize together with the ternary eutectic E.

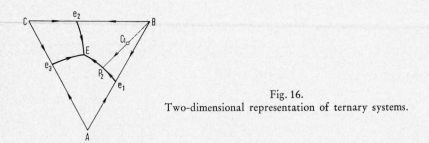

Fig. 16.
Two-dimensional representation of ternary systems.

The representation of complicated systems in three-dimensional diagrams is rather difficult to survey. For this reason, the two-dimensional representation of ternary systems mentioned above will now be discussed. The notation is the same as in Fig. 15.

The arrows in Fig. 16 indicate the direction of change in melt composition as crystallization proceeds, and so always point towards lower temperatures. In other respects the analysis of the crystallization process is the same. As a melt of composition c_1 cools, the content of B in the melt falls until the cooling curve (the extension of BC) meets the eutectic line e_1E. Beyond the point P_2, a mixture of A and B crystallizes out, and the composition of the melt follows the eutectic curve from P_2 towards E, where the ternary eutectic separates.

3.2.1.2 *A Forms Simple Eutectic Systems with B and with C, whilst B and C Form a Compound with a Congruent Melting Point*

It can be seen from Fig. 17 that this system is really made up of two systems ABV and AVC. Consequently there are two ternary eutectics E_1 and E_2, consisting of mixtures of A, B, and the compound V on the one hand, and A, C, and the compound V on the other. The "binary" system AV gives a simple eutectic at e_5. In the composite system, the eutectic curves e_5E_1 and e_5E_2 arise at the point e_5 and proceed to meet the other eutectic curves at the ternary eutectic points E_1 and E_2 respectively. As shown by the arrows, the point e_5 on the line E_1E_2 represents a

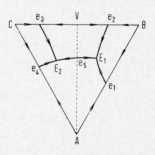

Fig. 17.
Projection of an equilibrium diagram for ternary mixtures forming a compound V with a congruent melting point. e_1 and e_4 =eutectics of the pure component A with B and with C, respectively. e_2 = binary eutectic B+V; e_3 = binary eutectic C+V. e_5 =binary eutectic A+V. E_1 and E_2 =ternary eutectics.

temperature maximum, but also a minimum with respect to the binary eutectic system AV. Any mixture of A, B, and C with a composition which lies on the line AV contains the substances B and C in the ratio of the compound V, and so behaves as a mixture of the binary system AV.

3.2.1.3 *A, B, and C Form a Ternary Compound with a Congruent Melting Point (Fig. 18)*

This system is regarded as one in which the compound V formed from the components A, B, and C forms a binary system with each of the components. Each of these systems has its own binary eutectic e_4, e_5 and e_6. The compound V also forms a ternary system with each pair of components, i.e. with A and B, B and C, and A and C. There are therefore three ternary eutectics E_1, E_2, and E_3, which are joined to the binary eutectics by eutectic curves. The arrows indicate the direction in which the composition of the melt changes as crystallization proceeds.

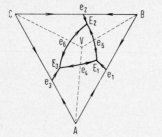

Fig. 18.
Projection of an equilibrium diagram for ternary mixtures forming a ternary compound V with a congruent melting point. e_1, e_2, and e_3=binary eutectics of the pure components A, B, and C. e_4, e_5, and e_6=binary eutectics of the pure components and the compound V. E_1, E_2, and E_3=ternary eutectics of V with the binary mixtures A/B, B/C, and A/C.

3.2.1.4   Two of the Substances A, B, and C Form a Compound with an Incongruent Melting Point (Fig. 19)

In Fig. 19, substances B and C form a compound V which is stable in equilibrium with a melt of composition p (see the equilibrium diagram of Fig. 6). A forms simple eutectic systems as shown in Fig. 4 with both B and C (e_1 and e_3). E is the ternary eutectic of A, C, and the compound p. P is a peritectic curve along which ternary melts of the appropriate compositions can exist in equilibrium with solid compound and solid B.

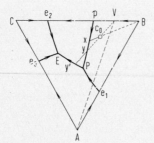

Fig. 19.
Projection of an equilibrium diagram for ternary mixtures, two components of which form a compound V with an incongruent melting point.

At the ternary peritectic point P, a ternary melt of this composition can exist in equilibrium with solid A, B, and compound V. If heat is withdrawn from such an equilibrium mixture, the solid B which is present reacts with the C in the melt to form the compound V. For this to happen, however, it is necessary for solid A to separate and for B which is present in the melt to enter into the compound formation; in this way the melt maintains the composition corresponding to the point P.

The peritectic reaction, which proceeds at constant temperature, is complete when all solid B has been converted to compound V, provided that B is not present in excess. Where excess B is present, some solid B remains. On further cooling, the composition of the melt follows the curve PE, solid A and compound V crystallizing out together until the ternary eutectic of A, C, and V finally separates out at E.

A peculiarity of this system is that the melting or crystallization of mixtures of compositions lying within the triangle VpP (not drawn) cannot yield a melt with a composition corresponding to the point P. The reason for this is that, e.g., an overall composition c_0 cannot consist of A, V, and B. Instead, the composition of the melt follows the line xy, whilst the B which has separated is converted to the compound. Since, at the point y, the only solid which can exist is V, the composition of the melt can change towards y′ with separation of the compound, and then towards the ternary eutectic point E with simultaneous separation of both V and A.

The system may exhibit other peculiarities if the positions of the points P, V, and p differ from those in Fig. 19. However, these will not be discussed here.

3.2.1.5 *A, B, and C Form a Ternary Compound with an Incongruent Melting Point (Fig. 20)*

Each pair of the components forms a simple eutectic. Point V in Fig. 20 gives the composition of the ternary compound $A_xB_yC_z$, which decomposes on melting, i.e. has an incongruent melting point. E_1 and E_2 are ternary eutectic points at which solid A, B, and V or B, C, and V exist in equilibrium with melts of these compositions. The region E_1E_2P gives all compositions of the melt which can exist in stable equilibrium with solid compound; the lines bounding the region represent crystallization paths along which the solid compound is formed or decomposed. P is a ternary peritectic point at which a melt of the composition given by P can exist in equilibrium with A, C, and V.

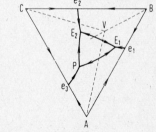

Fig. 20.
Projection of an equilibrium diagram for ternary mixtures which form a ternary compound V with an incongruent melting point.

If the equilibrium mixture existing at P is cooled, the component A reacts, initially at constant temperature, with solid C and the melt to form the compound. The compound and C then begin to separate out together, and the temperature falls; the composition of the melt follows PE_2 until, at E_2, the ternary eutectic separates at a constant equilibrium temperature. It is unnecessary to discuss the processes which occur during the melting and crystallization of other mixtures, since these can be easily deduced from what has already been said on the basis of Fig. 20.

When crystallization processes are carried out for the separation and purification of such ternary systems, a large number of crystallization sequences are possible. Pure A, B, C, or compound V may be obtained depending on the initial concentration of the mixture. The components concentrated in the residual melt appear in the form of the binary and ternary eutectics of various compositions.

3.2.2   Ternary Systems with Mixed-Crystal Formation

In binary mixed crystal systems two curves were required to correlate the equilibrium concentrations in the melt and in the crystallizate of a mixture of two substances at a certain temperature. Similarly, in the three-dimensional representation of ternary systems, two surfaces are necessary in the simplest case to describe the equilibrium conditions. Furthermore, the projections of a number of isothermal sections are given in the interests of clarity. The components A, B, and C of a ternary mixed crystal system form binary systems with one another, of the type discussed in Section 3.1.2.

3.2.2.1   A, B, and C Form a Continuous Series of Mixed Crystals (Fig. 21)

In the three-dimensional diagram of Fig. 21, the melting points T_A, T_B, and T_C of the three components A, B, and C are joined by two surfaces, one above the other. The upper surface intersects the side faces of the prism in the liquidus curves and

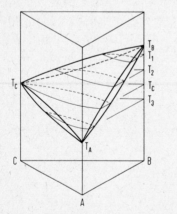

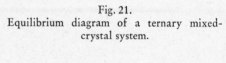

Fig. 21.
Equilibrium diagram of a ternary mixed-crystal system.

the lower one in the solidus curves of the binary systems. To every ternary melt in equilibrium with mixed crystals corresponds a point on the upper surface, and to every ternary mixed crystal in equilibrium with the melt corresponds a point on the lower surface. The corresponding compositions of the two phases are joined by tie-lines which lie in isothermal planes, i.e. parallel to the base of the prism. Fig. 21

shows four isothermal sections at temperatures T_1, T_2, T_c, and T_3, the projections of which on the base of the prism are reproduced in Fig. 22. The lines L—S are the intersections of the isotherms with the liquidus and solidus surfaces of the ternary system. The tie-lines are shown in the projections of the isothermal sections.

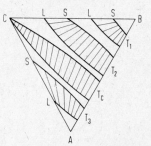

Fig. 22.
Projection of an equilibrium diagram for ternary mixed crystals, showing the isothermal sections T_1 to T_3. The lines connecting L and S are the tie-lines.

Special consideration is again given to crystallization in which ternary mixed crystals separate first from a melt of any arbitrary composition. If the temperature is reduced further, the quantity of crystallizate increases, whilst the quantity of the melt is decreased. However, the compositions of the two phases change, in accordance with the different course of the tie-lines in the various isotherms which describe the cooling.

Once again, however, we are primarily interested in fractional crystallization as a basis for the consideration of zone melting processes. This should lead to the pure substances A and B, as is to be expected from the course of the tie-lines. On the other hand, the substance whose melting point lies between those of the two others — in this case substance C — can be obtained in the pure form only with great difficulty, since, as shown in Fig. 22, the tie-lines in the neighborhood of C bend away towards A and B.

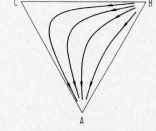

Fig. 23.
Projection of the "residue lines" of a ternary mixed-crystal system.

A clear picture of the course of a fractionation of ternary mixed crystal systems is obtained by projecting the so-called *residue lines* on the base of the diagram. These lines show the direction of the change in composition of the melt on cooling when the crystallizate is continuously removed from the equilibrium.

Fig. 23 shows the residue lines for the system represented by Figs. 21 and 22. The arrows point from higher towards lower temperatures. It can again be seen that the composition of the melt tends towards C at first, but then always bends away towards A. The change in the composition of the mixed crystals during the fractionation can also be represented by a similar series of curves.

3.2.2.2 *Two of the Substances A, B, and C Form a System with a Melting-Point Minimum (Fig. 24)*

This ternary system, in which the substances A and C form a minimum, can be readily recognized as a composite system. The minimum mixture M forms two systems, one with A and B and the other with A and C, similar to that described in

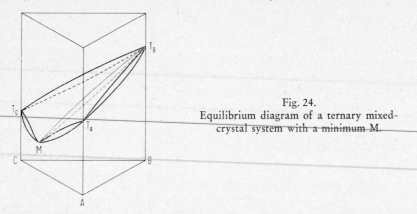

Fig. 24.
Equilibrium diagram of a ternary mixed-crystal system with a minimum M.

the last section. The system MB can therefore be regarded as a simple binary mixed crystal system.

The residue lines for the diagram of Fig. 24 are shown in Fig. 25. It can be seen that, depending on the composition of a mixture of A, B, and C, fractional

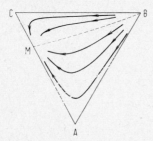

Fig. 25.
Projection of the "residue lines" of a ternary mixed-crystal system (see also Fig. 24) with a minimum M.

crystallization tends preferentially to yield substance B and the minimum mixture. In addition to these, it is also possible to isolate substance A or C, although only with difficulty.

3.2.2.3 *A Forms a Binary Minimum with each of Substances B and C (Fig. 26)*

This system, with the binary minima m_1 and m_2, is represented in Fig. 26.

The crystallization of various mixtures of A, B, and C can again be best illustrated by the course of the residue lines (Fig. 27). The equilibrium region of the mixture is

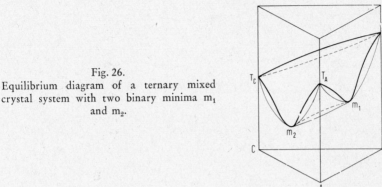

Fig. 26.
Equilibrium diagram of a ternary mixed crystal system with two binary minima m_1 and m_2.

divided into two parts by the line m_1m_2. Mixtures with compositions falling in the region Am_1m_2 give pure A and minimum mixture m_2 on fractionation, and the minimum mixture m_1 can also be fractionated out, but only with difficulty.

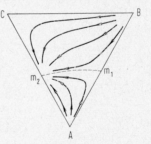

Fig. 27.
Projection of the "residue lines" of a ternary mixed-crystal system with two binary minima m_1 and m_2 (see also Fig. 26).

If the composition of the starting mixture falls in the region m_1BCm_2, fractional crystallization leads preferentially to substance B and minimum mixture m_2. It should also be possible to obtain minimum mixture m_1 and pure C.

3.2.2.4 *A, B, and C Form a Ternary Melting-Point Minimum*

Each of the three binary systems and the ternary system gives a minimum mixture which resembles a pure substance in its melting behavior; it melts and solidifies at constant temperature, without undergoing any change in composition.

The fractional crystallization of a ternary system of this type can be discussed with the aid of the residue line diagram of Fig. 29. Any mixture of the three substances leads to the ternary minimum mixture M and, depending on the overall

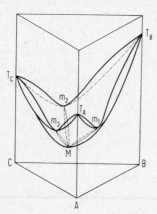

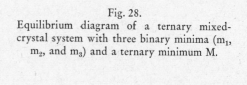

Fig. 28.
Equilibrium diagram of a ternary mixed-crystal system with three binary minima (m_1, m_2, and m_3) and a ternary minimum M.

composition, to pure A, B, or C. Whether the binary minimum mixtures m_1, m_2, and m_3 are also obtained depends on the degree of fractionation.

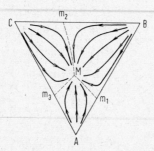

Fig. 29.
Projection of the "residue lines" of a ternary mixed-crystal system with three binary minima m_1, m_2, and m_3, and a ternary minimum M (see also Fig. 28).

3.2.2.5   C Forms a Binary Eutectic with each of Substances A and B

In the three-dimensional diagram of Fig. 30, the ternary mixture field contains a eutectic curve e_1e_2. Along this curve, melts of the compositions given by the curve exist in equilibrium with two types of ternary mixed crystals. The compositions of these mixed crystals are given by the intersections of the tie-lines with the curves (broken) on either side of e_1e_2. According to Fig. 31, fractional crystallization in concentration regions between e_1e_2 C yields pure C together with eutectic e_2 and — after more extensive fractionation — e_1. Mixtures with compositions falling within the region ABe_1e_2 give B and e_2, and, under favorable conditions, A and e_1.

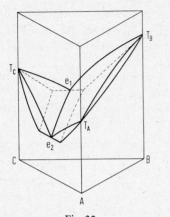

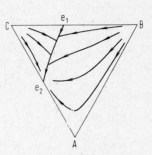

Fig. 30.
Equilibrium diagram of a ternary mixed-crystal system forming two eutectics e_1 and e_2.

Fig. 31.
Projection of the "residue lines" of a ternary mixed-crystal system forming two eutectics e_1 and e_2 (see also Fig. 30).

3.2.3 *Mixed Systems*

It is also possible in a ternary system that, instead of either only the pure components or only mixtures of these occurring in the solid form, pure substances and mixed crystals may form solid phases.

Fig. 32.
Equilibrium diagram of a ternary system. C and B form a continuous series of mixed crystals. A forms simple eutectics e_1 and e_2 with B and with C.

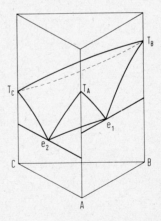

Suppose that one pair of substances C and B form a continuous series of mixed crystals, whilst the other two pairs, A with C and A with B, each form a simple eutectic system (Fig. 32).

e_1 and e_2 are the binary eutectics of A and B and of A and C respectively. Melts with compositions lying along the curve e_1e_2 crystallize to give mixtures of pure A with mixed crystals BC of varying composition. Solid solutions of B and C are also obtained on cooling melts with compositions falling in the region $T_B T_C e_2 e_1$.

Fig. 33 shows the residue lines for the region in which solid solutions are obtained from the melts.

It can be seen that fractional crystallization of appropriate mixtures yields pure B and the eutectic mixtures e_1 and e_2; pure C can also be obtained with sufficient fractionation. On the other hand, when a melt of composition falling within the

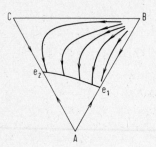

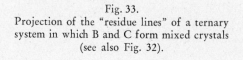

Fig. 33.
Projection of the "residue lines" of a ternary system in which B and C form mixed crystals (see also Fig. 32).

area Ae_1e_2 is cooled, pure A separates out first. When the composition of the melt finally reaches a point lying on e_1e_2, a mixture of A and mixed crystals BC separates, and the composition of the melt moves along e_1e_2. Fractionation into the two eutectic mixture can occur along this curve; the separation of components B and C proceeds as expected from the binary mixed crystal system of the two substances.

3.3 Higher-order Systems

In quaternary or higher-order systems, the complexity of the equilibrium relationships increases rapidly with the number of components. The difficulties encountered in the separation of multicomponent mixtures increase to the same extent. It is scarcely to be expected that all the constituents of mixed crystal systems containing four, five, or even more components, as best exemplified by the natural waxes, can be isolated at an acceptable expense by fractional crystallization; it has already been shown that in ternary systems the mutual correlation of individual fractions is subject to great difficulty or even impossible.

For this reason, crystallization is not so much the separation of a multicomponent system into its individual components, as the purification of a single substance.

Thus we can see the limitations to which crystallization methods are subject, but which by no means detract from their value, since these methods offer a valuable supplement to other separation techniques; conversely, the latter may lead to further improvement where the best results possible by crystallization have been achieved.

3.4 Determination of the Equilibrium Diagram for Binary Solid-Liquid Equilibria

3.4.1 *Microscopic Methods*

Most of the above remarks on the behavior of mixtures on melting and solidification also apply to zone melting. This means that, with a knowledge of the phase diagram, it is possible to make predictions regarding the freezing behavior during zone melting processes. If the equilibrium diagram is unknown, a picture of the characteristics which are of interest in this connection can be very rapidly gained with the aid of Kofler's micro-thermal analysis[7], which is the dew point - melting point method carried out on a hot stage.

This micro-method is fundamentally based on the observation of melting equilibria. All that has been said above again applies in this case. The method consists primarily in the exact determination of melting and freezing temperatures and the observation of crystalline forms and crystallized phases, and in the accurate establishment of their properties such as refractive index, etc.

Conclusions can sometimes be drawn as to the degree of impurity, and often even the nature of the contaminants, from the melting and freezing behavior. For example, mixed crystals are recognized by the existence of a longer or shorter melting and freezing range, and it is not difficult to distinguish this behavior from that which characterizes the formation of a eutectic melt. In this case the temperature at which melting begins is the eutectic temperature; if the material in question is not the pure eutectic, this temperature is often much lower than that at which the last crystal begins to disappear.

More accurate information can be obtained if something is already known of the qualitative composition. It is only necessary to know e. g. the class of substances to which the individual components belong to be able to study the melting behavior on the basis of model examples with the aid of the "contact method".

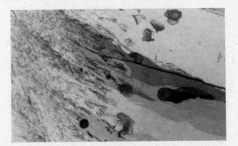

Fig. 34. Contact sample of stilbene (left) — azobenzene (right).

According to Kofler's method[7], the mixed zone of two substances in contact between a microscope slide and a cover glass is observed under the microscope as the temperature is altered. On heating on the hot-stage microscope, all the phenomena which are reflected in the equilibrium diagram of the binary system in question can be observed in the mixed zone.

Azobenzene and stilbene, which are well known for their miscibility in all ratios in the solid phase, give samples [10] such as that shown in Fig. 34. It can be seen that, with the same optical orientation, the stilbene crystals are growing unhindered and "isomorphously" into the azobenzene melt.

A eutectic can be particularly easily recognized if the contact sample is examined in polarized light. The eutectic melt then appears as a dark band framed by the light, crystalline compounds (Fig. 35) [11].

Fig. 35. Contact sample of angelic acid (top) and tiglic acid (bottom), photographed in polarized light at 25° C (center: eutectic melt).

mixed-crystal series β
(hexacosanol)

peritectic

mixed-crystal series α
(eicosanol)

Fig. 36. Contact sample of n-$C_{20}H_{41}OH$ and n-$C_{26}H_{53}OH$, photographed on the Leitz hot-stage microscope in polarized light.

Fig. 36 is a photograph of a contact sample of the two aliphatic alcohols eicosanol (n-$C_{20}H_{41}OH$) and hexacosanol (n-$C_{26}H_{53}OH$). The different types of crystals are clearly distinguishable on either side of a darker mixed zone[12]. It was therefore to be expected that a eutectic or a peritectic would be formed when the two alcohols were mixed. Only after the phase diagram (Fig. 37) had been plotted did it become certain that a peritectic was formed.

To establish the liquidus curve, nine mixtures of the alcohols taken in the weight ratios of 1 : 9, 2 : 8, 3 : 7, 4 : 6, 5 : 5, 6 : 4, 7 : 3, 8 : 2, and 9 : 1 were prepared and the temperatures at which crystallization started were determined under the microscope.

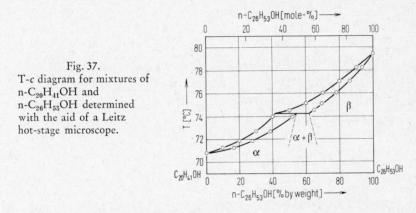

Fig. 37.
T-*c* diagram for mixtures of n-$C_{20}H_{41}OH$ and n-$C_{26}H_{53}OH$ determined with the aid of a Leitz hot-stage microscope.

The solidus curve cannot be determined from the points at which the mixtures begin to melt since the mixed crystallizate formed is not homogenous, even if the molten mixture is quenched; furthermore, it is difficult to observe the start of melting, so that the values obtained are not reproducible.

However, the use of normal freezing helps in this case[13], as will be explained with the aid of Fig. 38. Consider the cooling of a mixture of composition c_0; if it is

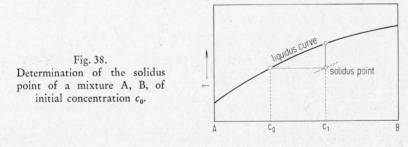

Fig. 38.
Determination of the solidus point of a mixture A, B, of initial concentration c_0.

possible to isolate the first mixed crystals to separate and their composition is found to be c_1, the temperature of their primary crystallization, which must lie on the liquidus curve can be determined. Thus two points on the liquidus curve are now known, namely that for c_0 and that for c_1. If a parallel to the concentration axis is drawn through the former and a parallel to the temperature axis through the latter, the point of intersection gives the required solidus point.

To isolate the first crystallizate, a suitable quantity of the mixture is placed in a melting boat (see p. 101) and is completely melted in a small annular furnace. If the boat is now withdrawn very slowly from the heating zone, the first crystallizate is obtained at the tip of the ingot. This is carefully removed and the temperature at which crystallization begins is determined under the microscope.

The reproducibility of the microscopic method is limited by the accuracy with which the freezing point can be read. If high accuracy is required, special attention must be paid to this point, and care must be taken to ensure a controlled supply of heat.

3.4.2 *Method of Measurement*

In the calorimetric method, a certain quantity of heat is supplied to a test mixture of known composition in an adiabatic calorimeter and the temperature is allowed to reach its equilibrium value. A plot of the temperature against the quantity of

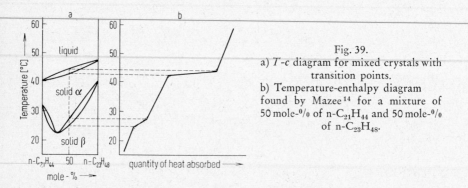

Fig. 39.
a) T-c diagram for mixed crystals with transition points.
b) Temperature-enthalpy diagram found by Mazee[14] for a mixture of 50 mole-% of n-$C_{21}H_{44}$ and 50 mole-% of n-$C_{23}H_{48}$.

heat supplied gives a temperature-enthalpy diagram (Fig. 39b) for a mixture of the composition in question. The combination of many such diagrams then leads to the desired phase diagram (Fig. 39a).

Mazee[14] has investigated long-chain paraffins by this method, and obtained the heating curve shown in Fig. 39b for a mixture of 50 mole-% of n-$C_{21}H_{44}$ and 50 mole-% of n-$C_{23}H_{48}$. From this curve and others obtained with similar systems over a wide range of concentrations, he was able to derive the T-c diagram shown in Fig. 39a.

The state of distribution of the two components can be estimated from the course of the plateaus in the heating curves. Moreover, a transition point can sometimes be observed (in our example between 25 and 27° C), indicating a transition in the solid phase. Such a transition is also found in mixtures of $C_{36}H_{74}$ and $C_{35}H_{72}$ (Fig. 40).

The equilibrium diagram of Fig. 40c is typical on account of its needle-shaped pair of curves. The mixture of 25 mole-% of n-$C_{36}H_{74}$ in n-$C_{35}H_{72}$ investigated by Mazee had a melting point only 0.4° C higher than that of the pure hydrocarbon n-$C_{35}H_{72}$.

Thus in comparison with the method of first crystallization, the calorimetric method gives additional information regarding transitions in the solid state. This information can also be obtained by the dilatometric method, in which the longitudinal expansion of the solid phase at constant cross-section is measured. Sudden changes in the longitudinal expansion indicate a phase transition.

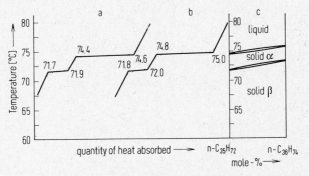

Fig. 40. Temperature-enthalpy diagrams for (a) pure n-$C_{35}H_{72}$ and (b) a mixture of 75 mole-% of n-$C_{35}H_{72}$ with 25 mole-% of n-$C_{36}H_{74}$. (c) T-c diagram for n-$C_{35}H_{72}$ and n-$C_{36}H_{74}$, according to ref. 14.

Finally, mention should be made of the oldest and most widely used method of determining phase diagrams, namely thermal analysis, or the method of heating or cooling curves. In these dynamic methods the substance is heated at a constant rate, and the rate of temperature increase is recorded; alternatively, the substance may be cooled and the rate of cooling recorded. The result is a temperature-time diagram.

4. Eutectic Systems

4.1 Normal Freezing of Eutectic Systems

A particular advantage of crystallization from the melt is that it is often possible by this method to obtain pure material in a single operation. This is due to the transition from the disordered liquid to the ordered crystalline state.

If the components of the mixture form a eutectic (cf. Fig. 4), the pure substance again crystallizes out first; sooner or later the eutectic mixture will however separate out, depending on the initial concentration of the impurity. This behavior is observed particularly in the case of aqueous solutions, since according to Brill[15], ice forms mixed crystals only with ammonium fluoride. All other organic and inorganic compounds investigated so far concentrate at the end of the bar of ice even after a single freezing pass. This assumes, however, that the solution contains not more than 1% of solute, since this would otherwise quickly be frozen in, despite vigorous mixing of the residual solution. Vigorous stirring is also essential to avoid a build-up of the solute in the aqueous phase immediately in front of the growing crystal front.

Fig. 41 shows the results of freezing 1.1 and 6.7% solutions of hydrochloric acid [16]. In the case of the 1.1% solution, the concentration of the hydrochloric acid in the first half of the ice bar (12 mm in diameter) to solidify, falls to 0.03 times its original value after only one pass at a rate of crystallization (rate of lowering; see p. 134) of 2 cm/h and with continuous mixing of the residual solution. The decrease in concentration in the first crystallizate was about 10 times smaller in the case of the 6.7% solution.

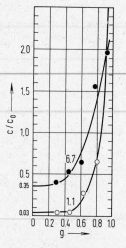

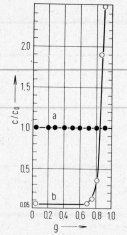

Fig. 41.
Concentration curve for HCl in 10 ml of water after normal freezing, for solutions initially containing 6.7 and 1.1% of HCl, respectively.
Stirring speed: 1100 rpm
Rate of lowering: 2 cm/h
Tube diameter: 12 mm
g = fraction of the ice bar
c_0 = initial concentration.

Fig. 42.
Concentration curves for dilute acetic acid after normal freezing.
(a) Without stirring of the liquid
(b) With stirring at 2200 rpm.

A 1% aqueous solution of acetic acid can also be concentrated by normal freezing, but only with vigorous stirring to prevent excessive concentration build-up at the phase boundary, as shown by the distribution curves a and b for the solidified charges (Fig. 42).

Thus even in the case of systems which do not form solid solutions and do not incorporate the dissolved components into the solid phase under equilibrium conditions, the rate of growth of the ice crystals and the diffusion and convection in the liquid phase during freezing must be borne in mind. For example, Table 1 shows that, at a constant rate of freezing of 6 cm/h, the segregation is twice as great at a stirring speed of 3000 rpm as at 1400 rpm. The segregation is measured by a factor k_A, which is defined as the ratio of the concentration c_E of the segregated substance (in this case $KMnO_4$) in the severed portion which solidified last, to its initial concentration c_A:

$$\text{segregation factor: } k_A = \frac{c_E}{c_A}. \tag{1}$$

Table 1. Accumulation of $KMnO_4$ in water at various stirring speeds.

c_A [%]	Stirring speed [rpm.]	End volume [ml]	c_E [%]	k_A
0.1	1400	0.089	1.1	11
0.1	2200	0.075	1.3	13
0.1	3000	0.045	2.2	22

The freezing process is naturally also affected by the rate of crystallization. For example, Fig. 43 shows the concentration curves for a 1% ammonia solution at three different rates of crystallization. The best result is obtained when charge moves at a speed of 2 cm/h.

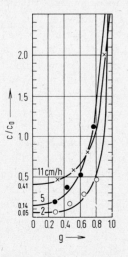

Fig. 43.
Concentration curves for an aqueous ammonia solution (1%) after normal freezing at three rates of lowering: 11 cm/h, 5 cm/h, and 2 cm/h.

The effects of the initial concentration and the rate of freezing on the segregation are shown in Fig. 44.

A 0.05% aqueous solution of KMnO₄ can still be efficiently segregated by freezing at a rate of 10 to 15 cm/h, whilst a 0.1 or 0.5% solution cannot. Thus a 0.05% solution gives a segregation factor of 7 at a freezing rate of about 6 to 11 cm/h, and the same factor is found for a 0,1% solution at 4 to 5 cm/h and a 0,5% solution at 1 cm/h [16].

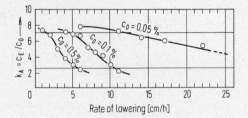

Fig. 44. The segregation factor k_A as a function of the rate of lowering for three different initial concentrations of an aqueous solution of potassium permanganate.

4.2   Zone Melting of Eutectic Systems

Zone melting is subject to the same laws as normal freezing. Consequently, pure material will continue to separate from a system which can form a eutectic, until the concentration of the mixture reaches the eutectic point. Pure A will crystallize first from a solution of concentration c_1 (see Fig. 4), and pure B from a solution of concentration c_2. During zone melting, owing to the fact that the size of the liquid portion is limited, the second component accumulates in a narrow zone, and not in the residual solution as in normal freezing. If the molten zone is very narrow, its composition after travelling a relatively short distance will correspond to the eutectic mixture, which will be transported to the end of the ingot by further movement of the zone. Meanwhile, the substance which crystallizes out behind the molten zone is no longer the pure component, but the starting mixture, which is simultaneously being melted at the leading face of the zone. Further separation of the substances in the ingot can only be achieved by the passage of a subsequent zone. The number of such zone passes required for complete separation of the pure substance from the eutectic mixture depends therefore on the length l of the molten zone and on the length L of the ingot. This separation may be achieved after one, or only after several passes, depending on the initial concentration, the position of the eutectic point, and the ratio L/l. Equations have been proposed for the calculation of the number of passes required for a constant zone length l on the assumption that no diffusion occurs in the solid and that the equilibration of concentration in the melt is complete [12].

In Fig. 45 consider the concentration of substance A (which separates first). The quantity of substance, n_A, in the molten zone of length l at the point $x = 0$ of the ingot, which has a constant cross-section q, is given by:

$$n_{A0} = l \, q \, c_s = l \, q \, c_0$$

c_0 [mole/l] = initial concentration
c_s [mole/l] = concentration in the molten zone
c [mole/l] = concentration in the separated crystallizate
c_e [mole/l] = concentration in the eutectic mixture
c_A [mole/l] = concentration of pure A.

If the molten zone now proceeds along the ingot, c_s will change as a function of x. The change in the quantity of A in the molten zone for a step dx is

$$dn_A = q \cdot c_0 \cdot dx - q \cdot c_k \cdot dx \qquad (2)$$

The first term on the right of eq. (2) is the increase, and the second term the decrease in the quantity of A in the melt. Multiplication of eq. (2) by $1/lq$:

$$\frac{dn_A}{l \cdot q} = \frac{c_0 \cdot dx}{l} - \frac{c_k \cdot dx}{l}$$

and insertion of $c_s = n_A / l \cdot q$ gives the change in concentration in the melt:

$$dc_s = \frac{c_0 - c_k}{l} \, dx. \qquad (3)$$

Integration of eq. (3) between the limits c_0 and c_s, i. e. between $x = 0$ and $x = x$, gives

$$\int_{c_0}^{c_s} dc_s = \int_0^x \frac{c_0 - c_k}{l} \, dx$$

$$c_s - c_0 = \frac{c_0 - c_k}{l} \, x,$$

or

$$c_s = \frac{c_0 - c_k}{l} \, x + c_0. \qquad (4)$$

Since pure A separates out first ($c_0 = c_A$), the melt ultimately reaches the point x_e at which the composition corresponds to that of the eutectic mixture c_e

$$c_e = \frac{c_0 - c_A}{l} \, x_e + c_0,$$

The position of x_e is given by: $\qquad x_e = \frac{l \cdot (c_e - c_0)}{c_0 - c_A} \qquad (5)$

If the molten zone has not yet reached the end of the ingot, new material of composition c_0 melts as the zone proceeds further, and an identical quantity of material freezes at the same time. Since the composition of the melt cannot however fall below c_e, c_s remains constant at c_e, and $dc_s = 0$. Hence, from eq. (3),

$$\frac{c_k}{l} \, dx = \frac{c_0}{l} \, dx, \text{ and thus } c_k = c_0.$$

This means that the concentration of the crystallizate becomes equal to the initial concentration.

When the molten zone finally reaches the end of the ingot, with $x = L - l$, then since

$$\frac{c_0 \cdot dx}{l} = 0$$

eq. (3) gives

$$dc_s = -\frac{c_k}{l} \, dx.$$

Since the molten zone disappears at $x = L$, integration between $x = L - l$ and $x = L$ gives

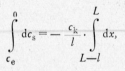

$$\int_{c_e}^{0} dc_s = -\frac{c_k}{l} \cdot \int_{L-l}^{L} dx,$$

and hence $c_k = c_e$.

Thus the eutectic mixture separates out at the end of the ingot,
After one pass, therefore, the ingot consists of three regions:

1. from $x = 0$ to $x = x_e$: pure A
2. from $x = x_e$ to $x = L - l$: initial composition
3. from $x = L - l$ to $x = L$: eutectic mixture.

The center section disappears when

$$x_e = L - l = \frac{l \cdot (c_e - c_0)}{c_0 - c_A}$$

or

$$\frac{L}{l} = \frac{c_e - c_0}{c_0 - c_A} + 1. \tag{6}$$

If c_A, c_0 and c_e are known, eq. (6) can be used to find the ratio L/l which permits complete separation of pure A from the eutectic in a single pass.

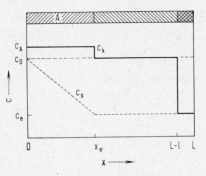
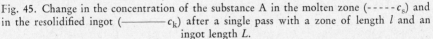

Fig. 45. Change in the concentration of the substance A in the molten zone (-----c_s) and in the resolidified ingot (——— c_k) after a single pass with a zone of length l and an ingot length L.

4.3 Separation of Eutectic Mixtures by Crystallization Techniques

As we have seen, the mixture crystallizing from a multicomponent system frequently corresponds in its composition to a prominent point in the equilibrium diagram. Consequently, such mixtures cannot be separated by crystallization techniques, no matter how often these are repeated, and in cases of this type only a part of one component can be obtained in the pure form, while the other component remains in the mixture. An attempt must then be made to separate the substances by other methods. Thus it may be possible to convert one or both components into derivatives from which they can readily be regenerated, and to separate the derivatives by crystallization.

Binary eutectic mixtures can be at least partly separated by the addition of a third component (cf. Fig. 46).

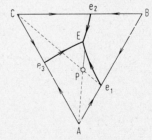

Fig. 46.
Ternary system with three binary eutectics
e_1, e_2, and e_3, and a ternary eutectic E.

If e_1 is the eutectic of the substances A and B which are to be separated, the straight line e_1C gives all ternary compositions at which A and B exist in the eutectic ratio together with a third substance C. The substance C should form simple eutectic systems with both A and B. E again represents the ternary eutectic. If C is added in the proportion given by the point P to the binary eutectic e_1 which is to be resolved, and the molten ternary mixture is allowed to crystallize out, then pure A will separate first. When the melt reaches a composition which lies on the eutectic curve e_1E, the composition follows this curve, until the mixture finally crystallizes out at E as the ternary eutectic. Whether A or B is obtained in the pure form, and in what quantity, naturally depends on the added substance C and on the ternary system resulting from this addition.

5. Zone-Melting Behavior of Crystallizing Phases with Mixed-Crystal Formation

5.1 The Equilibrium Distribution Coefficient k_0

When mixed crystals are formed, a solution exists even in the solid phase. The solid and liquid phases in equilibrium with each other very often have different compositions. This difference in the concentrations of solutes in the coexisting phases can be expressed by the equilibrium distribution coefficient k_0, i. e. by the ratio of the concentrations of one of the components of a solution in the crystallizate and in the melt:

$$k_0 = \frac{c_{\text{solid}}}{c_{\text{liquid}}}. \tag{7}$$

k_0 is constant only when Raoult's law is valid, i. e. only at "ideal dilutions". This concentration range, in which the solidus and liquidus curves may be regarded as linear, is marked by a circle in Fig. 47, and is shown enlarged in Fig. 48.

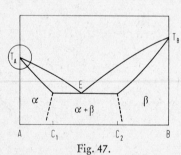

Fig. 47.
Equilibrium diagram of a binary system with mixed-crystal formation and a eutectic E. α and β are two types of mixed crystals.

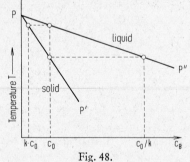

Fig. 48.
Section of the equilibrium diagram for a mixed phase A,B. For B, $k_0 < 1$.

If the concentration of B in the liquid phase is c_0, then that in the solid phase is $k_0 \cdot c_0$, where k_0 is the distribution coefficient of B. For the case shown in the diagram $k_0 < 1$. Conversely, k_0 determines the relative positions of the equilibrium curves PP″ and PP′, i. e. the liquidus and solidus curves, but not their absolute gradients. k_0 can therefore be deduced from a phase diagram only for the range of compositions in question, by taking two values of c joined by a line parallel to the c-axis, and dividing one by the other, as follows:

$$\frac{c_1}{c_0} = \frac{k_0 \cdot c_0}{c_0}$$

Thus for each value of k it is also necessary to state the appropriate concentration, since the solidus and liquidus curves can generally be represented by straight lines

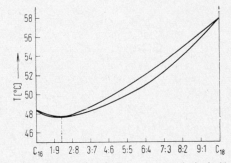

Fig. 49. Equilibrium diagram for the system stearyl alcohol/cetyl alcohol [17]
(minimum: 86% by wt. of $C_{18}H_{37}OH$; m. p.$_{min}$ 47.65° C).

only over very narrow ranges of concentration. For example, in the phase diagram for the system stearyl alcohol/cetyl alcohol (Fig. 49), $k_0 = 0.7$ for cetyl alcohol dissolved at a concentration of 4% in stearyl alcohol.

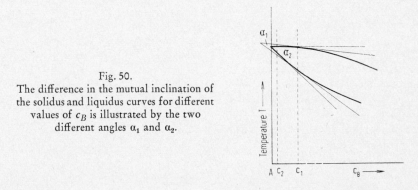

Fig. 50.
The difference in the mutual inclination of the solidus and liquidus curves for different values of c_B is illustrated by the two different angles α_1 and α_2.

The importance of specifying the concentration range in giving a k-value is more clearly shown in Fig. 50. In this case the angle α_2 between the tangents at the lower concentration c_2 is greater than that (α_1) between the tangents at the higher concentration c_1. The greater the angle, the greater is the k_0-value.

The concentration-dependence of the distribution coefficient is shown still more clearly in Fig. 51, in which the k_0-values for eicosanol and hexacosanol, obtained from the phase diagram recorded by Kofler's method (Fig. 37), are plotted against

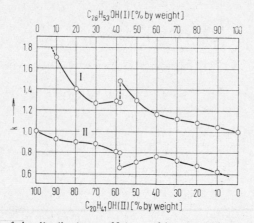

Fig. 51. Dependence of the distribution coefficients of hexacosanol (curve I) and eicosanol (curve II) on the concentration [12]. - - - - - Peritectic jump.

the composition of the mixture. The lower the concentration of the substance in question, the greater is the deviation of the k_0-values from 1, and hence the more favorable are the conditions for zone melting (the phase diagram is of the type IV in Roozeboom's classification).

5.2 The Effective Distribution Coefficient k (k_{eff})

It is not sufficient to know how the distribution coefficient varies with concentration to be able to predict the course of a crystallization process. It must also be borne in mind that the value of k_0 is greatly influenced by the diffusion conditions at the crystallizing phase boundary.

For example, if owing to its higher melting point substance A separates out in preference to B on slow cooling of the melt, B will accumulate in the phase boundary layer. Consequently, however, it will also be built into the solid phase at a concentration higher than the equilibrium value when B is constantly removed from the boundary. The change in the concentration in the growing crystal is governed by the concentration in the phase boundary, where B accumulates particularly when the rate of solidification is greater than the rate of diffusion in the melt, since in this case the impurities cannot escape sufficiently rapidly into the melt by diffusion. Under certain circumstances, the concentration in the solid phase will then become equal to that in the melt, i. e.

$$c_{[B]} = c_{(B)}.$$

The effective distribution coefficient k_{eff} (abbreviated to k), as opposed to the equilibrium value k_0, is then equal to unity, so that separation of the components is no longer possible.

To avoid unnecessary delay in the separation it is therefore necessary to ensure efficient concentration equilibration with the surrounding melt, e. g. by stirring or by a convection current (strong heating in addition to efficient cooling). However, it is impossible to avoid a narrow, non-homogeneous boundary layer δ (cf. Fig. 52).

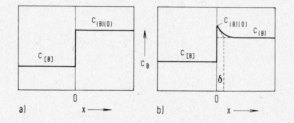

Fig. 52. Concentration of an impurity with $k < 1$ in the solid and liquid phases.

a) Rate of crystallization $\gtrsim$ rate of diffusion
b) Rate of crystallization $\gg$ rate of diffusion

$$\frac{1}{k_0} = \frac{c_{(B)\,(0)}}{c_{[B]}} \qquad\qquad \frac{1}{k} = \frac{c_{(B)}}{c_{[B]}}$$

$c_{(B)}$ = concentration in the body of the liquid phase.
$c_{(B)\,(0)}$ = concentration in the liquid phase at the phase boundary (distance = 0).

It is therefore necessary to use in calculations an effective distribution coefficient k (k_{eff}), which depends on the rate of freezing. The relationship between k_0 and k, and the effect of the rate of freezing f on k have been expressed by Burton, Prim, and Slichter[18] in the following equation:

$$k = k_{eff} = \frac{k_0}{k_0 + (1 - k_0)\, e^{-f \cdot \delta/D}}. \tag{8}$$

As a simplification, k_0 is assumed to be independent of f. D is the diffusion coefficient of B in the melt and δ is the thickness of the boundary layer, in which the transport of matter is due to diffusion alone.

Fig. 53 shows k as a function of the k_0-values. In the freezing experiments, the rate of crystallization f (= freezing rate) was fixed. The diffusion coefficient D was generally unknown, but it is often between 10^{-5} and 10^{-4} cm²/sec (cf. Table 2). Molecules larger than those listed in Table 2 have smaller diffusion coefficients (e. g. for human serum albumin $D = 6.1 \times 10^{-7}$ cm²/sec at $20°\,C$[28]). The thickness of the boundary layer δ may vary over a wide range, e. g. 10^{-1} cm for poor stirring and 10^{-3} cm for good stirring; it therefore depends on convection in the melt, as well

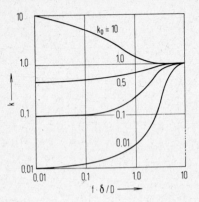

Fig. 53.
k as a function of $f\delta/D$ for various values of k_0 (ref. 27).

as on the rate of freezing f. The quantity δ can be found by determining k at various freezing rates, all other quantities being kept constant.

Table 2. Diffusion coefficients of a number of substances in various solvents.

Substance	Solvent	Concentration [mole-%]	Temperature [°C]	D [cm²/sec]	Ref.
Cd	Hg	0.1	15	$1.81 \cdot 10^{-5}$	19)
Si	Fe		1480	$2.4 \ \cdot 10^{-5}$	20)
C_2H_5OH	H_2O	0.09	9.4	$0.82 \cdot 10^{-5}$	21)
KCl	H_2O		25	$1.9 \ \cdot 10^{-5}$	22)
I_2	C_6H_6		20	$1.67 \cdot 10^{-5}$	23)
n-Heptane	C_6H_6	44	25	$2.47 \cdot 10^{-5}$	24)
$NaNO_3$	$AgNO_3$		330	$4.57 \cdot 10^{-5}$	25)
B	Ge		936	$3 \ \ \cdot 10^{-4}$	26)

In agreement with the discussion so far, experiments on the germanium/antimony and germanium/gallium systems have shown that k-values lying below unity become larger with increasing freezing rate[29] (e.g. from 10 to 80 μ/sec). This of course means that the separation is less effective. The melt must therefore be allowed to solidify as slowly as possible (this obviously also applies to impurities with $k > 1$).

The influence of the freezing rate of germanium/boron mixtures on the distribution of boron between the melt and the single crystals drawn from it was studied by Bridgers and Kolb[26]. The effective distribution coefficients obtained (Table 3) are subject to an inaccuracy of $\pm$ 15%. A value of 17.4 was found for k_0 of boron in germanium.

Table 3. Effective distribution coefficients of boron in germanium for increasing rates of crystallization [26].

Rate of growth of Ge crystals (cm/sec) $\times 10^3$	k, k_{eff}
0.38	15
0.94	11
1.60	5.8
1.70	6.9
3.05	4.2
3.30	4.8
3.56	4.1
6.05	3.5
6.09	3.3
6.19	2.6
6.35	2.9
8.38	2.4
8.40	2.4
8.63	2.4

5.2.1 Determination of the Distribution Coefficient

As was pointed out above, the ideal distribution coefficient can be found from the phase diagram. Unfortunately, the phase diagrams have only rarely been determined accurately over the whole range of concentrations, and it is just in the neighborhood of the melting points of the pure components that satisfactory values are often lacking. However, if the k-values obtained at higher concentrations are plotted against the concentration, the k-values can be extrapolated graphically to low concentrations.

Thurmond and Struthers [30] found that log k depends on the reciprocal of the temperature:

$$\log k = B - \left(\frac{A}{T}\right) \tag{9}$$

where A and B are constants which can be determined empirically.

For example, Table 4 shows the constants A and B for the additives antimony and copper in germanium and silicon.

Table 4. Constants of equation (9), according to ref. 30.

System	B	A
Sb/Ge	6.75	11.050
Cu/Ge	2.59	9.200
Cu/Si	0.69	7.120

The log k curves were calculated from the phase diagrams given in the literature [38, 32, 33] and the melting points of germanium (1209°K) [34] and silicon (1703°K) [35]. The distribution coefficients extrapolated from these curves for the additives in germanium and silicon and their melting points are in good agreement with experimentally determined values (cf. Table 5).

Table 5. Comparison of the values of k for germanium and silicon alloys, obtained by extrapolation from eq. (9) and measured experimentally.

	k (extrapolated)	k (measured)
Sb/Ge	$4.0 \cdot 10^{-3}$	$3 \cdot 10^{-3}$
Cu/Ge	$0.98 \cdot 10^{-3}$	$1.5 \cdot 10^{-3}$
Cu/Si	$3.2 \cdot 10^{-3}$	$4.5 \cdot 10^{-3}$

The experimental values were obtained by drawing single crystals of germanium [36] and silicon [37] from melts to which radioactive antimony (^{124}Sb) or copper (^{64}Cu) had been added.

The agreement between calculated and experimental k-values is not always satisfactory, since the experimentally determined phase diagrams sometimes differ from ideality. This is because thermodynamic equilibrium is not established between the solid and the liquid. However, a necessary condition for complete equilibrium between the crystallizate and the melt is that the rate of crystallization or melting should be pratically zero, a condition which naturally cannot be satisfied in practice.

5.2.1.1 Determination of k by Zone Melting of a Homogeneous Mixture

In the practical evaluation of crystallization processes such as zone melting, effective values of the distribution coefficient are sometimes more valuable than the ideal values. It is particularly interesting in this respect that k can be determined by a zone-melting process itself (cf. also k (measured) in Table 5).

According to Pfann [38], the concentration of a substance at any point x of an ingot of a solid solution after the passage of a molten zone of length l can be calculated from the equation:

$$\frac{c}{c_0} = 1 - (1-k)\, e^{-kx/l} \tag{10}$$

This equation does not apply to the last zone of length l, which crystallizes by normal freezing. Thus, if the concentration c of an impurity B along the ingot is determined by a suitable analytical method and plotted against x/l, the resulting curve will be similar to that shown in Fig. 54. (This curve was calculated for an initial concentration $c_0 = 45\%$ in the bar before melting and for $k = 0.42$. The experimental curve will differ from the theoretical one owing to the dependence of the distribution coefficient on concentration). k_B can now be calculated from each point of this experimental curve, using eq. (10).

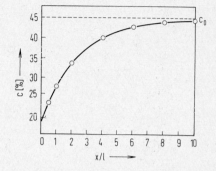

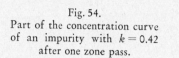

Fig. 54.
Part of the concentration curve
of an impurity with $k = 0.42$
after one zone pass.

However, k_B is better calculated from the concentration c_B in the first crystal-lizate, which is obtained from the curve of c against x/l by extrapolation to the point $x/l = 0$. Insertion of $x/l = 0$ in eq. (10) gives

$$\frac{c}{c_0} = k$$

5.2.1.2   Determination of k by Zone Leveling

In contrast to zone melting, zone leveling leads to the uniform distribution of a substance B in an ingot of A. This process can also be utilized for the determination of k-values. In this method the zone melting tube is filled with pure substance A, and the solute B is introduced at the end of the ingot, either in the pure form or as a solution in A (Fig. 55). Corresponding to the zone melting equation (10), we then have

$$c = k \cdot c_0 \, e^{-k \, x/l} \tag{11}$$

where c_0 is the concentration of the solute in the first zone-length.

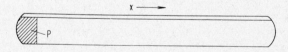

Fig. 55. Original situation in zone leveling.
P = drop of an impurity B.

Extrapolation to $x/l = 0$ is simpler in this case than in zone melting since eq. (11) gives a linear plot of log c against x/l (Fig. 56). This line was calculated in the same manner as Fig. 54, for $c_0 = 45\%$ and $k = 0.42$, so that it represents an ideal case, which cannot be realized in practice. The point $x/l = 0$ again gives the composition of the first crystallizate at the tip of the ingot, where eq. (11) becomes $c = k \cdot c_0$, so that k can be found from the calculated value of c_0 and the value of c obtained from the graph.

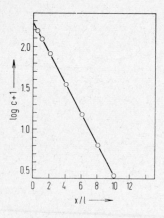

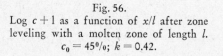

Fig. 56.
Log $c + 1$ as a function of x/l after zone leveling with a molten zone of length l.
$c_0 = 45\%$; $k = 0.42$.

5.3 The Normal Freezing of Mixed Crystal Systems

If a homogeneous melt of a mixed crystal system of Fig. 7 or Figs. 46 and 48 is allowed to solidify under the conditions of normal freezing, a pure substance does not separate out immediately. Instead, we obtain crystals enriched in components A, for which $k > 1$. The concentration of A in the melt consequently decreases and that of B (with $k < 1$) increases, so that the melting point of the mixture is lowered. The equilibrium temperature therefore falls off, and the concentration of B in the mixed crystals separating out will be rather greater than $k \cdot c_0$ (Fig. 48); the concentration of A will however always remain higher than that in the liquid phase. As freezing continues, the composition of the liquid follows the liquidus curve (PP″ in Fig. 48), while the composition of the mixed crystals follows the solidus curve (PP′ in Fig. 48). The remaining liquid phase therefore becomes progressively richer in B, which becomes more and more incorporated in the solid material, until the solid finally reaches, and even passes, the original composition (cf. intersection of the vertical through c_0 with PP′ in Fig. 48). This is possible because the melt is always in equilibrium only with the crystals which have just separated, and these in turn are removed from the equilibrium by the deposition of new layers of crystals.

The concentration of the impurity B at any distance x along a frozen bar of total length L can be calculated from an equation proposed by Gulliver[39] in 1922 (cf. also [40, 41, 42]):

$$c_{B[A]} = k \cdot c_0 \left(1 - \frac{x}{L}\right)^{k-1} .$$

$$(12)$$

This assumes that neither k nor the density of the substance changes along the ingot on recrystallization. Fig. 57 shows a number of calculated concentration curves for B with various distribution coefficients.

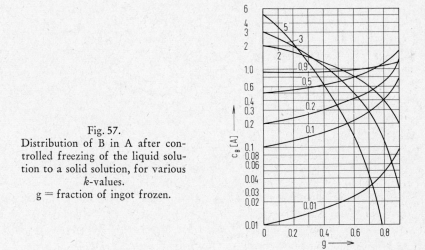

Fig. 57.
Distribution of B in A after controlled freezing of the liquid solution to a solid solution, for various k-values.
g = fraction of ingot frozen.

The various k-values give different concentration ranges for B: the greater the difference between k and unity, the more effective is the separation. Substances with $k > 1$ always accumulate in the first part of the ingot to solidify (left) and those with $k < 1$ in the end which solidifies last (right).

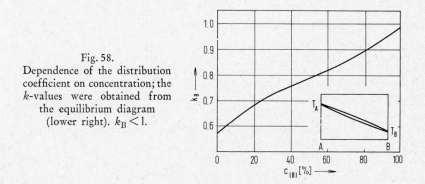

Fig. 58.
Dependence of the distribution coefficient on concentration; the k-values were obtained from the equilibrium diagram (lower right). $k_B < 1$.

Eq. (12), and hence also the curves in Fig. 57, do not describe the complete freezing behavior for the whole length of the ingot. Fig. 59 shows a complete concentration curve which was calculated by Hamming's method [43], taking into account the dependence of the distribution coefficient on concentration (cf. Fig. 58).

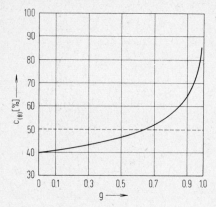

Fig. 59.
Concentration curve of a substance A along a bar B which has solidified by normal freezing, taking into account the dependence of k on concentration as shown in Fig. 58; $c_0 = 50\%$ A.
g = fraction of ingot length.

The distribution of B in the frozen solution is however governed not only by the equilibrium conditions but also by the rate of freezing (cf. p. 39) and the convection conditions in the melt, and hence also by differences in temperature between the liquid and the crystalline portions of the ingot. The extent to which this can influence the separation is shown by the concentration curves in Fig. 60.

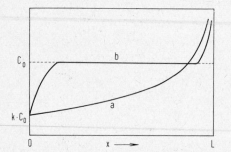

Fig. 60.
Distribution of B along the frozen bar A for $k_0 < 1$.
a) With complete mixing in the melt.
b) When transport of material in the melt is by diffusion only.

Tiller et al.[44] have also discussed the freezing of a mixed crystal system. These authors found that the phase boundary was preceded by a liquid zone in which the concentration of the impurity fell off exponentially from the phase boundary to the remainder of the liquid in proportion to D/f (D = diffusion coefficient, f = rate of freezing). The concentration distribution in an ingot solidified by normal freezing can then be given by (cf. Fig. 52b):

$$\frac{c}{c_0} = 1 - (1 - k_0) e^{-k_0 \cdot f \cdot x/D} \tag{13}$$

assuming that the equilibrium distribution coefficient k_0, the initial concentration c_0, and the ratio D/f are known.

5.4 Zone Melting of Mixed-Crystal Systems

To describe the freezing behavior during zone melting, it is only necessary to replace D/f in eq. (13) by the length of the molten zone l (see eq. (10)).

The reason for this is that in zone melting the solid is not melted as a whole, but only at separate zones heated by a series of furnaces mounted a certain distance apart. Consequently, the variation of the concentration of an impurity B in the melt and in the solid ingot differs from that found in normal freezing (cf. Fig. 61).

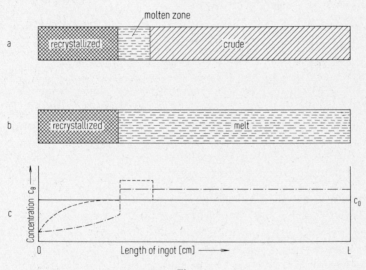

Fig. 61.

(a) Zone melting with a narrow molten zone.
(b) Solidification of a rod-shaped melt.
(c) Concentration of impurity B (initial concentration c_0) - - - - - during zone melting (a)
and - - - - - - - - - during normal freezing (b).

The concentration of B is higher in the narrow molten zone than in the long melt, and it is therefore always greater in material which has been recrystallized by zone melting than in material solidified by normal freezing. Thus normal freezing gives a better separation than the passage of a single molten zone through the ingot.

Fig. 62 shows the distribution curves for the impurity B in the system of Fig. 7, after normal freezing and after zone melting using one pass and using 15 passes.

The normal freezing curve (NF) is flatter and is always concave, whilst that for multipass zone melting is steeper and becomes convex in the second half. Thus the advantage of zone melting lies in the possibility of carrying out several recrystallizations at the same time. As can be seen from the curve for 15 passes, this results in a distinct improvement of the separation.

Let the initial concentration of B in the solid ingot be c_0; if $k < 1$, B will accumulate in the melt, and the farther the molten zone has progressed from its starting point, the greater will be $c_{B (A)}$, i.e. the concentration of B in the melt. Thus as the

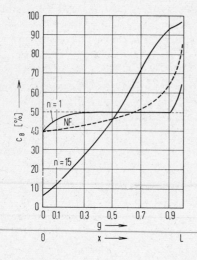

Fig. 62.
Concentration curves for a component B of a mixed-crystal system as represented in Fig. 7 for normal freezing NF and for zone melting with $n = 1$ and $n = 15$ zones. $g =$ fraction of ingot.

molten zone traverses the ingot, B is transported to the end which solidifies last. The distribution process proper occurs at the melt/crystal phase boundary, where the molecules migrate only as a result of a concentration gradient caused by the different tendencies of the various substances in the mixed phase to separate. If the first crystallizate, which is rich in A, is left in contact with the melt for a long period, e.g. by allowing the molten zone to move very slowly, the reverse exchange can take place; the molecules of B which have accumulated in the melt return to the solid phase, so reversing the separation. This reversed effect does not occur in zone melting, however, since even the optimally low rate of migration of 1 mm/h is too high for an exchange of this type, and furthermore, the crystals which have already separated out are screened from the melt by further deposition. Thus a new equilibrium state is always being frozen in during zone melting as the crystal front advances relatively slowly.

This is expressed in the phase diagram (Fig. 48) by the course of the line PP″. The concentration of B in the solid recrystallized part of the ingot (see course of PP′) increases only until the concentration reaches the original value c_0, since B is then being melted into the zone at the leading phase boundary at exactly the same rate as it is separating out at the freezing end. Only when new material is no longer being melted, i.e. when the zone reaches the end of the ingot, does the rate of incorporation of B in the solid phase increase. Thus the concentration of B tends towards a maximum at the end of the ingot. After the passage of one molten zone ($n = 1$), therefore, the ingot can be divided into three regions according to the change in the concentration of B in A, (cf. Fig. 62):

1. the region at the beginning, with $c < c_0$, starting with the concentration kc_0;

2. the long region in the middle, with constant concentration c_0;

3. the region of normal freezing, which has exactly the same length as the molten zone, and which exhibits a concentration distribution similar to that found in normal freezing.

In the first two regions, the concentration at any point x of the recrystallized ingot is given [38] by eq. (10) for a zone length l. The complete concentration distribution can again be calculated by Hamming's method.

The curve of the k-values (cf. Fig. 58) is first determined from an equilibrium diagram of Type I in Roozeboom's classification (see pp. 7 and 8). If we consider an ingot consisting of 50% of A and 50% of B traversed by a molten zone of length l such that $L/l = 10$, and let the zone advance in individual steps of 0.1 L,

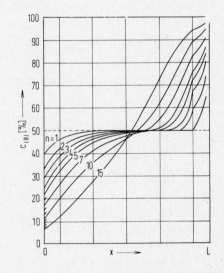

Fig. 63.
Concentration curves for a substance B after zone melting with 1—15 zone passes. Initial composition: 50% of A + 50% of B.

it is possible to calculate the concentration in the solid phase at any point, using the k-value obtained from the curve of Fig. 59 for the concentration in the melt. A simple though laborious method thus gives the concentration curves shown in Fig. 63. These curves are specific for the case chosen, and are not valid for other initial concentrations, owing to the dependence of k on concentration.

5.4.1 Distribution of Impurities with $k < 1$ and $k > 1$ along the Ingot as a Function of the Number of Zone Passes and the Zone Length l

Braun and Marshall [45] also give equations which permit the calculation of the distribution of impurities with any values of k at any point in the ingot after n zone passes. The distribution after the previous pass and the initial concentration for the zone in question must be known, and the concentration curves are calculated in succession for increasing numbers of passes. The initial concentrations can be obtained for a semi-infinite ingot from Lord's equation [46] if

$$n < N \text{ for } x = 0 \text{ to } x = N - n$$

where n is the number of molten zones of length l and N is the ratio of the overall length of the ingot to the zone length. The concentration distribution in an ingot of finite length is an analytical function up to $x = N - n$. Beyond this point the function must be calculated in steps, since it exhibits peculiarities at the end points of each region.

The authors illustrate their numerical calculations with curves for

$$N = 10; \quad k = 0.1; \quad n = 1; 2; 3 \text{ and}$$
$$N = 5; \quad k = 0.3; \quad n = 1 \text{ to } 10$$

The dependence of the concentration distribution on the number of zone passes and on the ratio of the zone length to the overall length of the ingot has been studied by Burris, Stockman, and Dillon [47]. The curves were calculated under the following assumptions:

1. uniform composition of the liquid phase,

2. no diffusion in the solid phase,

3. constant distribution coefficient,

4. constant zone length,

5. concentration of the impurity less than its solubility.

A liquid phase of uniform composition is not always guaranteed, for reasons connected with diffusion; i.e. condition 1 is difficult to satisfy. Moreover, condition 5 is often not satisfied, since a solid mixed phase consisting of impurity and principal substance sometimes separates as a result of unexpected compound formation in certain concentration ranges. Finally, the distribution coefficient is not always constant (condition 3); for a given concentration of the impurity, it depends not only on the rate of crystallization [48, 49], but also on the temperature gradient at the phase boundary and on the crystal faces [26] which are being formed; however this only gives a 10% variation in k, in agreement with Burton's findings [50].

As the number of zone passes is increased, in this case up to 9, the concentration of the impurity decreases, particularly at the beginning of the ingot (cf. Fig. 64).

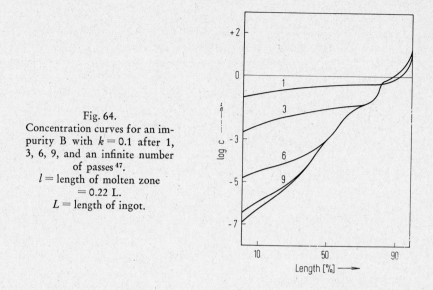

Fig. 64.
Concentration curves for an impurity B with $k = 0.1$ after 1, 3, 6, 9, and an infinite number of passes [47].
l = length of molten zone
= 0.22 L.
L = length of ingot.

A finding of theoretical interest and of extreme practical importance is that the improvement in separation becomes insignificant beyond 9 zone passes. The last curve represents the final concentration distribution after an infinitely large number of passes.

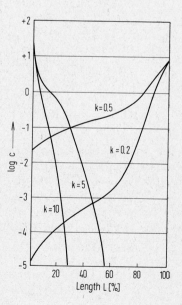

Fig. 65.
Distribution of the impurity B in an ingot of length L ($l = 0.1\ L$) after 10 zone passes [47], for the distribution coefficients $k =$ 0.5, 0.2, 5 and 10.

Fig. 65 shows the concentration distributions for four different values of k. It can be seen that all substances with $k > 1$ concentrate at the beginning of the ingot and those with $k < 1$ at the end. The greater the difference between k and 1, the greater will be the quantity of extremely pure substance obtained after the same number of passes (in this case 10).

The effect of the zone length on the distribution of substances with $k > 1$ is shown in Fig. 66. For $k = 5$, the most favorable distribution after 10 passes is obtained with a relatively long zone ($l = 0.2 L$). If the zone length is only 5% of the total length of the ingot, the concentration remains unchanged over a fairly long distance. Since substances with $k > 1$ accumulate in the solid phase, and so move in the opposite direction to that in which the zone moves, the only transport path available to them is the length of the molten zone. Thus the longer the zone the smaller is the

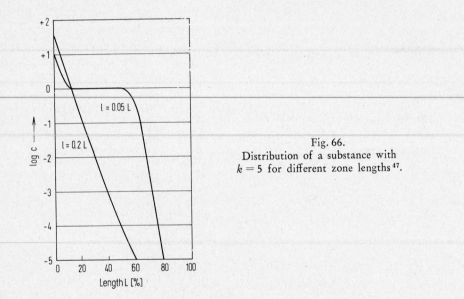

Fig. 66.
Distribution of a substance with
$k = 5$ for different zone lengths [47].

number of passes required to transport these substances to the beginning of the ingot. This result was also obtained by Matz [51] from purely mathematical considerations, using an extended theory of zone melting. The ultimate distribution is however better with short zones than with long ones, although this is only achieved after several passes (cf. Fig. 67).

The best enrichment in a relatively short time is probably obtained when e. g. 7 wide zones are followed by 2 narrow zones (Fig. 68). This gives a better separation than 10 narrow zones. Even better results are obtained if the whole bar is melted and allowed to solidify by normal freezing before the zone melting proper is started. The first "zone" in this case is a zone of the "maximum" length.

Substances with $k < 1$ accumulate in the melt, and consequently travel in the same direction as the molten zones. No further improvement in the separation can therefore be achieved by variation of the zone length. The beginning of the ingot is purest when a narrow zone is used.

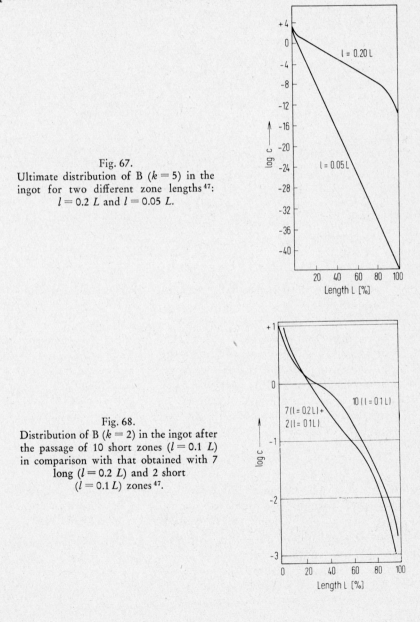

Fig. 67.
Ultimate distribution of B ($k = 5$) in the ingot for two different zone lengths [47]: $l = 0.2\ L$ and $l = 0.05\ L$.

Fig. 68.
Distribution of B ($k = 2$) in the ingot after the passage of 10 short zones ($l = 0.1\ L$) in comparison with that obtained with 7 long ($l = 0.2\ L$) and 2 short ($l = 0.1\ L$) zones [47].

It can be seen from Fig. 69 that, for $k = 0.1$ and a zone length $l = 0.1\ L$, a good separation is obtained with 10 passes. If k is close to 1, however, the separation becomes very difficult, and one hundred passes or more are often required to achieve the same separation as with $k = 0.1$.

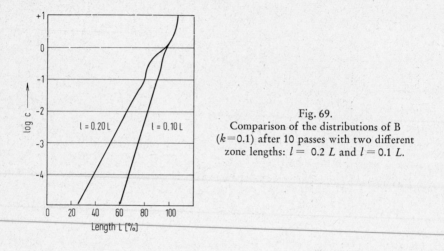

Fig. 69.
Comparison of the distributions of B
($k = 0.1$) after 10 passes with two different
zone lengths: $l = 0.2\ L$ and $l = 0.1\ L$.

5.4.2   Comparison of Zone Melting as a Steady-State Process with Distillation at Total Reflux

After a number of zone passes which depends on the length L of the ingot and the length l of the molten zone, we obtain a limiting distribution which does not change further on continuation of zone melting under the same conditions. In this limiting state, zone melting may be compared with distillation at total reflux.

The height equivalent to a theoretical plate of a packed column (HETP) is related to the total number of theoretical plates n and the length L of the column by the following simple expression:

$$\text{HETP} = L/n \qquad (14)$$

The HETP is the length of column along which the concentration in one and the same phase just changes by one equilibrium step given by the separation factor α. This step extends from any point x in the column to $x + \text{HETP}$, and can be expressed mathematically by the equation

$$\alpha = \left(\frac{\xi_A}{\xi_B}\right)^{\text{vapor}}_{x + \text{HETP}} \Bigg/ \left(\frac{\xi_A}{\xi_B}\right)^{\text{vapor}}_{x} \qquad (15)$$

in which ξ_A and ξ_B are the mole fractions of the substances A and B in the vapor phase. In order to calculate n, and hence the HETP, it is necessary to know α and the concentration ratio of the two substances in the uppermost vapor space and in the lowermost liquid of the distillation column. The relationship between these quantities is:

$$\alpha^n = \left(\frac{\xi_A}{\xi_B}\right)_{top}^{vapor} \bigg/ \left(\frac{\xi_A}{\xi_B}\right)_{bottom}^{liquid} \tag{16}$$

Eq. (16) may also be assumed to be valid for the equilibrium between the liquid and solid phases in zone melting, so that if the separation factor is known it is possible to calculate n, and hence also the HETP, for an ingot of a given length. For a given separation factor, a lower value of the HETP would again indicate a greater efficiency of the zone-melting arrangement. However, the required steep concentration distribution along the ingot is most readily obtained with short zones, although often only after a very large number of passes. This means that it takes longer to reach the ultimate state, and the time required at low rates of travel becomes even longer. This limiting factor is not encountered in distillation, and this is why a zone-melting apparatus is best characterized not by the number of theoretical plates or the HETP, but by the "number of passes" Z, which is proportional to the ratio L/l:

$$Z = x \cdot \frac{L}{l} \tag{17}$$

Experiments carried out with micro-equipment [12] have shown that, depending on the conditions, $2\,L/l$ or more zone passes are required to approach the ultimate distribution which can be achieved in practice.

Pfann [38] gives the value $Z = 14$ for a ratio $L/l = 10$. His calculation was based on the consideration that each zone pass reduces the initial concentration at that time, c_0, to the value $k \cdot c_0$ (where $k < 1$). Thus it must be possible to calculate the number of zone passes from the lowest concentration reached at the beginning of the ingot fort $k < 1$.

The ultimate distribution for various values of k is then given, according to Pfann [38] by

$$c = A \cdot e^{Bx} \tag{18}$$

The quantity B is related to the distribution coefficient k and the zone length l by

$$k = \frac{B \cdot l}{e^{Bl} - 1} \tag{19}$$

while A is related to the initial concentration c_0 by

$$A = c_0 \cdot L \cdot \frac{B}{e^{LB} - 1}. \tag{20}$$

Fig. 70 shows the ultimate distributions calculated from eq. (18) for substances with various k-values.

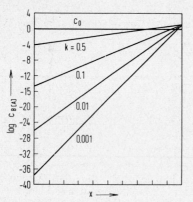

Fig. 70.
Ultimate distributions of substances
with distribution coefficients
$k = 0.5, 0.1, 0.01,$ and 0.001.
$L/l = 10$. The curves are calculated
from eq. (18).

According to Fig. 70, even after a very large number of zone passes, the concentration at the left-hand end of the ingot does not fall below 10^{-4}, taking an arbitrary value of 1 for the initial concentration and assuming a distribution coefficient $k = 0.5$. This concentration is reached after 14 passes, since, according to the above discussion, the initial concentration is reduced by a factor k after each pass; thus

$$c = c_0 \cdot k^Z . \tag{21}$$

It follows, therefore, that Z is given by

$$\frac{\log c - \log c_0}{\log k} = Z . \tag{22}$$

The ultimate concentration distribution in a recrystallized ingot has been qualitatively and quantitatively described on the basis of a large number of zone-melting experiments. This does not require complete separation into the individual components. It is sufficient to divide the ingot into several pieces and to remelt the pieces separately until the ultimate distribution is again achieved. This may be repeated any desired number of times, transferring from a larger to a smaller apparatus, where necessary, and mixing together corresponding fractions. This process is carried out discontinuously, like adsorption chromatography, in which the column is also divided up and the resulting fractions possibly chromatographed again.

5.4.3   Zone Melting of Complex and Multi-Component Systems

We have so far dealt mainly with systems in which the components form a continuous range of mixed crystals. In principle, the conclusions reached are naturally also valid for other types. However, the distribution after zone melting is different. In the case of types II and III, which are more frequently encountered than type I, only one of the substances, depending on the initial composition, can be obtained in a very pure form. If the initial concentration of one of the components is very low, the loss of pure material will be insignificant. Thus if, in a system of type III, 100 g of starting material A is contaminated with 1 g of B, and if the minimum is to be expected with a 50% mixture, the resulting loss of A is only 1 g. (The 2 g of mixture at the end of the recrystallized ingot cannot be separated further even by repeated zone melting.) In practice, however, a complete separation cannot be expected since ultimate purification is achieved only after a very large number of zone passes.

5.4.3.1   Zone-Melting Behavior of Peritectic Systems

The rather complex type IV, which can form a peritectic, often occurs in practice. Whereas the components of types I to III are miscible in all proportions, the miscibility is limited in types IV and V. Two types of crystal are formed instead of one, and each of these exists only over a certain range of concentrations.

The behavior of type IV mixtures is shown in Fig. 71.

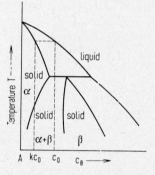

Fig. 71.
T-c diagram for mixtures of substances which form mixed crystals and a peritectic.

For example, let the substance A contain a little of B, and let the initial concentration be c_0. Freezing of the melt leads to separation of mixed crystals with a concentration $k \cdot c_0$. Thus B accumulates in the melt as the zone traverses the ingot. Corresponding to this increase, more and more B freezes out behind the melt. Initially, therefore, we have the same result as in the case of type I. After a certain distance, however, the mixed crystals separating at the crystal boundary react with the adjacent melt, and a new phase β is formed, with a sudden jump in the concentration of B. After this jump, the process continues steadily: B accumulates still further in the melt, and its concentration in the newly-formed β-phase also increases, so that the melting points of samples taken from the recrystallized ingot steadily decrease towards the end of the bar which solidifies last. The concentration distribution in an ingot of this type after zone melting is shown in Fig. 72. As the number of zone passes is increased, the peritectic jump moves closer to the end of the ingot.

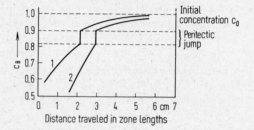

Fig. 72. Distribution of B along the solid ingot after 1 pass and after 2 passes, when the mixture (A, B) forms a peritectic.

Substance B is being added to the melt at a constant rate by the melting of new material. A large quantity of B is consumed at the instant of formation of the β-phase as a result of the peritectic reaction, and the concentration of A in the melt therefore increases in the immediate neighborhood of the phase boundary. However, this causes an increase in the melting point of the material which now crystallizes, and a change in the crystal habit. The β-phase is again formed immediately after the separation of the material which is richer in A, and which naturally crystallizes in the α-form. This would again lead to a deficiency of B in the melt, unless this defi-

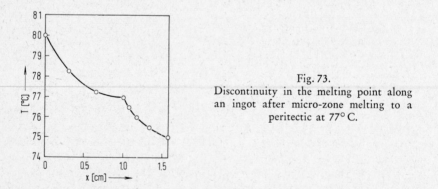

Fig. 73.
Discontinuity in the melting point along an ingot after micro-zone melting to a peritectic at 77° C.

ciency is made good in the meantime owing to an increasing concentration in the part which has not yet melted. For the same reason the melting point curve, which is obtained by melting point determinations on samples lying close together in the recast fractions, will show a small jump only after a number of zone passes (cf. Fig. 73).

The experimental results will not always agree with theory, since they may also be influenced by unpredictable factors, such as anomalous diffusion, etc. However, the results of the zone melting of mixtures of alcohols (discussed in greater detail further on), have largely confirmed that it is possible to predict the expected result of zone melting from the phase diagram.

5.4.3.2   Zone-Melting Behavior of Multi-Component Systems

5.4.3.2.1   Low-Concentration Impurities

In practice, it is often necessary to deal with multi-component systems which can no longer be described by simple equilibrium diagrams, if these are known at all. Nevertheless, zone melting can still be used since the yield of pure components is not very greatly reduced, provided that the impurities are present in small concentrations. The true melting behavior of two principal components, e. g. hexacosanol and eicosanol, is scarcely affected, as has been shown by zone-melting experiments on this mixture[12]. The higher-melting impurities were found to accumulate in the ingot before the hexacosanol, and the low-melting impurities in the lower-melting eicosanol.

It will normally be necessary to assume the presence of multi-component systems, even when pure starting materials are used; this is particularly so, however, in the case of isotopically labeled compounds, even if they are supplied in solution by the manufacturers. Autodecomposition[52] is certainly less in this case, but it is still sufficient to cause an appreciable change in the distribution coefficient of the labeled compounds. Thus cetyl alcohol labeled with ^{14}C migrates more rapidly than the unlabeled alcohol in stearyl alcohol[17]. In this case the impurities formed by autodecomposition act like a solvent.

This effect can also be brought about artificially to improve the purification of the principal substance, by introducing a suitable solvent into the molten zone before the zone melting begins; as the zone passes along the ingot, the solvent carries the undesirable impurities along with it[53]. The solvent must then be removed at the end of the ingot. There is naturally a danger of further contamination, as in recrystallization from solution, since the mode of purification is the same in both cases; however, better yields can be expected in zone melting.

It is even possible, in zone melting, to introduce a saturated solution of the principal substance[54], and to pass the suspension of crystals in a tube through a number of heating and cooling zones. Everything is dissolved in the hot zones, and the compound to be purified crystallizes out again in the cooler zones. An interesting point is that it is possible to maintain zones of clear solution in contact with zones of a crystalline suspension. This method can therefore be used for the resolution of diastereoisomers on the basis of their different solubilities[55].

Another example of recrystallization by zone melting is the process suggested by Pfann[56] for the purification of silicon with the aid of tin. The silicon forms the end

of an ingot of tin through which a molten zone passes; when the zone reaches the end
of the ingot, some silicon is dissolved and, as the zone advances, separates out again
in the pure form at the end of the zone. The result is that, after a large number of
zone passes, the silicon has been transferred to the beginning of the ingot, whilst the
impurities are found at the end. It must be borne in mind, however, that the silicon
now contains a small quantity of dissolved tin, a disadvantage which is difficult to
avoid in any recrystallization technique.

Süe et al.[57] carried out a detailed investigation of the possibility of purifying
volatile inorganic substances which are unstable in the molten state, with the idea of
forming a eutectic, and so lowering the melting point to such an extent that
decomposition would become impossible. Lead nitrate decomposes on melting, but
not after potassium nitrate has been added, since the resulting eutectic melts at
$207°$ C. This mixture is formed by 4.7 g of Pb $(NO_3)_2$ and 5.3 g of KNO_3. The best
results with this mixture were obtained in the removal of cesium nitrate (cf. Table 6).
In each case, the authors added the cation as the radioisotope; in this way they
could follow the progress of the zone melting more easily, by recording the intensity
of the radiation.

Table 6. Purification of lead nitrate as a eutectic melt with potassium nitrate;
$c_n(0) =$ concentration of impurity at the beginning of the ingot after $n = 4$ zone passes.
$k_R = c_0/c_n$ for the beginning of the ingot.
Initial concentration $c_0 =$ quantity of impurity/quantity of Pb$(NO_3)_2 = 10^{-3}$.

Impurity	$NaNO_3$	$CsNO_3$	$Sr(NO_3)_2$	$La(NO_3)_3$
Isotope	^{22}Na	^{134}Cs	^{90}Sr	^{140}La
$c_n(0)$	$2.5 \cdot 10^{-4}$	$2 \cdot 10^{-4}$	$7 \cdot 10^{-4}$	$9.5 \cdot 10^{-4}$
Purification coefficient k_R	4	5	1.4	1.05

Considerable further improvement in zone refining can be achieved by the zone
melting of cryohydrates. Süe et al.[57] demonstrated a particularly elegant purification
of potassium chloride by this method (see Table 7).

Table 7. Results of zone melting of the cryohydrate with potassium chloride.
(Initial concentration $c_0 = 10^{-3}$; rate of zone travel $v = 5.6$ mm/h)

Impurity	NaCl	NaCl	$SrCl_2$	$SrCl_2$
$c_n(0)$	$7.0 \cdot 10^{-5}$	$3.5 \cdot 10^{-5}$	$1.0 \cdot 10^{-4}$	$1.5 \cdot 10^{-5}$
Number of passes n	8	10	10	20
Purification coefficient k_R	14	28	10	65

5.4.3.2.2 High-Concentration Impurities

If however, the various components of a multi-component system are not present
as impurities, but in comparable concentrations, their separation is much more

difficult. Unfortunately, no experimental work has been carried out in this direction, and we can only conclude from theoretical considerations that a zone separation could again be achieved by using a known substance as the charge, as will be discussed later. A satisfactory solution to such problems will probably be found only by combining zone melting with another method of separation, zone melting being carried out only on the binary mixture resulting from this other method.

An example of a suitable auxiliary method would be the "amplified distillation" which enabled Weitkamp et al.[58] to isolate 32 acid components from wool wax. These authors distilled a small quantity of fatty acid esters together with a large quantity of a hyrocarbon mixture, the boiling range of which included that of the esters. When the boiling point of a component was reached, the substance distilled over with a larger quantity of the hydrocarbon with the same boiling point. This excellent method has not become established, simply because it is difficult to isolate the small quantities of fatty acid from the large quantities of the carrier substances. However, this could be achieved by zone melting, since similar boiling points do not imply similar melting points [59].

6. Modified Zone-Melting Methods

6.1 Zone Freezing

Zone freezing (cf. Fig. 74) is really the reverse of zone melting. Thus, instead of passing a narrow molten zone through a crystalline ingot, a narrow crystalline zone is passed through the melt. There is no fundamental difference between this process and zone melting. In each case, the separation depends on a difference in the distribution of an impurity between the solid and liquid phases, and the only difference is that in zone freezing the melt is the principal phase. Substances which lower the

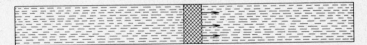

Fig. 74. Zone freezing. The diagram shows a narrow solid zone in the middle of a long molten or liquid sample.

melting point accumulate in the liquid in front of the crystalline zone. The concentration of these substances is lower in the solid zone itself, and lowest of all in the liquid behind the zone (see Fig. 75).

After a certain time the concentration of the impurities in the liquid at the trailing face of the solid zone will reach a steady level, which slowly rises as the zone advances (cf. Fig. 75 c). Conversely, substances which have separated out preferentially during the passage of the solid zone are redistributed in the liquid behind the zone. Normal freezing is preferable to zone freezing with one solid zone in that the concentration differences are frozen in the former case, and not partially cancelled out again. Thus the only possible reason for using zone freezing with a single zone in preference to normal freezing would be the apparatus required.

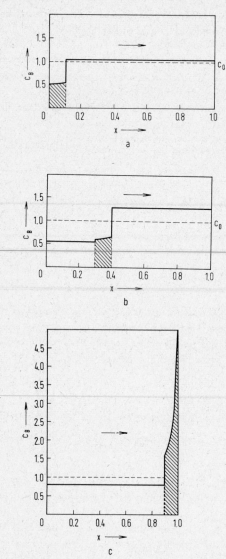

Fig. 75.
Distribution of B $(k = 0.5)$ in the liquid and solid phases (a) at the beginning and (b) as a narrow crystalline zone passes through a liquid charge A $(L = 1.0, l = 0.1)$. (c) The zone has reached the end of the liquid charge, bringing with it most of the impurities.

The situation is rather different if several short solid zones are passed through the liquid. However, this procedure is superior to zone melting only when thorough mixing of the liquid phase is ensured and when the substances enriched have k-values >1. Substances with k-values <1 again accumulate at the end which freezes last (cf. Fig. 76).

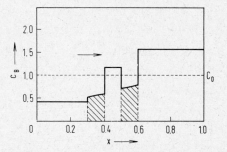

Fig. 76. Distribution of B in the liquid and solid phases during the passage of two narrow crystalline zones through a liquid charge A
($k = 0.5$, $L = 1.0$, $l = 0.1$).

6.2   Zone Leveling

One of the most common methods of modifying the properties of a substance is to mix it with other substances. It is particularly easy to mix two components when both are liquid and miscible in all proportions. For this reason, solids are preferably mixed in the liquid state, e.g. molten metals. It is simply necessary to ensure that not even partial separation occurs on solidification, since this would give rise, e.g. in the case of molten metals, to "non-homogeneous mixed crystals", the centers and outer layers of which differ in composition, or which might even exhibit a zonal structure.

Crystals of this type can be made uniform again by a zone-melting method. Pfann has coined the expression "zone leveling".

6.2.1   *Discontinuous Zone Leveling*

No new considerations are required for the theory of zone leveling. According to Fig. 77, as a molten zone traverses an ingot, the concentration returns to its original level after a certain distance, following an initial stretch of lower concentrations. Consequently, this center portion becomes substantially more homogeneous, since the concentration c_0 now exists also in the smallest region. The depleted portion which solidifies first is particularly large when k is much smaller than 1. The region with the increased concentration at the end of the ingot, on the other hand, is only as long as the molten zone itself (see Fig. 77). If it is now desired to distribute the material as uniformly as possible over the whole ingot, i.e. over the initial and final regions, it is allowed to migrate in the reverse direction, i. e. from right to left, in a zone of the same width. The loss of concentration at the left-hand end of the ingot is thus partly compensated once more.

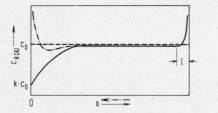

Fig. 77.
Distribution of B after the passage of one molten zone (———) and after a second pass in the opposite direction (-·-··-·-··-). Initial concentration c_0 (-----); $k_B < 1$.

The more often the zone is passed backwards and forwards the more uniform will be the final distribution of the impurity. In this process the molten zone is made as short as possible in relation to the overall length of the ingot. The only inconvenience is the need to reverse the direction of a long boat.

6.2.2 *Continuous Zone Leveling in a Ring*

It is very much more convenient to use a boat in which the substance forms a continuous ingot, so that the molten zones move round in a circle (Fig. 78).

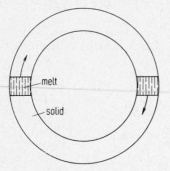

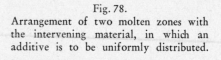

Fig. 78.
Arrangement of two molten zones with the intervening material, in which an additive is to be uniformly distributed.

The continuous cyclic process is used whenever nothing is known about the nature of the impurities to be distributed so that the distribution coefficient cannot be accurately given. However, if k can be determined from the distribution of material between the melt and the crystal, using suitable analytical methods, it will be possible to homogenize a mixture with an average impurity concentration c_0 by a single zone pass. For this purpose, the concentration in the molten zone must be brought from c_0 to c_0/k right at the beginning of the zone leveling. In this way, the conditions for a uniform transfer of the impurity to the crystallizing solid phase are provided from the outset, and it is unnecessary to wait first for the rise in concentration of this impurity (with $k < 1$) in the molten zone. This avoids the transition region with the concentration rising from $k \cdot c_0$ to c_0 which is found at the beginning of a straight ingot.

The distributions of the impurity before and after the zone pass are shown in Fig. 79. The broken line close to c_0 shows only an average value, and does not take into account the maxima and minima which may well occur.

Fig. 79.
Distribution of an impurity before (-----) and after (———) zone leveling with a single zone; $k_B < 1$.

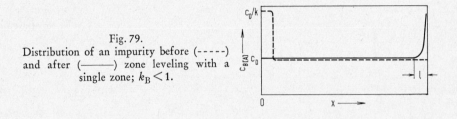

6.2.3 Zone Leveling Using the Pure Components

Suppose that instead of starting with solid solution, as in the two zone-leveling methods described above, and homogenizing this with or without an added impurity, we start with a pure material, again in the form of a rod or ingot, and place the desired additive in the molten zone at the beginning. The resulting concentration distribution will be as shown in Fig. 80. After the substance has been melted and transported as the molten zone through the ingot of pure material, the supply will

Fig. 80.
Distribution of the pure compound before (-----) and after (———) zone leveling with a pure ingot. c_0 = initial concentration of B; $k_B < 1$.

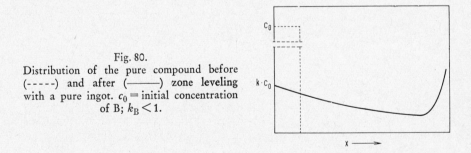

diminish at a rate which will be greater, the greater is the tendency for the additive to separate in preference to the principal substance, i. e. the greater is its distribution coefficient. Similarly, substances with little tendency to separate can be transported along the whole ingot without appreciable loss; however, they are blended with the ingot only to a slight extent.

Compounds with very small k-values (e. g. 0.01) in particular can be very uniformly distributed (i.e. with no sharp concentration gradients), throughout the
ingot. If it is desired to avoid even slight changes in the distribution, the fall in the
concentration in the molten zone is stopped by reducing the length of the zone in
proportion to the distance covered. The additive will then be uniformly distributed
throughout the ingot corresponding to the concentration in the zone at the start of
the zone leveling.

Pfann[2] has proposed formulas to describe the zone leveling starting with two
pure compounds only qualitatively discussed here. He deduced that, after one zone
pass, the concentration in the ingot of an additive is related to the distribution
coefficient k and the initial concentration c_0 by

$$c = k \cdot c_0 \cdot e^{-kx/l} \tag{23}$$

where x is again the distance covered and l the zone length.

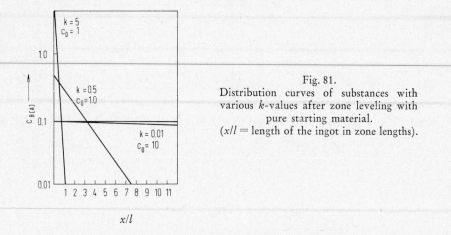

Fig. 81.
Distribution curves of substances with
various k-values after zone leveling with
pure starting material.
(x/l = length of the ingot in zone lengths).

Fig. 81, which was calculated from eq. (23), shows that, even in the case of low
k-values, e. g. 0.01, the concentration decreases towards the end. As has been
mentioned, this decrease can be avoided by reducing the length of the molten zone
or by reducing the cross-section of the ingot. To maintain the concentration at the
value $k \cdot c_0$, the length of the molten zone must be reduced from its initial value l_0 to l

$$l = l_0 - kx \tag{24}$$

or, alternatively, the cross-section must be reduced from q_0 to q

$$q = q_0 \cdot e^{x/G} \tag{25}$$

G is related to k and l by eq. (26):

$$G = \frac{l}{\log_e (1-k)} \tag{26}$$

Eq. (26) can only be applied to ingots of length l_0/k, and (24), (25), and (26) are valid only for $k < 1$.

Another method of zone leveling starting with pure substances is to fuse one component into a ring-shaped ingot as a "plug", through which several zones are allowed to pass. This form of zone leveling has been studied [17] in detail for the

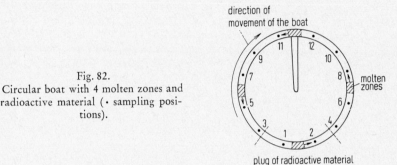

Fig. 82.
Circular boat with 4 molten zones and radioactive material (· sampling positions).

system stearyl alcohol/cetyl alcohol, using zone-refined radioactive cetyl alcohol labeled with ^{14}C as the additive. The process could thus be followed quantitatively by carrying out activity measurements at various points (marked by dots in Fig. 82). The zone-melting apparatus required is described on p. 129.

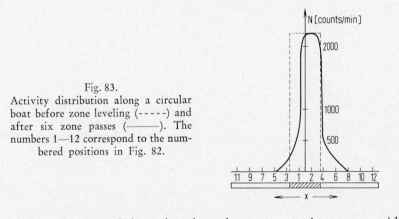

Fig. 83.
Activity distribution along a circular boat before zone leveling (-----) and after six zone passes (———). The numbers 1—12 correspond to the numbered positions in Fig. 82.

It was to be expected that, when the molten zone came into contact with the "active plug", the first portion of cetyl alcohol would be dissolved out of the plug

and would bleed out to the left in the diagram. As the molten zone advances into
the radioactive region, the concentration of the lower melting alcohol rises in the
melt and hence also in the recrystallizing material. However, as soon as pure stearyl
alcohol is melted in at the leading face of the zone again, the dilution of cetyl
alcohol solution will result in a decrease in the radioactivity in the solid phase which
separates out. This behavior is illustrated in Figs. 83 and 84 for a substance with
$k < 1$. The greater is $| 1 - k |$, the farther compounds with $k < 1$ will be carried
along with the zone. The value of k for cetyl alcohol was 0.7. It can be seen from
Fig. 84 that the plug of active material was displaced in the direction of travel of
the zone. The asymmetry of the activity curve (Fig. 83) must also be interpreted in
this sense.

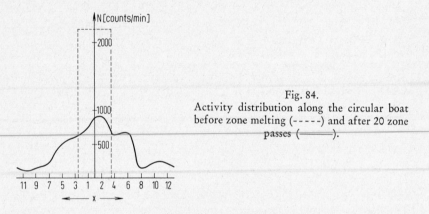

Fig. 84.
Activity distribution along the circular boat
before zone melting (- - - - -) and after 20 zone
passes (————).

The abscissa of Figs. 83 to 85 represents the linear length of the ring-shaped boat.
The boat itself is shown "opened up" below the abscissa of Fig. 83, the shaded area
representing the "active plug". The leveling process steadily progresses as the

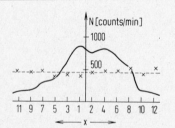

Fig. 85.
Activity distribution along the circular boat after 28
(————) and after 58 zone passes ($\times$); the latter
correspond to complete zone leveling (- - - - -).

number of zone passes increases (see Fig. 84), until finally, after 58 passes, all of
the radioactive alcohol is uniformly distributed in the stearyl alcohol (Fig. 85).

The activity along the boat after complete leveling out of 2200 counts/min was
about 460 counts/min, corresponding to a cetyl alcohol content of about 0.8 wt.-%.

6.3 Zone Separation

As can be seen from the distribution curves in Figs. 83 to 85, it must be possible to separate the components of a mixture by zone alloying the mixture to be separated with a pure substance. As the mixed zone travels through the pure ingot, the compound with the distribution coefficient $k > 1$ should initially remain behind, whilst the substance with $k < 1$ is carried forward (see Fig. 86). Naturally, a quantitative separation cannot be achieved with a single zone pass, since a small quantity of the substance with $k < 1$ also crystallizes out at the beginning. However, the smaller its distribution coefficient, the lower its concentration in the crystallized material, and hence the more successful is the separation.

To achieve further separation, it would be time-consuming to pass the molten zone which has reached the end of the ingot over the same path once more. On the other hand, a large number of molten zones, as used in zone refining, would take up the distributed material again and carry it further towards the end of the ingot,

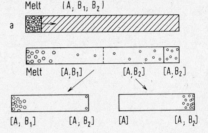

Fig. 86.
Process of distribution when two substances (with $k > 1 = B_1 = \circ$ and with $k < 1 = B_2 = \circ$) are melted into an ingot of pure material.

leaving behind all the components having a greater tendency to separate out; it is then advantageous to divide the ingot into two or three portions and to subject these portions to the normal zone-melting process (see Fig. 86).

Zone separation really differs from conventional zone-melting methods only in the first operation. Instead of an ingot with uniformly distributed impurities, we start with a pure substance and the molten zone, which initially contains all the components. The ultimate distribution after several zone passes is the same in both cases, except that, in zone separation, the substances with $k > 1$ immediately appear at the position which they could normally only reach after the passage of several wide zones.

Another question which arises is whether the mixture should not simply be separated by zone melting, without first adding a third substance; thus two substances whose k values with respect to a third substance differ so much that they lie above or below 1 could also differ greatly between themselves in their melting behavior. Mixtures which are available in sufficiently large quantities will undoubtedly be zone refined as such, but the above more complicated process is in fact more favorable from the point of view of apparatus for the separation of small or very small quantities of material. The length of the molten zone must be chosen to suit the available quantity of the material, and the length of the ingot to suit the composition of the mixture to be separated. The additive is chosen to give a suitable melting point and suitable solvent properties for the components of the mixture. It is also important to ensure that the added components can be easily removed after the separation. In this respect, the process resembles chromatography or, still more closely, extraction.

Another point about zone separation is that the substances must have different melting points, since the distribution of a material in the ingot is governed by the relative position of the melting points of the substance and the ingot.

7. Anomalies in Zone Melting

It has frequently been found in zone-melting experiments [60] that, contrary to the rule, the highest melting point after zone melting was not at the beginning of an ingot (Fig. 87a), but at the end, i. e. in the part which solidified last (Fig. 87b).

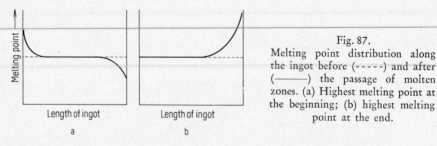

Fig. 87.
Melting point distribution along the ingot before (-----) and after (———) the passage of molten zones. (a) Highest melting point at the beginning; (b) highest melting point at the end.

The external conditions of the experiments in which abnormal behavior was observed were always the same as for those in which normal behavior had been observed. On closer examination, however, characteristic differences could be observed in and at the edge of the molten zone. For example, examination of a mixture of eicosanol and hexacosanol at a low magnification showed visible turbulence (recognizable from the brisk motion of the dust particles which are always present) throughout the molten zone while molten "caterpillar wax" is fairly calm [12], and becomes turbulent only at elevated temperatures. The simplest explanation for this is probably that the "caterpillar wax" must contain less mobile compounds with higher molecular weights, which may also be more highly associated than the smaller alcohol molecules.

This behavior was observed in melting experiments with docosyl behenate and methyl arachate in comparison with a mixture of eicosanol and hexacosanol (1 : 9). It was necessary to supply more heat to the esters than to the alcohol mixture to produce the same movement in the melt, although the melting point of the alcohol mixture was higher, as is shown by the increase in the heating current required and by the increase in the width of the molten zone, with constant cooling. It may therefore be assumed that, owing to the differences in the diffusion behavior in viscous melts, smaller molecules migrate preferentially to the cold phase boundary, where they separate out, even if they have a lower melting point than the higher-molecular weight portion. In other words, even where the melting points are relatively low, small molecules have an advantage over the larger, less mobile molecules in making up concentration deficiencies in the phase-boundary layer. This effect is further intensified by the tendency of long polar molecules to form clusters which are slowly driven forward ahead of the crystal front.

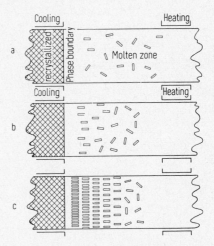

Fig. 88.
Schematic diagram of zone melting. The isolated liquid-crystal regions (a) accumulate in the advancing zone (b), and then pass from the nematic into the smectic state (c).

Such ordered states in melts are spoken of as liquid crystals, and the phenomenon is known as mesomorphism. The states vary according to the temperature. Thus, in considering the solidification process in the molten zone, it is also necessary to take into account the possibility of various pre-orientations. This may be the case, e. g. with natural waxes, which quite frequently contain the ester together with the corresponding alcohol and acid. The melts of these mixtures may initially contain the mesomorphic compound at a concentration high enough only for the formation of a few isolated groups. As the molten zone proceeds along the ingot, however, these steadily increase in number in the liquid phase, until they are finally pressed together. The liquid-crystal microregions may then be packed too closely together, so that they first form double layers, then occupy larger regions, and finally lose their freedom and become frozen in as an immobile "liquid-crystal" layer (cf. Fig. 88).

As a result of preorientation, therefore, compounds with higher melting points may be carried by the zone to the end of the ingot during zone melting. Moreover, the critical concentration at which the mesomorphic compounds form their own lattices may be reached before the end of the ingot; in this case, a short zone in which one substance is accumulated is found in the middle of the ingot, and can be recognized by a maximum in the melting point curve.

7.1   Influence of the Melting Temperature on the Distribution of Material in the Ingot

As was pointed out on p. 38, the concentration distribution in the molten zone differs substantially from that found at static equilibrium between the liquid and solid phases. The impurities may build up at the crystallizing boundary of the zone to a greater or lesser extent, depending on the convection conditions, and the concentration in the crystal will show a corresponding variation. Thus the concentration varies along an irregularly solidified ingot, and the properties (e. g. the melting points) in various sections of the ingot will naturally also differ (cf. Fig. 89).

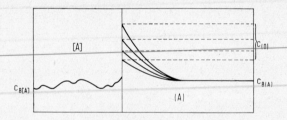

Fig. 89. Concentration curves with various convection conditions in the liquid adjacent to the solid phase.

These changes in the concentration distribution of the solid phase can best be described as a dependence of the effective distribution coefficient on the length of the ingot. It is quite possible for k to vary in the course of a zone pass; poor separation effects are generally balanced out again by subsequent more stable zones, and the separation process is achieved. The situation is different when the limiting distribution is already attained by the passage of several zones, and k approaches unity owing to poorer convection in the zone. A new limiting distribution is then reached and the separation which has already been achieved is cancelled out.

As an illustration, consider attempts to fractionate a mixture containing 20% of eicosanol and 80% hexacosanol by zone melting (cf. also p. 188). These alcohols were introduced into the ring-shaped boat of the apparatus described on p.129 in such a way that neither end of the ingot butted on a boundary. The ingot, which was traversed by a total of 219 zones, could move freely in the boat. The molten zones were not always of the same length (cf. Fig. 90).

The curves of Fig. 90 show a connection between the separation effect (expressed by a concentration difference Δc) and the length L of the ingot. The change in the length of the ingot is probably due to the surface- and boundary-active properties of the mixture. L is proportional to $1/\Delta c$.

The efficiency of the separation also decreases with decreasing length l of the molten zone. Since the molten zone was shortened by reducing the heating current and keeping the cooling unchanged ($-10°C$), the convection in the molten zone also deteriorated

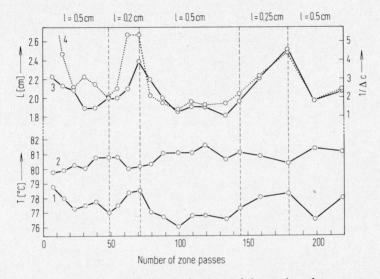

Fig. 90. Zone-melting parameters as functions of the number of zone passes.
Curve 1: lowest melting point observed in ingot.
Curve 2: highest melting point observed in ingot.
Curve 3: length L of ingot.
Curve 4: reciprocal of the separation effect Δc, where Δc is the difference between the highest and the lowest hexacosanol concentrations in the ingot.

appreciably. This explains why the maximum values of $1/\Delta c$ are observed in the region of $l = 0.2$ cm. The maxima are most pronounced when the new, but poorer, final state is reached after several zone passes.

If the rate of travel of the molten zone is comparable with the rate of diffusion, the effective distribution coefficient can change under certain experimental conditions. It is very likely that, at the zone lengths shorter than 5 mm used in this series of experiments, the diffusion distance became larger and an effective distribution coefficient nearer to 1 became active; this would explain the decline in the efficiency of the separation at shorter zone lengths. The fact that the change in the effective distribution coefficient could not be compensated by decreasing the zone length l, and so increasing the ratio L/l, shows the great importance of diffusion in zone melting.

7.2 Transport of Matter

When one or more molten zones are passed through an ingot of material, it is repeatedly observed that e. g. organic compounds migrate as a whole in the direction opposite to that in which the zone travels (cf. Fig. 91). This is due to the wetting behavior of the melt towards the crystals [61].

If the boundaries of a molten zone are examined before and after melting, a small trough can often be observed at the position of the melt on solidification. The material missing from this position accumulates at the two boundaries (cf. Fig. 92b and 92c). As the molten zone advances, the increased level of the material behind

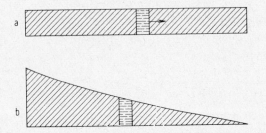

Fig. 91. Distribution of matter (a) before and (b) after the passage of molten zones through an organic charge.

the zone is frozen in, whilst the dam in front of the zone is always melted in again. With the passage of each subsequent zone, fresh material is added to that which has already separated, leading to an increase in the level of the left-hand portion of the ingot. This must be accompanied by a corresponding decrease in the quantity of

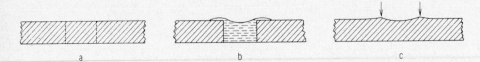

Fig. 92. Distribution of matter (a) before melting, (b) during melting, and (c) after melting in and at the edges of a narrow molten zone.

material in the right-hand portion. The above process can proceed to the stage where one half of the boat is free of the material. In this case, insoluble particles of impurities which are conveyed by the molten zone to the end of the boat frequently accumulate on the bottom (Fig. 93).

Goodman and Bradshaw [62] seek the cause of this behavior in the different densities of the melt and the crystal. These authors derived an equation from which the extent of transport could be calculated. According to this equation, substances which expand on melting must accumulate at the beginning of the ingot, and those which contract on melting at the end. It was found [56], however, that many organic compounds migrated to the end at which the molten zone entered the ingot, irrespective of whether the density of the melt was greater or smaller than that of the crystals.

Fig. 93. Quartz boat showing the distribution of matter (wax) after zone melting.

The behavior predicted by Goodman and Bradshaw has never been observed in the zone melting of ice[63]. In many aqueous solutions, in fact, the opposite effect is observed, i. e. a light but distinct accumulation of ice at the beginning of the charge.

It is therefore much more likely that the transport of matter is due primarily to the interfacial forces of the melt/crystal system (and possibly also the melt/container system), and only to a small extent to the density difference between the liquid and

Fig. 94. (a) Incomplete wetting of a solid by a drop of liquid (contact angle $\vartheta < 90°$).
(b) Molten zone in an ingot; the liquid wets the solid, but does not spread.

the solid phases. The molten zone in a horizontal ingot can be compared e. g. with a liquid in a vessel. If the wetting of the solid phase by the liquid is incomplete, the contact angle $\vartheta < 90°$, and the surface of the liquid is concave (cf. Fig. 94).

If the molten zone now migrates in the direction of the arrows, the crystal is built up layer by layer from the liquid phase at the left-hand boundary, with a volume increase which exactly corresponds to the contraction on melting; consequently the ice ingot will solidify with the same cross-section throughout after the passage of the zone.

If surface-active substances are dissolved in the water, however, the surface tension may be so greatly reduced that the liquid will spread[58]. The aqueous solution will then also cover part of the solid surface adjacent to the molten zone; it will not extend far, however, since this extremely thin film of liquid is frozen by the cooler at a distance of only a few millimeters from the molten zone. In this way, matter can be transported opposite to the direction of travel of the zone, although the liquid may be more dense than the solid.

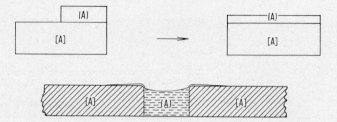

Fig. 95. Advance of a liquid over a solid as a result of spreading.

This transport can be even more easily observed in the case of compounds whose melt is less dense than the adjacent solid, and so lies between the side faces like a small "pillow" with a convex surface, projecting beyond the liquid/solid boundaries (see Fig. 96).

Fig. 96. Molten zone in an ingot with a density higher than that of the melt ($\vartheta < 90°$).

The wetting angle is again $< 90°$, and is a measure of the "overlap of material". As the zone advances, the melt again freezes layer by layer, but this time with a decrease in volume. Owing to the proximity of the cooler, the melt lying on the solid is too viscous to flow back when the zone freezes again; it therefore remains where it is, freezes, and the hot mobile melt from the interior of the zone follows.

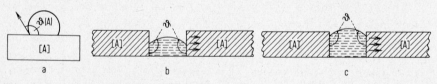

Fig. 97. Molten zones in substances in which the melt does not wet its own solid ($\vartheta < 90°$).
    (a) Phase scheme.
    (b) Density of the melt greater than that of the crystals.
    (c) Density of the melt less than that of the crystals.

Consequently the height of the ingot becomes progressively greater to the left of each successive zone, the effect being more pronounced the greater the tendency of the liquid to spread on the solid. Thus the material migrates opposite to the direction of zone travel when the liquid phase wets the solid, irrespective of whether the volume is increased or decreased on melting.

If the melt does not wet the solid, whether the density of the former is greater or smaller than that of the latter, material is displaced in the same direction as that in which the zone moves (cf. Fig. 97). The contact angle ϑ in this case is $>90°$, measured in the liquid phase. The quantity of material crystallizing at the left-hand crystal boundary is governed by the contact angle and by the density of the melt, i. e. in the last analysis, by the area of contact between the crystal and the melt (cf. Fig. 98).

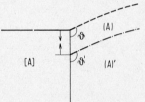

Fig. 98.
Melt (A) in contact with solid [A]. (A)' density of melt greater than that of solid [A]. (A) density of melt less than that of solid [A].

If this melt freezes from one side, e. g. from the left, there is an accumulation of matter in the center of the molten zone which is carried steadily towards the right.

Table 8. Transport of matter for different conditions of wetting between melt and crystal.

Phase scheme	Difference in density	$\vartheta_{(A)[A]}$	$\beta_{(A)[A]}$	$\delta_{(A)[A]}$	Direction of travel of zone	of matter	Final distribution
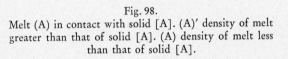 [A] (A)	$d_{(A)} > d_{[A]}$	$< 90°$	< 0	> 0	$\longrightarrow$	none	▭
[A] (A)	$d_{(A)} > d_{[A]}$	≈ 0	< 0	< 0	$\longrightarrow$	$\leftarrow$	▭
[A] (A)	$d_{(A)} > d_{[A]}$	$< 90°$	< 0	> 0	$\longrightarrow$	$\longleftarrow$	▭
[A] (A)	$d_{(A)} > d_{[A]}$	≈ 0	< 0	< 0	$\longrightarrow$	$\longleftarrow$	◁
[A] (A)	$d_{(A)} > d_{[A]}$	> 0	> 0	$> 90°$ $\gg 90°$	$\longrightarrow$	$\longrightarrow$ $\longrightarrow$	◁
[A] (A)	$d_{(A)} > d_{[A]}$	> 0	> 0	$> 90°$ $\gg 90°$	$\longrightarrow$	$\longrightarrow$ $\longrightarrow$	◁

$\vartheta_{(A)[A]}$ = contact angle between melt and crystal
$\beta_{(A)[A]}$ = work of wetting (melt/crystal)
$\delta_{(A)[A]}$ = work of spreading (melt/crystal)

Where the density of the melt is greater than that of the solid, the former (A′) will expand upwards; if on the other hand the melt is less dense (A), it will contract. This is indicated by the two arrows pointing towards one another in Fig. 98. This expansion or contraction in the immediate neighborhood of the interface is more pronounced as the contact angle tends towards 180°.

The influence of the contact angle and the difference in the densities of the melt and of the crystal on the observed and presumed transport of matter is summarized qualitatively in Table 8.

EQUIPMENT

1. General Considerations

The most important requirement for the zone-melting process is a sharply bounded molten zone, which should be as narrow as possible, flanked on both sides by crystalline solid. Such a molten zone is formed if a small part of a rod of crystalline material is melted with the aid of a furnace. However, only as much heat should be supplied as is required to liquefy the zone. It is not easy to confine the molten region within definite limits simply by regulating the temperature of the furnace. Small coolers are therefore fitted in front of and behind the furnace; this is necessary in particular where it is desired to melt several closely-spaced regions of one and the same ingot.

The boat containing the charge is passed through this battery of heaters and coolers with the aid of a motor. Coolers are not required in the case of high-melting metals; one or more heaters can then also be passed over the ingot. In any case, the molten zones travel through the charge in this way.

It has already been explained that the rate of travel of the zone, i.e. the rate of freezing f of the melt, strongly affects the efficiency of the separation. This fact was expressed in the effective distribution coefficient k_{eff}, which lies between the ideal distribution coefficient k_0 and 1, and which can be calculated from the Burton-Prim-Slichter equation if the diffusion coefficient D and the thickness δ of the phase boundary layer are known. The greater f becomes, the more closely k_{eff} tends towards unity, i.e. the less effective will be the separation achieved by zone melting. At low rates of travel, however, the time required becomes very great, particularly when several zones are necessary to achieve the desired effect. Thorough mixing of the melt is therefore ensured by vigorous stirring or by providing strong thermal convection, and in this way, it is possible to increase the rate of travel.

The efficiency of zone-melting processes is thus determined by the following parameters:

k = distribution coefficient
L = length of the ingot
l = length of the molten zone
f = rate of freezing
D = diffusion coefficient of the impurity in the melt
ϑ = thickness of the phase boundary layer in which transport of material takes place only by diffusion.

We are indebted to Pfann for considerations which, together with the conditions indicated, can serve as rules for the construction of zone-melting equipment which will operate economically. However, this does not mean that it is possible, with the aid of these rules, to build a piece of apparatus which will be capable of universal application; it is first necessary to establish the zone-melting problem to which it is to be applied.

We must first consider the desired degree of purity. The equilibrium distribution coefficient k_0 must then be known or determined. Only at this stage can we calculate the effective distribution coefficient k_{eff}, having decided on a definite rate of travel f of the zone. The greater the value of f, the more rapid is the operation; at the same time, however, k becomes less favorable, so that a larger number of zone passes n are required than for a lower value of f. We must therefore strive to keep n/f, i.e. the ratio of the number of zone passes to the rate of travel, as small as possible. This minimum value of n/f is found with the aid of zone-melting calculations (see p. 50). These calculations naturally include all the simplifications involved in the approximate equations, and their practical value is consequently often limited. For manufacturing processes with known starting materials and definite end products, the principal use of such considerations is probably the estimation of the time required.

According to Pfann[56], the time t after which zone melting should be complete is related to the maximum ingot length L_m, the ratio $R = L/l$, the number of passes n, the rate of freezing f, and $R' = i/l$ (the ratio of the interzone distance i to the zone length l), as follows:

$$L_m = \frac{Rft}{R + (n-1)\,(R' + 1)} \tag{27}$$

However, it is not possible to build a new apparatus for each run. It is generally sufficient simply to change the relative settings of the heaters and coolers to suit the substance in question. On the other hand, the dimensions of the apparatus should be such that one unit is only suitable for the zone melting of quantities e.g. between 1 mg and 100 mg, whilst another may only be suitable for quantities between 10 g and 200 g.

1.1 Heat Conduction

This is the principal problem in zone melting. For this reason, theoretical considerations on the temperature gradient in the melt and heating and cooling methods are discussed in some detail.

1.1.1 *The Temperature Gradient*

The magnitude of the temperature gradient depends on the temperature difference, on the distance between the heater and the cooler, and on the thermal conductivity of the substance. The efficiency of the separation is sometimes greatly affected by the temperature difference, since this may cause convection in the melt to increase to the point of turbulence, with the result that pure diffusion processes can be neglected. In this case, the situation is rather complex, and a quantitative theoretical treatment of these processes, similar to that given for pure diffusion, is impossible. A review of this field is given in the monograph "Diffusion" by W. Jost, which includes references to further publications [64].

If the temperature of the heater is increased, whilst that of the cooler and the distance between the heater and the cooler are kept constant, the temperature gradient in the melt becomes steeper and the molten zone becomes wider (cf. Fig. 99).

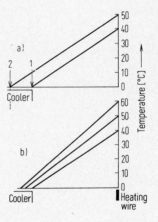

Fig. 99a.
Temperature change in a molten zone from the point of maximum temperature to the point of minimum temperature, i. e. up to the solid/liquid interface, for two cooler position 1 and 2, and for two temperatures (e. g. 40 and 50° C) in the molten zone.

Fig. 99b.
Temperature change with a single cooler position. In this case the length of the molten zone was increased by raising the temperature.

Thus the point at which the first crystals appear moves closer to the end of the cooler, and turbulent flow occurs in a larger region of the melt. This generally favors the separation. At the same time, however, the differentiation of the temperature-dependent crystallization of the various components decreases. The narrower the temperature range over which a component crystallizes, the narrower will be the crystallization zone, but also the more closely will the regions for the various substances be spaced.

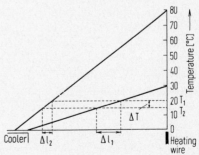

Fig. 100.
Difference in the width and position of the melting range Δl with the same temperature drop ΔT, as a result of differences in the temperature gradients, i. e. in the heating temperatures.

In any case, it is necessary to ensure that the crystals, once they have separated out, do not re-establish equilibrium with the surrounding melt. A steep temperature gradient can only be an advantage in this respect. It can be seen from Figure 100 that the linear distance Δl corresponding to the temperature range ΔT decreases as the temperature gradient in the melt is increased; at the same time, the position at which this temperature range occurs lies closer to the cold end of the molten zone.

On the other hand, the increase in the length of the molten zone which necessarily accompanies a change in the composition of the melt during zone melting can be greatly reduced by the use of a steep temperature gradient (see Fig. 101). As has already been explained, compounds which lower the freezing point of the mixture

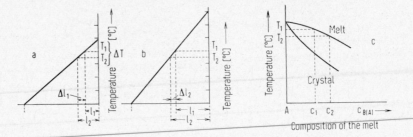

Fig. 101. Increase in the length of the molten zone, shown schematically for a smaller (a) and greater (b) temperature gradient in the melt. Note the difference between Δl_1 and Δl_2. (c) The difference between the freezing points at both ends of the ingot assumed for the increase in length in Fig. 101 a and b can be explained from the equilibrium diagram of the substance A which is to be purified and the impurity B which it contains, if the concentration of the latter is first c_1, and then becomes c_2.

accumulate in the molten zone as it traverses the ingot. If ΔT is the difference between the freezing points T_1 and T_2 of the melt at the beginning and at the end of the ingot, the increase in the length of the molten zone will be Δl_1 for small temperature gradients and Δl_2 for large gradients. Although this widening of the molten zone is convenient as the first indication of an effective purification, it is undesirable in directed zone melting, as it brings with it very complex effects.

The heating temperature cannot be chosen as high as is desired in order to obtain the greatest possible temperature gradient and strong convection, since the substance may decompose at higher temperatures. It is better to keep the cooling temperature as low as possible; this generally also shortens the molten zone and so reduces the diffusion path.

The diffusion conditions can be further improved in favor of a more effective separation by the use of low rates of travel; for organic compounds, however, the required rates may be inconveniently low (frequently between 1 and 2 mm/h).

The concentration changes steadily in the two phase boundaries and gradually assumes a constant value in the middle portion of the molten zone. In the case of low-viscosity melts, e.g. metals, convection begins at a temperature only slightly above the melting point. Owing to the temperature gradient, however, the convection zone does not extend right to the phase boundary, but is separated from the latter by a more or less wide diffusion zone. In many cases, there is no convection at all, so that the width of the diffusion zone is equal to the zone length. In this case, the rate of equilibration of concentration again varies from one section of the molten zone to another, since the diffusion coefficient depends on the temperature and the concentration. Diffusion is least at the phase boundaries and increases with temperature to assume a maximum value in the middle.

Fig. 102 shows the assumed concentration distribution along the ingot for a rate of travel which guarantees adequate equilibration of concentration by diffusion. It is assumed that the zone has reached the region where the starting material and the crystallizate have

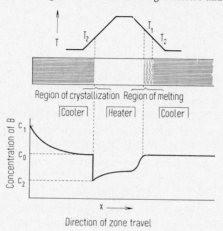

Fig. 102. Molten zone in an ingot of a mixture A, B corresponding to Fig. 103, with the temperature distribution in the zone and the distribution of B in the recrystallized material and in the zone.

the same composition (see p. 46). The fall in concentration may be assumed to be linear in the region of the melt where the temperature is highest. Diffusion is inhibited close to the phase boundaries, i.e. in the low-temperature regions.

So far, the only part of the molten zone which has been considered as decisively affecting the separation is the crystallization zone. To complete the picture however, it is necessary to consider also the melting zone (see Fig. 102).

Crystals begin to melt beyond the point T_2, first a few and then in increasing quantities, until finally, at T_1, we have a completely clear melt. Thus, between T_2 and T_1 the quantity and composition of the steadily disappearing crystals change from c_0 to c_1, as can be seen from the equilibrium diagram (Fig. 103) for a pair of substances A and B.

According to the microscopic observations made by Vetter [12] on melting films of mixed crystals, it may be assumed that diffusion in the molten zone is negligible between T_1 and T_2. Melting begins with a slow disintegration of the crystal structure, the melt remaining trapped in the spaces between the remaining crystals; only at higher temperatures does the liquid form a continuous film in which the last remaining crystals are distributed separately. Thus local equilibria, which change continuously following the rise in temperature, arise along T_1–T_2. Only in the neighborhood of T_1 do the crystals begin to crumble away, and an exchange of matter with the clear molten zone becomes possible by diffusion. The composition of the clear molten zone close to the region in which melting is taking place is then c_0, since the solid is quantitatively incorporated into the melt. The change in the concentration of the melt as a result of exchange of matter with the region lying in front

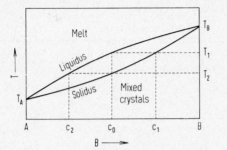

Fig. 103.
Equilibrium diagram of two substances, A and B, which form a complete series of mixed crystals.

of the molten zone is only negligible since the length of the molten zone is large in comparison with the length of the zone in which such an exchange can occur.

The most important requirement in the design of zone-melting equipment is therefore to make the coolers and heaters as adaptable as possible. It is often necessary first to find the optimum conditions for a given mixture. For example, if no cooling is provided in working with high-melting substances, stirring is necessary under certain conditions to ensure thorough mixing. However, it is generally impossible to use more than one or two zone stirrers in one ingot, so that the great advantage of zone melting, i. e. the possibility of passing many zones along the ingot at the same time, is again lost. Another suggestion, proposed by Pfann, was to mix the melt by pumping.

2. Heating

2.1 Electrical Resistance Heating

Electric furnaces which can be easily made by the operator himself are readily controlled. The required resistance wire is available in all diameters; it can be shaped to suit the container, or made into a circular heating element (cf. Fig. 104).

The heating current can be varied continuously to give a wide range of temperatures, by the application of various voltages tapped off directly from a variable transformer and possibly reduced still further by a voltage divider circuit. Each heater should be individually adjustable to allow control of the zone length at any time. The heaters are therefore connected in parallel, and each is fitted with a potentiometer. To avoid excessively high currents, however, it is better to connect, for example, four heaters in series. In the case of multistage units with heaters connected in series, it must be possible to use at least one heater alone. Electric heaters are very versatile as regards shapes and arrangements.

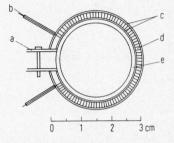

Fig. 104.
Cross-section of a 30 W circular heater fitted around a glass tube. a = Fastener; b = current supply; c = ring made from a copper strip; d = resistance wire; e = glass tube through which the zone-melting boat slides.

In many cases, simple electric resistance heating will be found to be quite adequate and suitable for the purpose in question. It has the disadvantage however, that the wall of the container is often so strongly overheated in the middle of the heated zone that the substance decomposes or becomes contaminated with material from the container. Plastic boats readily lose plasticizers, polymerization accelerators, or stabilizers. There is little danger of undesirable side-effects of this type in the case of narrow zones, but the risk increases with increasing current.

Bohl and Christy[65] have suggested a melting method for the purification of silver bromide, which combines the advantages of continuous zone melting in a ring with those of a long straight ingot. The sample of silver bromide is melted into an

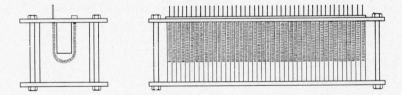

Fig. 105. Heating battery in an apparatus for the zone refining of silver bromide (Bohl and Christy[65]). Each heater consists of a coil bent into the form of a U.

evacuated glass tube and placed in a furnace containing a succession of closely spaced loops of resistance wire. A molten zone is passed slowly along the ingot by supplying current to each of the loops of wire in turn with the aid of a ring switch, each loop of wire being connected to one contact of the ring switch. To pass two molten zones through the ingot simultaneously, current is supplied to two diametrically opposite contacts.

The unit shown in Fig. 105 contains 44 heating coils, each bent into a U-shape (19×31 mm), situated at intervals of 3.1 mm. Each heater was made by winding enough 0.5 mm chrome steel wire on a drill shank 1.5 mm in diameter to give a resistance of 4.5 to 4.2 ohms. The heaters were insulated from one another by plates of mica.

2.2 Thermostat Heating

If it is desired to use the same heater to produce very narrow zones as well as wide zones, it is better to use thermostat heating instead of resistance heating. The current-carrying heater wire is then replaced by heated metal plates or wires. These metal plates can be easily fitted to the container for the ingot, can be arranged side by side as often as desired, and can then be brought into close contact with one another to form narrow or wide heaters. However, a heat thermostat is also required, and if running water no longer gives adequate cooling, a cold thermostat as well. The cost is repaid by the fact that, once the correct temperature has been reached, it can be maintained and controlled over long periods. Thus the same structural units are used for heating and cooling in this case; naturally this is not possible with resistance heating.

Versatile units can be very easily contructed with metal tubes, lead tubes being preferred because of their ease of bending and their resistance to acids. The coolers consist of groups of two or three loops, each group being separated from its neighbors by a single winding of another metal tube, through which hot liquid or hot air is passed. The length of the molten zone is then slightly greater than the diameter of the heating tube. Further improvement can be achieved by painting the cooling tubes black and fitting the heating tubes with reflectors.

2.3 Radiation Heating

Handley and Herington [66] have proposed an original, if costly, solution to the heating problem by the use of infrared heating. The light from the incandescent filament of a 100 W projector lamp is focussed, with the aid of parabolic and spherical concave mirrors, on the central axis of a blackened tube, 100 to 150 mm long, fitted with an infrared filter glass window. The authors later [67] simplified the apparatus by replacing the combination of mirrors by a single ellipsoidal reflector. The lamp was placed at the focal point nearer the mirror, and the sample at the other. No provision was made for cooling. In spite of this simplification, the apparatus has the disadvantage that only a single molten zone can be used.

Radiation energy was also used by Nicollian, Weisberg, and Gunther-Mohr [68] to melt germanium. Tuddenham [69] has even used a conventional solar furnace [70] for the zone melting of copper and high-melting oxides.

Mullin and Hulme [71] produced the molten zone with a "Kanthal heater". To permit an increase in the rate of travel in the case of metals with low melting points (e. g. indium, m. p. 156° C), which consequently often give viscous melts, these authors used electromagnetic agitation, in which the melt was made to rotate by an electromagnetic field. This field was produced by an oil-cooled stator of a three-phase induction motor supplied with 400 c/s a-c. The axis of rotation of the 300 gauss magnetic field was the longitudinal axis of the ingot. The decrease in the thickness of the phase boundary layer resulting from the electromagnetic mixing led to the same zone melting effect at a rate of travel of 20 cm/h as was otherwise possible only at a rate of travel of 5 cm/h.

Still shorter zones can be achieved by the application of Pfann's principle of temperature-gradient zone melting [72], in which a temperature gradient is simply

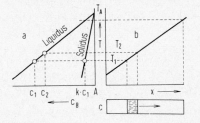

Fig. 106. (a) Part of an equilibrium diagram for two substances A and B. (b) Temperature gradient along a length x of an ingot. (c) Ingot with molten zone.

imposed along the ingot. For example, according to Pfann, it is possible to pass a narrow Al-Si zone through a silicon rod if a thin disk of aluminum is inserted into the ingot of silicon and two different temperatures are imposed at the ends of the ingot. The substance B (Al) should lower the melting point of A (Si), and the two should be miscible in both the solid and the liquid states. (cf. Fig. 106).

We next assume that a thin disk of B is sandwiched between two portions of an ingot of A. A temperature gradient is then set up in the ingot, and sufficient heat is supplied to the layer of B to raise its temperature above the lowest melting point of the mixed system. A will then dissolve in B until a wider zone is formed, with a concentration c_1 at its cooler end corresponding to the saturation concentration of A at T_1. At the warmer interface, A continues to dissolve until the melt is also saturated with A at this point. In this way, a concentration gradient is set up, and A diffuses from the hot interface to the cold, where it separates out.

Braun, Frank, and Marshall [73] also used a rotating magnetic field to supplement thermal convection in the zone refining of aluminum. The ingot was 44 cm long and 9.4 mm in diameter, and was placed in an alumina boat lined with fused aluminum oxide. Three water-cooled copper coils at an angle of 120° to one another were fitted around the furnace. These were supplied with three phases of a 50 c/s current in such a way that each coil produced the same magnetic field at the peak voltage. The resulting field of about 100 oersted was sufficient to cause visible convection in mercury. In zone melting, the axis of rotation of the field was perpendicular to the axis of the ingot, to ensure good convection at the phase boundary.

In the cases described, the hydrodynamic flow has been produced indirectly by induced electric currents; however, it is also possible to connect the ingot as a conductor in an electrical circuit, and to place one bar magnet vertically above and

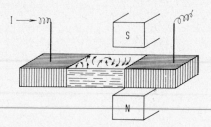

Fig. 107. Arrangement for electromagnetic agitation of a molten zone [74].

another vertically below the phase boundary, as shown in Fig. 107. It is assumed that the magnetic field decreases along the normal from the phase boundary into the molten zone, with the result that the convection shown in the illustration is produced. The greater the current in the ingot and the greater the magnetic field gradient in the zone, the more vigorous is the stirring effect.

2.4 Heating by an Arc Discharge

Heating by an arc discharge is particularly recommended for high-melting materials. The required high temperatures are produced with the aid of an electric arc burning in argon. One of the electrodes is made of graphite, tungsten, or the same material as the ingot. The second electrode is the ingot itself (see Fig. 108).

The ingot is placed in a boat or directly into a channel of a copper vessel through which flows a cooling agent, and passes at a distance of 1.5 to 1.4 mm below the tungsten electrode at a speed of 0.35 to 125 mm/h. The arc is produced with a few kilovolts d-c. The argon pressure in the closed system is usually less than one atmosphere ($^1/_3$ to 1 atm). Movement of the arc can be prevented by increasing the argon pressure or by imposing a magnetic field of 2000 gauss.

In 1956 Burch[75], and Burch and Young[76] used a method similar to that described by Geach and Jones[77] to carry out zone melting of thorium/zirconium alloys (0.1 to 1.0% of Zr) and thorium/uranium mixtures (3 and 16 wt.-% of U) with a travel rate of 125 mm/h.

Cabane[78] used an electric arc in argon at $^1/_3$ atm for the zone melting of uranium, zirconium, vanadium, and thorium. In this work, the copper trough and the tungsten electrode (which was also water-cooled) were placed in a closed tubular steel container. The externally mounted motor moved a water-cooled copper pipe on which the trough

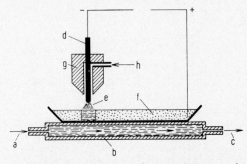

Fig. 108. Heating by a flame arc. *a* Water inlet for a cooled copper boat *b*; *c* water outlet; *d* tungsten electrode; *e* flame arc; *f* ingot; *g* cooled holder for electrode; *h* argon inlet.

carrying the ingot was placed. The ingot was preceded by a sample of zirconium metal or a titanium-zirconium alloy (30×5×400 mm) to facilitate ignition of the arc. The molten zones produced were 20 to 30 mm long and 30 mm wide.

Gerthsen[79] has attempted the zone melting of high-melting oxides with the aid of an arc discharge. The ingot was used as an electrode for two arcs, i. e. as the anode for one and the cathode for the other. This arrangement made use of the appreciable conductivity of the melt. It can be used with air and other gases, oxygen being preferred in the case of oxides having a high oxygen partial pressure. To ensure a radially symmetric molten zone, the two ends of the ingot are rotated synchronously and in the same direction at a maximum speed of two revolutions per second. It should be noted that in this process, the power supplied to the molten zone at relatively low current intensities (3 to 4 a) is about 150 W; this is sufficient for the zone melting of ingots 6 to 7 mm in diameter, made of a material with a melting point of about 2000° C.

A further improvement in the reproducibility of the conditions is achieved by the use of a "wall-stabilized" discharge, which is produced in a cooled nozzle with an internal diameter of about 4 mm. It is ignited by short-circuiting the electrodes with the ingot and then lifting them off. This contact ignition is still possible up to specific resistances of about 10^4 ohm.cm at a voltage of 200 V. In the case of substances with extremely high resistances, the arc is first ignited between the opposite electrodes and the ingot is thus preheated by the positive column of the discharge, so that a liquid, satisfactorily conducting zone is formed. The double arc is then struck by contact ignition, as described above.

2.5   Heating by Electron Bombardment

In analogy with the work of Geach and Summers-Smith[80] and of England and Jones[81], the ingot is again melted in a copper trough, but in this case it is heated by bombardment with highly accelerated electrons[82]. It is important in this process to maintain a very good vacuum. A monocrystalline ingot is more easily obtained by this method than by the use of an arc discharge.

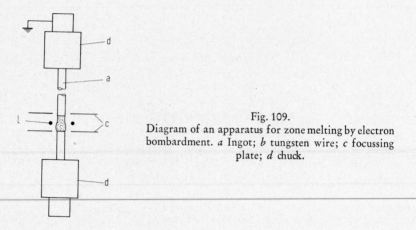

Fig. 109.
Diagram of an apparatus for zone melting by electron bombardment. *a* Ingot; *b* tungsten wire; *c* focussing plate; *d* chuck.

Similarly to the arc discharge method, the electron bombardment method is suitable for the zone refining of high-melting substances (e. g. rhenium which melts at 3160° C) owing to the local concentration of heat. According to Keck and Golay[83], this method can also be used without a container, as has been shown by Calverley, Davis, and Lever[84, 85]. The electrons emitted by a strongly heated tungsten wire (cf. Figs. 109 and 110) are accelerated towards the ingot (as the

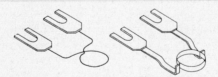

Fig. 110. Tungsten wire (0.03 mm) and plate (2 mm × 0.03 to 0.06 mm) for the cathode in zone melting by electron bombardment[85].

anode) by a potential difference of several kilovolts, and are focussed by a circular shield at or below the cathode potential. The energy consumed in this process, with a maximum current of 300 mA at 5 kV, is relatively small, as has been reported by Carlson[86]. The electric circuit of the furnace used by this author is shown in Fig. 111.

There is always a danger, when electron furnaces are used, of contamination of the charge with tungsten. This can be avoided in part by suitable positioning of the wire with respect to the ingot, and by the use of low wire temperatures and high

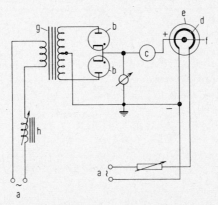

Fig. 111. Circuit diagram of the electric power supply of an electron heating furnace for zone melting. *a* 110 volt a—c supply; *b* Valvo DCG 4/1000 G; *c* ammeter (0—300 mA); *d* wire; *e* concentrator; *f* sample; *g* high-voltage transformer; *h* choke.

accelerating potentials. Where possible, the emitting wire is best made from the material to be purified. The samples to be purified need only have a low conductivity, and even aluminum oxide can be zone refined by electron bombardment if its surface conductivity is increased by marking it with graphite.

Geach and Jones[87] reported that, in zone melting with highly accelerated electrons, loss by evaporation becomes excessive at travel rates of less than 1 mm/min (the vapor pressure of metals at their melting points is generally $\approx 10^{-3}$ mm Hg). On the other hand, in zone melting under the high vacuum of 10^{-4} to 10^{-5} mm Hg required for electron bombardment, the zone purification may be accompanied by a (frequently higher) purification by vaporization. However, this effect can only be utilized when the output of the pump unit (rotary pump + diffusion pump) is such that the gas liberated does not affect the vacuum. For a 10 l vacuum tank and a zone length of 6 mm, the average rate of pumping must be 20 to 30 l/sec. This figure is no longer applicable in the case of highly volatile materials, and the emission current also changes in this case. According to Allenden[87], electron bombardment of the escaping gases gives rise to ions, which in turn bombard the wire thus raising its temperature. However, this results in an increase in the rate of electron emission, so that the whole process readily speeds up and gets out of control.

Allenden gives two methods of stabilization. Where the sample of high-melting material is very small in diameter, the ratio of the wire diameter to the diameter of the sample should be as small as possible, e. g. less than 3.1 for a potential of 4 kV. Geach and Jones used a 19 mm coil of tungsten wire having a diameter of

0.5 mm, and the applied potential with respect to the sample was − 4 kV. The potential of the molybdenum focussing screen was the same. The samples were mounted in a water-cooled support which could be moved at a speed of 0.3 to 13 mm/min with respect to the heating coil.

2.6 Induction Heating

The heating method generally used in the zone melting of metals is high-frequency induction heating, with the aid of which high temperatures can be readily achieved. A suitable arrangement is shown in Fig. 112. In the illustration, the molten zone

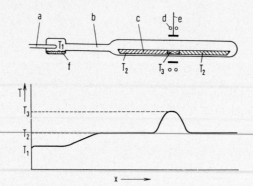

Fig. 112. Zone-melting equipment with inductively heated circular radiator. The lower diagram shows the temperature distribution. *a* Thermocouple; *b* quartz tube; *c* ingot; *d* induction coil; *e* circular radiator; *f* sample of material.

produced by an inductively heated circular radiator has moved along to the middle of the ingot. The ingot is fixed in a quartz tube, whilst the induction coils move together with the circular radiator.

In the zone melting of compounds which dissociate, it is necessary to maintain a certain vapor pressure in the closed quartz vessel; this is achieved by the use of a sample maintained at a certain temperature.

Indirect induction heating could naturally also be used for organic compounds. It would be necessary to melt the substance into a metal or graphite boat and to heat sharply delineated zones of the container with the aid of induction coils carrying a current of suitable frequency. The induction coil generally consists of copper tubing (Fig. 113) through which cold water is passed to remove the heat generated in the coil itself.

Zone-melting arrangements of this type are expensive to operate. Six induction coils in series require a 10 kW high-frequency generator (450 kc/s)[88]; the more closely the induction coils encircle the ingot, the more efficient is the generator[89].

Tuning of the generator to the material of the charge, which is already difficult, then becomes even more critical. However, Buehler[90] has found a satisfactory solution for the zone melting of silicon.

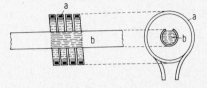

Fig. 113. Arrangement for zone melting with induction heating.
a Induction coil (water-cooled copper tube); *b* substance in a metal or graphite boat.

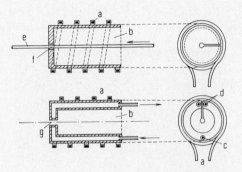

Fig. 114. Arrangement for the zone melting of narrow zones with induction heating.
Above: without cooling; below: with cooling.
a Induction coil; *b* concentrator; *c* inlet; *d* outlet for cooling liquid; *e* boat; *f* molten zone.

A concentrator consisting of a simple copper cylinder (Fig. 114) could be used for narrow molten zones, and this would also serve as an effective cooler if it were hollow and supplied with a cooling liquid (Fig. 114b).

It may be even better if the cooler is independent and the induction coil is fitted at a distance from the boat, as shown in Fig. 115.

Analogously to the arrangements described, it should be possible to heat organic materials in alternating elecric fields instead of magnetic fields. Experiments have shown[91], however, that even for small quantities of material, a 1000 W generator is required for the high-frequency capacitance heating. Weaker generators, e. g. a 100 W generator (21 000 c/s), cannot be used, especially if the field is to be produced between two metal coolers. Considerably better results were obtained in preliminary experiments with a microwave generator. Dielectric heating with microwaves would be particularly advantageous for the zone melting of ice, since it would avoid any unnecessary heating of the cold space. It would be attractive at this point to use stationary waves.

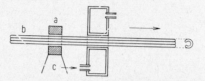

Fig. 115. Longitudinal section of a cooled zone-melting arrangement.
a Inductor; *b* metal or graphite boat; *c* cooling water.

Metals can also be inductively melted directly without a heating ring. An arrangement of this type was used by the Centre d'Étude de Chimie Métallurgique de Vitry — C.N.R.S. for the zone melting of iron in a calcium oxide boat[92]. In

Fig. 116. Zone melting of iron without a container.
(The photograph was kindly supplied by the Centre d'Étude de Chimie Métallurgique de Vitry — C.N.R.S.).

this arrangement, the quartz tube containing the boat is mounted on a trolley, which is drawn through the two water-cooled induction coils.

Iron can also be zone melted without a container (see Fig. 116), by drawing the charge through the coil, which is wound round a quartz tube. This elegant method of zone melting without a container (see p. 103) can also be used for copper, if

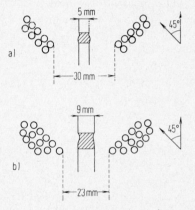

Fig. 117. Arrangement of the conical induction coils in the zone melting of copper rods 5 and 9 mm in diameter.

a) Two "induction funnels".
b) Three "induction funnels"; electrical supply from a 12 kW generator (350 kc/s), according to Le Hericy [93].

instead of one coil, several are used in the form of a cone. The object of this arrangement is to support the surface tension, which is too low in the case of dense melts, by the induced opposing force, i. e. to raise the melt. The optimum angle of the cone was found by Le Hericy [93] to be 45° (cf. Fig. 117).

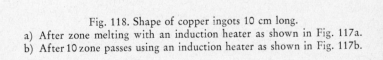

Fig. 118. Shape of copper ingots 10 cm long.
a) After zone melting with an induction heater as shown in Fig. 117a.
b) After 10 zone passes using an induction heater as shown in Fig. 117b.

The "induction funnels" are fixed, and the ingot again moves vertically downwards, in a sealed Pyrex glass tube filled with extremely pure argon. In the case of a
copper rod 9 mm in diameter, it is necessary to reduce the diameter at the neck of
the "induction funnel" and to use more windings; this can be clearly seen from
Fig. 118, which shows the outline of a copper ingot 10 cm long after interrupted
zone melting under the conditions of Fig. 117a, and after the passage of 10 zones
under the conditions of Fig. 117b.

As early as 1957, Mataré[94] used the force associated with induction heating to
stabilize a molten zone in silicon bars. To make this force act against gravity,
another conical coil, which was electromagnetically tuned only to the molten zone

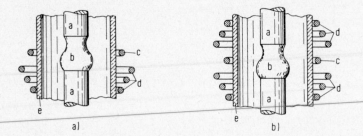

Fig. 119. Mataré's arrangement of induction coils[94] for zone melting without a container,
(left) with one heating coil *c* and one stabilizing coil *d*, and (right) with one heating coil
and two stabilizing coils; *a* ingot; *b* pear-shaped molten zone; *e* quartz-glass cylinder.

at a low frequency (500 kc/s), was used in addition to the induction coil melting
the charge. A third induction coil, of the same shape and the same frequency as the
second, permits an increase in the diameter of the rod, which is normally limited to
1 to 2.5 cm. Fig. 119 shows the relative positions of the induction heaters. The bases
of the stabilizing coils, which are shaped like truncated cones, are coplanar with the
upper and lower interfaces of the zone.

Wernick, Dorsi, and Byrnes[95] have obtained stable zones, with optimum energy
utilization, by suitable arrangement of the induction coils. The coils used for nickel,

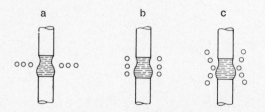
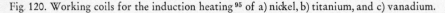

Fig. 120. Working coils for the induction heating[95] of a) nickel, b) titanium, and c) vanadium.

titanium, and vanadium (cf. Fig. 120) were made from a 5 mm copper tube. Buehler[96] has used a similar shape of coil for the zone melting of molybdenum, tungsten, and niobium without a container.

3. Cooling

Coolers are unnecessary in the case of high-melting substances or in the growing of single crystals by zone melting, since in this case uniform crystal growth occurs only with a gentle temperature gradient in the solid phase. In single crystal growth, the ingot is sometimes even protected by a jacket to prevent excessively fast cooling; alternatively, gentle after-heating may be applied.

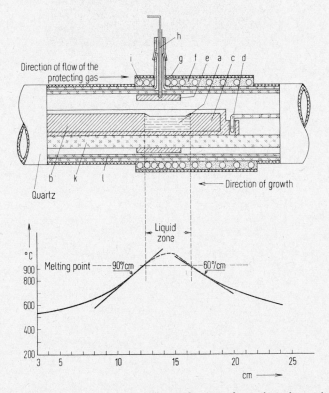

Fig. 121. Zone-melting arrangement for the purification of metals and growing of single crystals. Below: temperature distribution in the solid ingot and in the molten zone. An inductively heated graphite ring is used as the heater.
a Melt; *b* polycrystalline ingot; *c* nucleus (single crystal); *d* quartz glass holder; *e* graphite ring; *f* quartz wool; *g* asbestos; *h* thermocouple; *i* water-cooled copper coil (6 mm in diameter); *k* quartz slide bar; *l* protective tube.

For example, Figs. 121 and 122 show a zone-melting arrangement as used by Messrs. Standard Elektrik Lorenz AG, Bauelementewerk SAF, Nürnberg, for the melting of germanium. A nitrogen current is used for cooling and as a protective atmosphere; it is blown in through nozzles in a collar.

Fig. 122. Apparatus for the zone melting of germanium (Standard Elektrik Lorenz AG, Bauelementewerk SAF, Nuremberg).

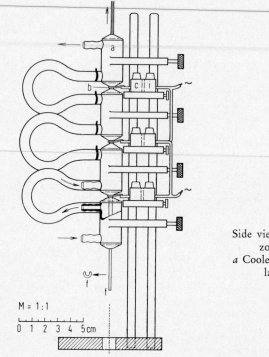

Fig. 123.
Side view of the three-stage micro zone-melting apparatus.
a Cooler; *b* heating coils; *c* porcelain insulator; *f* boat.

M = 1:1

0 1 2 3 4 5 cm

This type of cooling is still used in other zone melting units. However, the cold zone is not very accurately delineated. But this is unnecessary in melting large ingots of raw material.

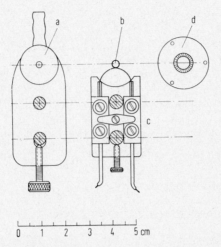

Fig. 123 a. Top view of a cooling and heating element of the microzone-melting apparatus, *a* Cooler; *b* heating coil; *c* porcelain insulator; *d* holder for boat.

Since cooling generally increases the efficiency of the separation at a relatively small cost in apparatus, coolers are usually fitted in front of and behind a single heating zone, or between zones where several are used.

Liebig condensers, which can be made in various sizes from glass, are very simple in their construction. Metal Liebig condensers are used in the zone-melting micro-apparatus described by Hesse and Schildknecht[97] (cf. Fig. 123). Both the condensers and the heating coils are arranged so that they can be moved along a supporting bar, so that the length of the molten zone can be controlled not only by heating and cooling but also by the distance between the condenser and the heater.

Modified Liebig condensers connected together by flexible hoses were also used for the zone-melting apparatus described on p. 98. The distance between these condensers can again be varied. However, Liebig condensers have the disadvantages that they are too long for time-saving operation, and that the connecting hoses are subject to deterioration, particularly as a result of operation below room temperature.

Fig. 124b shows 10 units for 15 g charges and one unit for 100 g charges. These are mounted on a wall, and have a common safety switch which disconnects the current supply if the cooling water is cut off.

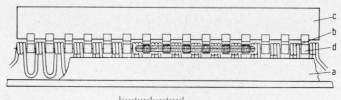

Fig. 124 (a). Diagram of a multistage zone-melting apparatus described by Schildknecht
and Hopf [98].
a Fixing rail for coolers *b; c* fixing rail for heaters *d*.

A cooler made of lead tubing with the windings arranged in groups of up to three
appears to be more advantageous (see Fig. 124a). The cooler is held in position by
metal strips, and the heaters are fitted between the groups of windings on a sheet of
eternite. Using this cooler, it is obviously also possible to operate below room
temperature using brine; the entire zone-melting apparatus must then be efficiently
insulated.

Frigen (F 22) is used directly for temperatures down to $-70°$ C; this is passed
from a refrigerator through ring-shaped cooling segments (Fig. 125). In multistage

Fig. 124 (b). Ten zone-melting units for 15 g samples and one unit for 100 g samples
(installed in the Organisch-Chemisches Institut, Universität Heidelberg).
This apparatus is now available commercially from Messrs. Desaga, Heidelberg (Germany).
Photograph by G. Klose.

units, the cooling elements are divided into at least two groups to ensure that the parts of the cooler nearer to the refrigerator are not colder than the other parts.

For freezing temperatures below $-70°$ C, the cooling is best carried out with cooled air. Liquid air has so far been used only for the normal freezing of methylene chloride, chloroform, and carbon tetrachloride. Cooling brine can also be used in this method, which is used to purify solvents and to concentrate compounds

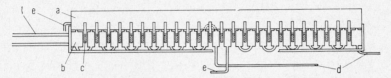

Fig. 125. Diagram of a multistage ice zone-melting apparatus without thermal insulation[98]. *a* Fixing rail; *b* cooler; *c* heaters; *d* inlet and evaporation tubes for Frigen F 22; *e* return tube; *f* freezing channel.

dissolved in them. Röck[99] employed this method to freeze benzene for zone refining, and Ball, Helm, and Ferrin[100] have purified 3-methyl-pyridine by freezing.

4. The Container

No difficulties are encountered in moving a solid rod through coolers and furnaces. It is only when the substance melts that the rod loses its strength, even when, in the case of short zones, the melt adheres to the solid phase and cannot flow away. For this reason, it is customary to use a container of some kind. The only requirement is that the substance must not be contaminated by the material of the container during the melting process, as was found to occur with copper in a graphite boat.

Zone melting of higher-melting crystals can be carried out in boats made of quartz or oxides such as lime and alumina. The surface of the container is often treated to reduce wettability and to increase its life. Glass is the best container material for low-melting substances. Even at low temperatures, synthetic materials tend to give up their plasticizers or other additives, and readily contaminate the substance; the only synthetic which has been found satisfactory is unplasticized silicone rubber, and in fact this material is essential when the zone melting is to be carried out in sealed tubes. The thermal conductivity of metal is too high, so that even small variations in the heater temperature cause relatively large changes in the length of the molten zone. Besides glass, quartz[60] is also very suitable for containers of various shapes.

For substances with low vapor pressures, such as waxes, it is possible to use open boats, and this also permits easy observation of the separation during the melting (Fig. 126). Micro-boats can be made from thick-walled glass tubing.

A length of tubing sealed at one end is heated from one side with a fine flame until the glass begins to soften and the point which was heated most strongly is almost liquid. Air is then sucked out the open end of the tube until a portion about 1 cm long has collapsed, and the tube is immediately drawn out to give a very narrow glass channel (Fig. 127).

Fig. 126. Zone-melting boat 15 cm long, filled with wax.

The dry substance is pressed into the channel with a spatula and fused over a hot-plate. It is important that the substance should be placed a number of centimeters from the ends of the boat, since it changes its position in the boat as a result of the transport of material.

Fig. 127. Glass micro-boat (diameter 1 mm) with glass rod and hook.

However, it is better, even in micro-zone melting, to use sealed tubes. Alternatively, the boat may simply be surrounded by a glass sheath (see Fig. 128).

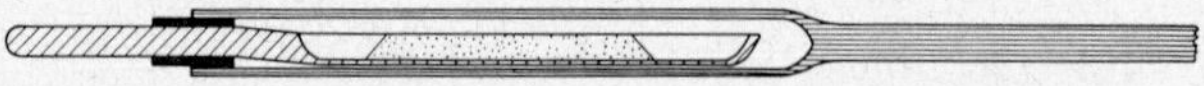

Fig. 128. Microzone-melting boat inserted into a glass tube.

Many substances tend to overflow at the ends and sides of open glass boats. This difficulty can be avoided by melting the substance close to the forward end of the sealed glass tube with a suitable silicone rubber stopper in front of the charge[156] (see Fig. 129). This stopper prevents gas bubbles from entering the molten zone at

Fig. 129. Sealed microzone-melting tube.
a Pull-rod; *b* silicone plug; *c* tube for sample; *d* sample.

the forward end, and also prevents the loss of volatile substances by sublimation; at the same time, since it can move inside the tube, it ensures equalization of pressure on melting, so that the tube does not explode during zone melting.

Fig. 130 shows an open ring-shaped container for zone melting or zone leveling in a ring.

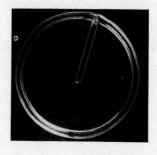

Fig. 130.
Circular glass boat for ring-zone
melting equipment [60]
(Ring diameter 70 mm;
channel diameter 4 mm).

4.1 Zone Melting Without a Container

In a method which is used above all to prepare extremely pure substances, it is obviously necessary to make sure that the removed impurities are not replaced by other contaminants, e. g. from the container. Many methods have therefore been proposed for zone melting without a container. As early as 1953, Keck and Golay [83] made use of the fact that a molten zone between two vertical rods is held in place by interfacial tensions, and that the molten zone ("floating liquid zone") is suspended between the fixed ends of the rod. In this work, the heat was transferred by an incandescent tantalum cylinder, e. g. for a round silicon rod. The moving zone remained stable even when the ingot was drawn through this cylinder.

The stability of the molten zone depends inter alia on the surface tension of the substance close to its melting point. This was determined from the radius and the weight of a drop of material melted from a rod. The values found for germanium and silicon were respectively 600 and 720 dyne/cm, with an accuracy of ± 5%.

Theoretical analyses of the stability of these vertical solid/liquid/solid two-phase systems have been carried out by Heywang and Ziegler [103], and later, in greater detail, by Heywang [104] alone. It was found that the maximum permissible zone length for rods with a radius $r < 2 \, (\sigma/\varrho g)^{1/2}$ (where σ is the surface tension, ϱ the density, and g the acceleration due to gravity) increases in proportion to the radius. For rods with larger radii, however, the maximum stable zone length is almost constant, and depends only on the material. The value found for gold and tin is 0.7 cm, and that for silicon, titanium, and zirconium about 1.5 cm. The floating zone method is best suited to metals with low densities and high surface tensions in the melt, i. e. metals for which the ratio σ/ϱ is large (e. g. Fe and Ti).

Pfann, Benson, and Hagelbarger [105] have described a method by which fairly large quantities can be zone-melted in spite of these limitations (cf. Fig. 131), in which the material is in the form of a plate (Fig. 131a and b) or a tube (Fig. 131c). The molten zone in (a) is a complete strip, whilst that in (b) does not extend right to the ends of the plate. The molten zone in (c) is in the form of a ring.

The zone melting of silicon in industry is nearly always carried out by the floating zone method (see Fig. 132); only one molten zone is used, and one end of the rod can be rotated by a technique developed by R. Emeis[106] in the Research Laboratories of Siemens-Schuckert-Werke A.G. (Pretzfeld Works) to improve mix-

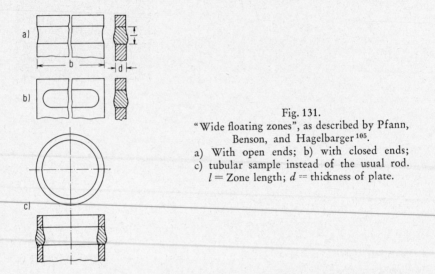

Fig. 131.
"Wide floating zones", as described by Pfann, Benson, and Hagelbarger[105].
a) With open ends; b) with closed ends; c) tubular sample instead of the usual rod.
l = Zone length; d = thickness of plate.

ing. The heat required for melting is supplied via an inductively heated ring of tungsten strip. This circular radiator moves either upwards or downwards. Several zone passes through a rod of sintered silicon powder gives well formed single crystals. These are no longer round like the original silicon ingot; instead, they are hexagonal, indicating the [111] axis as the approximate direction of growth.

Wroughton et al.[107] have suggested additional stabilization of the melt in inductive heating, by making use of the mutually opposing forces between the inducing and induced currents. Thus if the lower part of a vertical ingot is cooled, the center of gravity of the molten zone is displaced upwards, and the melt is levitated.

According to Pfann and Hagelbarger[108], a molten zone in a conductor can be stabilized in a magnetic field if a current is passed through the conductor. It is also possible to melt only part of the ingot, e. g. only on one side, so that the part which is not melted supports the melt. With a little skill, non-conducting substances can also be purified in this way without any additional equipment.

Brace et al.[109] provided the molten zones in titanium and iron ingots with further support (cage zone refining) by passing an induced current not through a long cylinder but through a long prism; the current melts only the interior of the rod. The corners and part of the surface remain solid and form a skeleton from which the molten zone cannot escape. When several zones are to be passed in this process, the heating efficiency is steadily reduced, so that the thickness of the ribs is built up by material which has already been partially purified. This avoids contamination of the pure melt by the skeleton (The prism may also be replaced by a round ingot onto which additional thinner rods have been fused). This method cannot be used for

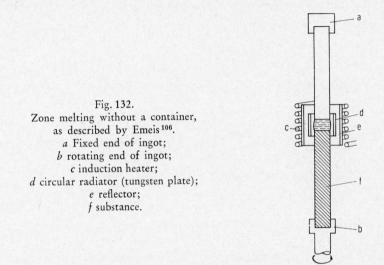

Fig. 132.
Zone melting without a container,
as described by Emeis [106].
a Fixed end of ingot;
b rotating end of ingot;
c induction heater;
d circular radiator (tungsten plate);
e reflector;
f substance.

growing single crystals, but it can be used for the purification of larger ingots. The experiment was carried out by passing 5 molten zones through a titanium ingot 30 cm long and 2 cm thick in an inert atmosphere.

5. Transport of the Charge

There are two basic methods of moving the molten zone: either the whole arrangement of coolers and heaters can be passed slowly over a fixed horizontal or vertical boat (Fig. 133), or the boat may be moved through a fixed heating unit.

In the case of vertical movement, it is not immaterial whether the tube moves

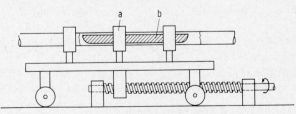

Fig. 133. Zone-melting arrangement with moving heater *a* and fixed boat *b*.

upwards or downwards. According to the author's own experiments [110], the zone melting effect is much more pronounced when the molten zone moves downwards (if it is in fact observed at all when the zone moves upwards). The reason for this difference is the more thorough mixing at the upper interface by thermal convection (cf. Fig. 134), since the upper diffusion layer (see p. 38) is narrower than the lower, and the distribution coefficient in the lower interface tends towards the value of unity, corresponding to laminar flow.

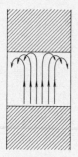

Fig. 134. Currents in a vertical molten zone.

One disadvantage of vertical zone melting, particularly in the case of substances with high vapor pressures and with occluded gases, is that bubbles of vapor are often formed during melting (cf. Fig. 135). Owing to the temperature equilibrium between the solid and liquid phases, the gas phase must also be formed at a certain point in the zone-melting tube, in accordance with Gibbs' phase rule. At this triple point, where three phases coexist, neither the temperature nor the pressure of the system can change, but only the quantity of vaporized substance. The pressure in the bubble remains the same, and its numerical value is given by the Clausius-Clapeyron equation, which is valid for melting, vaporization, and sublimation equilibria.

The size of the gas bubble is not, however, determined solely by the vapor pressure at the triple point. Many substances contain gases which are dissolved or occluded in cavities, and when the substance is melted these gases unite with the vapor of the substance itself; according to wetting relationships, a more or less large bubble is formed, and this often increases in volume as the zone passes along the ingot. In vertical tubes, this bubble is situated above the liquid phase, and separates this from the solid; consequently, if the zone moves downwards, this interferes with the recrystallization (see Fig. 135), so that the ingot may even be divided into individual, unconnected pieces. In the case of tubes with very small diameter (a few mm), a large number of small plugs of material can often be observed even after only 2 to 3 zone passes.

With tubes larger than 1 cm in diameter, if these are made of glass the walls must be thicker (about 1 mm) so that the tube can withstand the stresses imposed by melting and crystallization. According to Pfann [56], to avoid breakage of the tube the molten zone should if possible be moved downwards in the case of substances which expand on melting and upwards for those which contract on melting; in the latter case, therefore, there is a risk that no zone refining will occur.

These disadvantages are avoided if the tube is laid horizontally. In this case, volatile impurities can diffuse back into the purified material from the cushion of vapor lying over the substance, but on the other hand the liquid zone cannot be

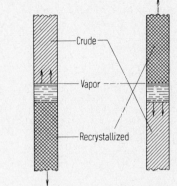

Fig. 135.
Possible directions of zone travel. Left: container moves downwards, zone moves upwards; right: container moves upwards, zone moves downwards.

separated from the solid by gas bubbles. Moreover, since mixing is equally thorough at the two interfaces, the efficiency of separation is independent of direction, so that purification can be expected even in the case of compounds which readily evaporate, or even sublime. However, the efficiency of separation appears to be better with vertical than with horizontal ingots.

Since the substance will accumulate at the forward end of the ingot after several passes, it is advisable to pack the material in obliquely, i. e. so that the forward end

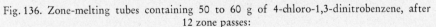

Fig. 136. Zone-melting tubes containing 50 to 60 g of 4-chloro-1,3-dinitrobenzene, after 12 zone passes:
a) uniformly filled;
b) uniformly filled, apparatus inclined at 2°;
c) charge packed obliquely.

of the tube contains no substance initially, whilst the level gradually rises towards the other end. After zone melting, we then obtain a uniformly filled tube. The same effect can be achieved by inclining the entire apparatus at an angle of about 2° during zone melting (see Fig. 136). The tubes shown in the illustration were removed from the apparatus while the zones were still liquid. The zones then solidified to polycrystalline regions, which are dark in appearance, and over which no crystals have grown in the tube.

As far as possible, the diameter of the tube should not exceed 5 cm for substances with low thermal conductivities. Even if the substance melts over its entire cross-

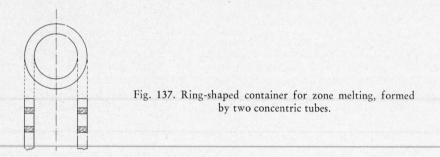

Fig. 137. Ring-shaped container for zone melting, formed by two concentric tubes.

section in wider tubes, the molten zones obtained are generally too long. If in spite of this limitation it is still desired to zone-melt a large quantity of material in a single charge, the operation is best carried out in a ring gap (see Fig. 137).

5.1 Transport Mechanisms

Since the separation of many mixtures requires a large number of very slow zone passes [111], the glass tube containing the charge is preferably placed over several heated points right at the outset. Several phase boundaries are thus formed simultaneously, and these move through the ingot as the latter is drawn through the heaters and coolers. Figs. 138 and 139 show how an impurity which accumulates in the melt is distributed along the ingot by the moving zones.

Fig. 138 shows the distribution after three zones have moved two zone lengths towards the right. In each of the three cases, the zone has given a first crystallizate in which the concentration of the impurity has fallen from 50% to 40%. B accumulates in the melt (as can be seen from the increase in concentration in the zone), so that its concentration in the crystallizate also increases, owing to the constantly changing melt equilibrium. When a zone enters the region which has already been partially purified by the preceding zone, the concentration of B in the melt suddenly decreases, with the result that the concentration in the separating crystal is also decreased (see Fig. 138 b). This yields an ingot of non-uniform composition which, if it were examined at this stage, would be found to contain sections in which the concentration of B was higher than the original value. A similar situation arises when new zones (4 and 5 in Figs 138 b and 139 b) enter the ingot. The striking features of these figures are the decrease in concentration in zone 5 of Fig. 139 b as compared with

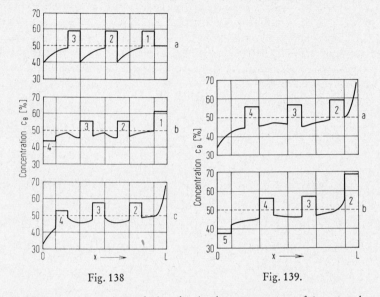

Fig. 138.   Fig. 139.

Concentration curves in an ingot during the simultaneous passage of 3 to 4 molten zones, for an impurity B with a fictive distribution coefficient smaller than unity (initial concentration = 50% of B).

Fig. 140.
Concentration curves for an impurity with a distribution coefficient smaller than one, after 3 (- - - - -) and after 4 (————) zone passes.
a) Starting position of the ingot corresponding to the final distribution ————.
b) Starting position of the ingot corresponding to the final distribution - - - -.

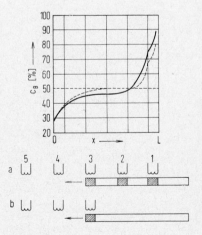

zone 4 in Fig. 138 b, and the large increase in concentration in zone 2, which is just leaving the ingot in Fig. 139 b.

The distribution of the impurity B after the passage of 5 zones, of which three were initially produced simultaneously, is shown by the continuous curve in Fig. 140. The broken curve, which represents a less effective separation, shows the distribution after zone melting in which each zone enters the ingot in succession (cf. Fig. 140 b).

When a large number of zone passes are to be used, it is more economical to arrange the heaters and coolers in a ring, and to place the charge in a boat having the form of a ring or a segment. The ring must not be closed (see Fig. 141 b), since the separation would otherwise be nullified after one revolution. However, a closed ring is essential for zone leveling (Fig. 141 a).

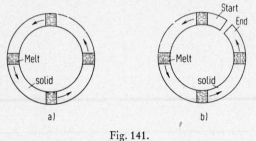

Fig. 141.
a) Zone leveling in a ring;   b) Zone melting in a ring.

Nevertheless, the "lengthways process" (see Fig. 143) can also be carried out continuously at regular intervals if, after a short but slow forward movement, the boat is rapidly returned to its starting position (see Fig. 142).

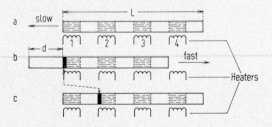

Fig. 142. Reciprocating zone-melting technique (according to [225]).
a) Actual slow zone-melting run along a distance d.
b) Rapid return of ingot to its starting position, which has been reached in c).
Examples of suitable parameters are: $L = 8$ cm, $d = 2$ cm, $L/d = 4 =$ number of molten zones. $d =$ Length of molten zone $+$ interzone distance (cf. ref. 56).

If the number of zone units is L/d (e. g. 4 in Fig. 142), then for a forward stroke of d cm, the number of strokes required for the first of N zones to traverse the ingot is

$$N + L/d - 1 \qquad\qquad (28)$$

The object of this process is that e. g. a compound which has accumulated in the first zone (black in Fig. 142) is suddenly passed on to the second zone on the backward stroke, and from the second into the third zone on the next stroke. At the same time, a new zone starts its journey at the beginning of the ingot. The reciprocating process should therefore give the same separation as the discontinuous process, but in a shorter time.

For an ingot 8 cm long, with a 1 cm zone every 2 cm along its length, the time required for the passage of N zones through the entire ingot at a travel rate of 1 cm/h is $(N + L/d - 1) d$ hours, assuming a starting position as shown in Fig. 143 (cf. Table 9).

Table 9. Time required for reciprocating and discontinuous processes.

Number of zones	Process		
	Reciprocating	Discontinuous	
N	hours		
10	26	32	37.5
100	206	320	375

One hundred zone passes by the discontinuous process requires 375 h (Table 9, column 4), assuming the initial and final positions to be as shown in Fig. 143. Even if the boat is initially laid across the whole set of heaters and coolers and then allowed to traverse slowly, 320 h are still necessary for 100 zone passes (Table 9, column 3), as compared with the 206 h required for the reciprocating process (Table 9, column 2).

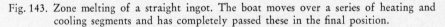

Final position   Starting position

Fig. 143. Zone melting of a straight ingot. The boat moves over a series of heating and cooling segments and has completely passed these in the final position.

The time required can be even further reduced by using the maximum possible number of zones along the ingot. If the total length L of the ingot is again 8 cm, but d in this case is only 1 cm instead of 2 cm, then $L/d = 8$ zones can now be used, and the time required for 100 zone passes becomes only 107 h.

For economical operation, therefore, it is extremely important to keep the zone length and the interzone distance as small as possible, and to make the maximum possible use of all zones by using the reciprocating or ring processes. The rate of travel, on the other hand, cannot be greatly varied for a given system, and so sets a lower limit to the time required.

5.2   Driving Mechanism

Both the normal lengthways process and ring zone melting require the use of a motor, coupled by a cord, a rod, or sometimes even a screw which is fixed to the shaft of the motor and propels the appropriate part of the apparatus with the aid of a moving nut (see Fig. 133).

Good service is obtained with highly geared down synchronous electric motors, preferably fitted with an additional continuously variable gear. It is however also possible to vary the rate of travel with pulleys of different diameters fitted to the shaft of the motor. Alarm clocks can also be used to advantage, particularly since they are cheap and efficient.

The travel rates for organic substances are slow between (1 mm/h and about 10 cm/h) so that in general no additional mechanism for reciprocating operation is necessary if a multi-stage apparatus is used. The ingot can be returned to the starting position by hand, thus saving on maintenance which is unavoidable in the equipment described by Ronald[112].

The need for electronic or electrical control devices, which are probably incorporated in the commercially available zone-melting apparatus made in the United States by Research Specialities Co.[113], can be avoided by simple mechanical methods. The usual pulley on the motor shaft is replaced by a spiral wheel on which

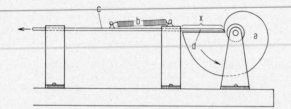

Fig. 144. Arrangement for automatic return of boat.
a: Elliptical wheel;   *b:* tension spring;   *c:* push-rod;   *d:* interrupter edge (length *x*).

a metal rod firmly fixed to the boat can slide. As the wheel turns anticlockwise (see Fig. 144), the push-rod moves to the left, taking the boat with it. After almost one complete rotation of the wheel, the boat moves through a distance *x*, extending a tension spring b, one end of which is fixed whilst the other end is attached by a hook to the push-rod. When the wheel completes its revolution, the spring contracts, bringing the boat rapidly back to its starting position, and the next forward stroke can then begin.

Maire and Moritz[114] used an electric motor which ran rapidly forward and slowly in reverse. The direction of the motor was reversed by markers on the driving cord, and moved the boat rapidly back by a fixed distance after each pass. The number of zone passes was recorded and could be preselected.

Revel and Albert[115] attempted to combine two operations with different speeds.

6. Zone Melting Apparatus

6.1 Apparatus for the Normal Freezing of Melts

Normal freezing can be used for growing single crystals, as has been shown in a review by Neuhaus[116]. The apparatus is very simple. A tube containing the melt

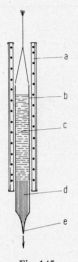

Fig. 145.
Normal freezing of a melt contained in a tube.
a: Heating mantle with resistance heaters;
b: container;
c: melt;
d: crystal;
e: point containing crystal nucleus.

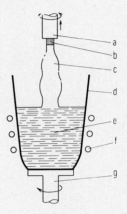

Fig. 146.
Growing a single crystal from the melt.
a: Holder;
b: crystal nucleus;
c: single crystal;
d: container for material;
e: melt;
f: induction coil;
g: platform for vessel.

may be lowered out of a heated jacket (Fig. 145), or the ingot may be drawn out of the melt, in which case both the melt and the single crystal may be rotated to avoid diffusion anomalies (Fig. 146).

6.2 Micro and Semimicro Zone-Melting Apparatus

The first micro zone-melting apparatus was described by Hesse and Schildknecht[97]; a three-stage version of this apparatus is shown in Fig. 123, but more stages can be added.

Schildknecht and Vetter[102] have described a micro-apparatus in which the inter-zone distance is almost the same as the zone length. The distance between the coolers was reduced by replacing the Liebig condensers with cooling loops made of copper wire. These loops, in conjunction with a tube through which a cooling liquid was passed, ensured adequate removal of heat. The heating was carried out in exactly the same manner. Hot oil was passed through the copper tube on which the heating loops were wound, or the tube was fitted with a heating coil. Fig. 147

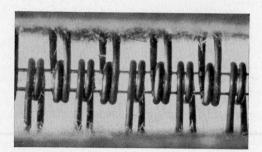

Fig. 147. Copper wire coils as the cooling and heating elements of a multistage micro-apparatus, with glass boat. Magnification about 6.5 ×.

shows the arrangement of the heating and cooling loops, and Figs. 148 and 149 show how they accommodate the boat. The tubes are embedded in mineral wool for insulation, and only the eyes of the wire loops are exposed.

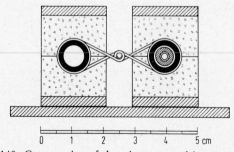

Fig. 148. Cross-section of the microzone-melting apparatus.

The heating and cooling loops are made of 0.5 mm copper wire. Other requirements are a length of tubing for the heating and cooling tubes and a knitting needle of the same diameter as the boat. A piece of wire 1 m long is wound round the knitting needle, starting at the middle of the wire, to form a loop similar to that in a safety pin. The two ends of the wire are then wound onto the tube pattern and the finished loop is removed from the tube. The cooling and heating elements themselves are easily made in this way. These are then screwed onto two threaded tubes 10 mm in diameter, with a fixed distance between the loops. One of these tubes forms the cooling system and the other the heating system (Fig. 149).

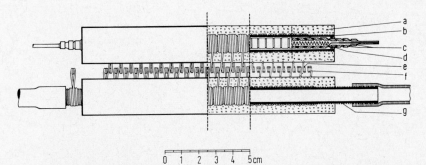

Fig. 149. Longitudinal section of the micro zone-melting apparatus described in ref. 102. *a:* Insulating material; *b:* copper heating tube; *c:* steatite beads; *d:* heating spirals made of resistance wire; *e:* copper wire heating coils; *f:* copper wire cooling coils; *g:* cooling tube.

To assemble the apparatus, the two tubes are placed parallel to each other in mineral wool, with the loops in a straight line so that the resulting passage can accommodate the boat (cf. Fig. 148).

This simple apparatus contains 18 cooling and heating loops in 18 cm, so that a large number of molten zones can traverse the micro-ingot in a relatively short time. Another advantage is that electrically heated apparatus can be immediately converted to a thermostatically heated unit.

These micro-units are mainly used for separation where only small quantities of substance are available. It is not unusual to divide a micro-ingot into small daughter ingots, which are themselves zone-refined once more to achieve ultimate separation. This technique requires a large number of similar units which can all be operated simultaneously, i. e. a zone-melting assembly (cf. Figs. 150 and 151[101]).

Handley and Herington[66], at the Chemical Research Laboratories, Teddington (Middlesex, England) used a semimicro zone-melting apparatus for the purification of 0.15 to 0.5 g of various organic substances, such as benzoic acid, pyrene, anthracene, and chrysene. The molten zone travels vertically downwards at a speed of 2.5 cm/h through the charge, which is contained in a glass tube 10 to 15 cm long and 0.25 to 0.62 cm in diameter. The heat is supplied by thermal radiation[67] from a projector lamp (Osram 12 volt, 100 watt), focussed by an aluminum reflector.

Mair et al.[117] zone-refined an ingot of bicyclo-3,2,1-octane, 57 cm long and only 2 mm thick, in a capillary tube made of borosilicate glass with 6 mm walls. The molten zone was moved vertically upwards at a rate of 7 cm/h by drawing the zone-melting tube through two electric ring heaters fixed to a glass tube (external diameter = 13 mm; internal diameter = 11 mm).

Ronald[112] has developed a semimicro zone-melting apparatus in which the movement of the molten zones is fully automatic, and with which 4 samples can be

Fig. 150. Zone-melting bench.
Ten electrically heated micro-units with a common motor, and with transmission pulleys on a single shaft[101].

zone-refined simultaneously. The containers are mounted vertically on a horizontal aluminum platform (25 × 60 × 0.10 cm), with which they are slowly moved upwards through the heater. A special electronic control ensures that, immediately on reaching its final position, the platform is returned with the containers to its start-

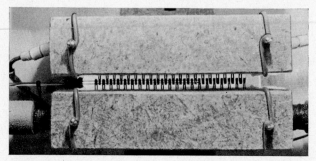

Fig. 151. Single unit of a zone-melting bench with glass boat;
wide loops = coolers; narrow loops = heaters ($^2/_3$ actual size).

ing position in 6 sec, and then begins to move slowly (3 cm/h) upwards again. The apparatus was tested with naphthalene contaminated with 1% and 0.1% of

2,4-dinitrophenylhydrazine (2,4-DNP); 500 mg samples were zone-refined in a capillary 25 cm long (external diameter 4 mm; internal diameter 2 mm). After 5 zone passes, the 2,4-DNP had migrated out of 90% of the naphthalene which had originally contained 1% of impurity, and had accumulated in a zone 1 cm long at the end of the ingot.

6.3 Special Zone-Melting Apparatus for Larger Quantities

6.3.1 *Zone-Melting Apparatus for Metals and Their Compounds*

The first zone-melting devices were designed for the purification of germanium and were originally intended for fairly large quantities. The purification is carried out in two stages. Germanium dioxide is first reduced with hydrogen, and the germanium powder is fused together in a graphite boat. This melt is partially purified by normal freezing, in which the metal is drawn from the furnace towards the cooling zone at a speed of 0.6 cm/min. The cooling zone, which still has a temperature of 400° C, is reached two hours after the metal has started moving. Details of the apparatus can be found in Olsen's discussion [88] of the zone refining of germanium.

After this preparation for zone melting, the germanium ingots weigh 0.45 kg. They are introduced, in the graphite boat, into a 3- to 6-stage zone-melting unit in such a way that the end of the ingot which solidifies first again forms the leading end in the second stage. The 10 kW high-frequency generator (450 kc/s) supplying six series-connected induction heaters is adjusted to give zones about 2.5 cm long in the germanium ingot, which is 30 cm long. (Owing to irregularities in the operation of the generator, the zone length varies between 2.5 and 5 cm, but this has no effect on the ultimate purification). With the graphite boat travelling at 0.4 cm/min, the zone refining takes about $3^3/_4$ hours. The boat is surrounded by a maximum of three water-cooled induction coils at the same time, and, to avoid loss of heat and for correct centralization, does not slide directly on the wall of the quartz tube (150 cm long, 5 cm in diameter), but on built-in quartz rods. One of these rods is replaced by a quartz tube, through which nitrogen is led into the apparatus. A movement of material, which in the case of germanium would proceed in the direction of movement of the molten zones, is avoided by tilting the apparatus through an angle of 5°. Moreover, the last drops of melt are allowed to drain into an overflow reservoir to remove the copper accumulated at the end of the ingot.

The ingots are always polycrystalline after purification but this is of no importance, since it is only after addition of, e.g., antimony or indium that the germanium is required as a single crystal for the preparation of transistors. The apparatus used for the zone alloying and single crystal growth has been described by Bennet and Sawyer [118]. It is similar to a zone-melting apparatus, but has only one induction furnace, consisting of copper windings and a graphite cylinder; it also has a so-called after-heater, which assists in the formation of a single crystal (see also Fig. 121). The single crystal grows adjacent to a crystal nucleus from the melt in a thin-walled quartz boat 40 cm long and 2.5 cm in diameter, to give an ingot 30 cm long and weighing 500 g.

The details of the procedure are given below.

The quartz boat is first roughened by sand-blasting with silicon carbide and is then cleaned with hydrofluoric acid, washed with very pure water, dried, and sooted several times. A small single crystal of germanium is then placed in the prepared boat with the [100] or [111] axis parallel to the longitudinal axis of the boat. Behind the single crystal is placed the germanium ingot, from which the contaminated end has been removed. Pellets of the desired impurities, either pure or in the form of alloys, are laid on the starting position of the molten zone. Before the boat is charged, the germanium ingot and the single crystal of germanium are superficially etched with a mixture of 150 ml of hydrofluoric acid, 150 ml of glacial acetic acid, 250 ml of nitric acid, and three drops of bromine. It is obviously essential that the crystal nucleus, from which the first molten zone (5.6 cm long) starts, should not be completely melted. The rate of travel of the quartz boat is usually 0.8 cm/h or, if the quality requirements for the semiconductor material are not great, 8.2 cm/h.

Following the zone leveling, cooling proceeds slowly (about 1 to 2° C/min) and, after the portion which crystallized last has been removed, the resulting single crystal is divided into portions 2.5 cm long. A crystal 25 cm long can be doped in 18 hours.

Silicon, which is another important raw material for semiconductors, has also been purified by a specially developed floating zone technique [106, 120, 121, 122] and grown into a single crystal (Fig. 152). The silicon ingot is zone-refined vertically without a container, and generally with induction heating (see Fig. 152 a). The molten zone divides the ingot into two parts, the lower of which is rotated to ensure thorough mixing of the zone.

According to Buehler, a purified single crystal is very readily obtained [123] from a silicon ingot 2 cm in diameter, using induction heating (5 Mc/s) with a zone length of 1.5 cm. The apparatus is fully automatic, and a number of zones can be passed through the ingot without interruption or supervision. Using a 500 kc/sec high frequency generator instead of the 5 Mc/sec generator, the forces acting between the inducing and induced currents can be used to such good advantage that it is possible to grow single crystals up to 25 cm in diameter [124].

In their first apparatus, Keck et al.[122] zone-melted silicon with an incandescent tungsten wire in an atmosphere of helium or argon. A cylinder of tantalum sheet was used to concentrate all the radiant heat into a narrow region. Owing to the relatively high surface tension (720 dyne/cm) and the low density (2.33 g/cm³) of molten silicon, it was possible to use 10 mm long zones at a diameter of 10 mm. However, since the incandescent tungsten wire has a relatively high vapor pressure at 2000° C, so that tungsten may be absorbed by the molten silicon, the authors changed to induction heating (cf. Fig. 153). The tubular melting chamber, which is

250 mm long, is firmly fixed in an iron frame, whilst a second frame moves vertically with the ingot. The mountings are inserted into the melting chamber as in the Wilson chamber.

Fig. 152 b.
Molten zone in a silicon rod heated with an induction coil (dark transverse band), examined through a dark magnifier *).

Fig. 152 a.

Zone melting of a silicon rod in a quartz tube with induction heating *).

Metal compounds which decompose on melting are zone-refined in an ampoule, which must be very uniformly heated to avoid condensation on the colder parts. Since the various components generally volatilize at different rates, this leads to a change in the composition of the starting material. New phases are formed, and one element may even separate out in the pure form. There are two possible methods of avoiding this effect in the zone melting of metal compounds.

1. The entire tube is kept so hot that the most volatile compounds cannot condense. The pressure in the tube is then given by the Clausius-Clapeyron equation, and may be uncomfortably high, particularly when the starting material is impure and is not stoichiometric in composition.

---

*) The photographs were kindly supplied by Standard Elektrik Lorenz AG., Bauelemente-Werk SAF, Nuremberg.

2. Folberth and Weiss [125], on the other hand, avoided this effect in the zone melting of gallium arsenide and indium phosphide by weighing in the components in quantities such that "stoichiometric" melts and stoichiometric crystals were formed and the vapor phase corresponded to the equilibrium vapor phase of the melt. It

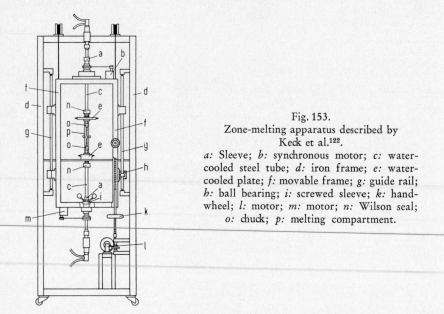

Fig. 153.
Zone-melting apparatus described by Keck et al.[122].
a: Sleeve; *b:* synchronous motor; *c:* water-cooled steel tube; *d:* iron frame; *e:* water-cooled plate; *f:* movable frame; *g:* guide rail; *h:* ball bearing; *i:* screwed sleeve; *k:* hand-wheel; *l:* motor; *m:* motor; *n:* Wilson seal; *o:* chuck; *p:* melting compartment.

does not matter if the temperature at certain parts of the tube is so low that the volatile components condense. The pressure in the tube is then equal to the vapor pressure of the most readily volatile component at the lowest temperature. The latter therefore provides a means of regulating the pressure. In this case, however, the temperature in the tube must rise as evenly as possible up to the heated zone. For this reason, Whelan and Wheatley [126] used the usual induction heating, together with long electric furnaces to heat the remainder of the zone melting space. In this way they maintained the interior of a quartz tube at 590° C and were able to zone-melt gallium arsenide without evaporation of the arsenic as a result of its relatively high vapor pressure at the melting point of this compound (1237° C ± 3° C).

In the apparatus shown in Fig. 154, the minimum temperature T_p, and hence also the pressure in the entire system, are regulated by a special heater. The mean temperature is adjusted with the aid of a graphite cylinder carrying a current. The cylinder is slotted so that an additional induced current will not be produced in it. If necessary, a small quantity of the most volatile component may be deposited in front of the sample to ensure stable conditions right at the outset.

If the components are not present in the stoichiometric ratio, and if in addition to the purification it is intended to remove the excess components by zone melting, it is difficult to predict accurately the changing equilibrium conditions during the melting and to take these into account in planning. Moreover, the stoichiometric

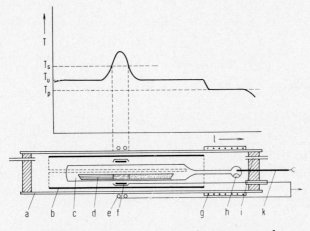

Fig. 154. Top: temperature distribution in a zone-melting apparatus for metal compounds which decompose readily. T_s = melting point, T_u = tube temperature; T_p = lowest temperature. Bottom: Zone-melting apparatus for compounds which decompose readily. *a:* Tube; *b:* slotted graphite cylinder; *c:* quartz tube; *d:* ingot in boat; *e:* induction heater; *f:* inductively heated graphite ring with reflector; *g:* resistance heater for temperature regulation; *h:* volatile component; *i:* inlet tube for protective gas; *k:* thermocouple. (According to Boomgard et al.[127]).

compound is not always the highest melting compound, and hence does not always crystallize first.

Simpler conditions are found when the equilibrium vapor pressure of the volatile component lies well below 1 atm. It is then possible to carry out the zone melting in an open tube, and the required partial pressure is maintained by a slow stream of an inert gas. Dissociating compounds of the volatile component which exist as gases can also be used, e. g. a mixture of hydrogen and hydrogen sulfide.

The apparatus shown in Fig. 154 is also suitable for doping with foreign substances. The desired impurities must be so volatile that a p-n junction can be produced in the ingot in a single operation, with the aid of different temperatures T_p.

Fig. 155 shows a zone-melting arrangement in which the heat of fusion is supplied by electron bombardment. The melting space is cooled and the ingot can be easily observed. A powerful pump unit maintains the pressure at 10^{-6} mm Hg. The rate of travel is adjustable between 0 and 350 cm/h, and the bombardment can be varied between 5 kW and a few milliwatts.

6.3.2   *Special Zone-Melting Apparatus for Organic Compounds and Salts*

In the zone-melting equipment used for high-melting, inorganic substances, the heating constitutes the greatest expense and frequently has to be matched to the particular separation problem at hand. This is not the case with apparatus for

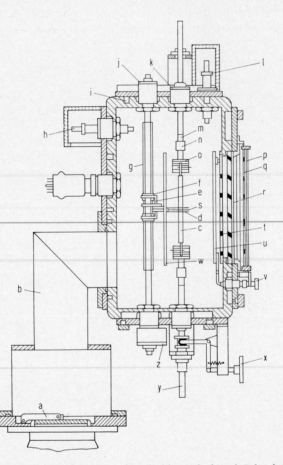

Fig. 155. Zone-melting apparatus described by Birbeck and Calverley [128].
a: Flap valve; *b:* pipe; *c:* sample; *d:* focussing plate; *e:* cathode bridge; *f:* nut; *g:* shaft; *h:* terminal 1; *i:* channel for cooling water; *j:* Wilson seal; *k:* seal; *l:* terminal 2; *m:* quartz distance piece; *n:* molybdenum gland; *o:* chuck; *p:* wire mesh; *q:* dark glass pane; *r:* quartz window; *s:* cathode; *t:* quartz glass; *u:* valve; *v:* operating knob for valve *u*; *w:* screening plate; *x:* handwheel; *y:* shaft; *z:* worm-drive housing.

relatively low-melting, organic compounds, where the main emphasis is placed on the cooling, since very many substances have low melting points or are even liquid.

The first and simplest experimental apparatus is due to Wolf and Deutsch [129], who slowly lowered a test tube 10 cm long filled with napthalene (purissimum pro usu interno, Merck), downwards through an electric ring furnace (1 cm/h). The molten zone which passed through the material carried the greater part of the anthracene, which was present as the impurity, towards the top of the charge. The process was repeated several times, and the anthracene content finally fell to less than 1 ppm.

Herington [130] also used a simple method for the purification of naphthalene in a vertical glass tube, through which a molten zone, produced by an external cylindrical heater, was passed in a downward direction at a speed of 5 cm/h (Fig. 156). A switch mechanism was later added to the apparatus to return the heater rapidly to its starting position at the end of each pass.

At the beginning of the zone melting, the substance is introduced in the liquid form into a tube, which is closed at the bottom by a glass stopper. The tube is 1.2 m long and has a diameter of 3.5 cm. (With larger diameters, the material does not melt over its entire cross-section). The stopper at the bottom is then replaced by a hollow glass connector, into which the highly contaminated melt can flow on reaching the bottom, so that the ultimate equilibrium state (see p. 69) is not reached so soon. For the zone melting of substances which melt below 40°C, the whole apparatus with the exception of the motor is surrounded by a cooling jacket at a temperature of -25°C.

This apparatus can be used for the zone melting of 1.5 kg samples of organic substances; the apparatus developed by Ball, Helm, and Ferrin [100] can be used for even larger quantities. The glass or metal tubes are 7.5 cm in diameter and 1.27 m long. The arrangement has an electrical return device, and is so designed that 5 vertical zone-melting tubes can be used simultaneously. The rate of travel of the molten zone can be varied between 105 and 25 mm/h.

In the zone-melting arrangements mentioned above, cooling was applied only when the compounds to be purified were low-melting or liquid. Schildknecht et al.[131], on the other hand, have included cooling elements on both sides of the resistance-wire heaters as a part of the design. As in the micro-apparatus described earlier (see p. 98), two brass tubes with internal diameters of 12 and 25 mm are brazed together to form a small Liebig condenser, and in this case the whole condenser was tinned for better sealing. Each cooler is fixed to a silver steel rod by a metal ring with a knurled screw.

Between the coolers lie the heating wires; these are not bent into a loop, however, but into a U-shape to fit the boat (cf. Fig. 157).

The heating wires were made from pieces of 0.8 mm wire (10 ohm/m) of exactly equal length. The ends of the pieces are forced into thin copper tubes, and these in turn are screwed into a porcelain insulator. In this way, the thin heating wires are permanently fastened and defective contacts are avoided. Like the coolers, the heaters are also fixed to the stainless-steel rod by a metal ring. The heater itself ensures very uniform heating, since it resembles a small chimney, formed by two asbestos disks cemented to the sides of the adjacent coolers.

To achieve independence of the external temperature, two 10 cm glass Liebig condensers with cooling liquid passing through them are fitted at the ends of the heating and cooling unit. Various zone lengths can be obtained with this apparatus, since the zone length is governed by the distance between the coolers and by the heating and cooling temperatures.

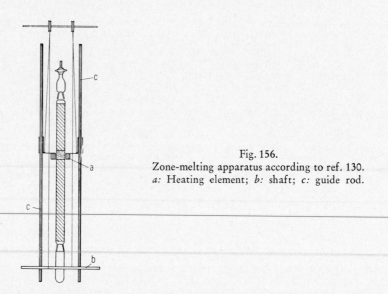

Fig. 156.
Zone-melting apparatus according to ref. 130.
a: Heating element; *b:* shaft; *c:* guide rod.

In the author's own experience, however, it is not always necessary to have such an adaptable apparatus for the zone melting of organic mixtures and in fact, particularly for routine work, a fixed arrangement may even be more suitable. The principal part of an apparatus of this type[98] is a long metal cooling tube, or rather

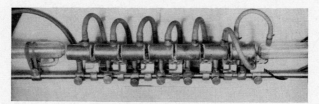

Fig. 157. Zone-melting apparatus for gram quantities (side view).
Heating wires held by porcelain connectors, between metal coolers.

a cooling spiral with the windings arranged in groups and surrounding the tube or boat containing the charge (cf. Fig. 158). This cooling spiral is made of soft 9 mm copper tubing which is wound, with heating, around a 2.2 cm steel rod to form groups of three windings. A 15 cm length of tubing is left free between the groups of windings, and the groups are pushed together to the required distance apart only during assembly. The whole cooling unit is fastened by the resulting loops to a block

Fig. 158. 15-Stage zone-melting apparatus.

of wood, and an electric ring heater is inserted between each pair of groups. The heaters themselves are screwed onto an eternite sheet (see Fig. 158). The ring heaters are connected in parallel, and each heater can be switched on and off independently and can be controlled by a potentiometer. The cooling is carried out with water or brine.

The cooling tube may also be made of lead, which is easier to work with but which must be more carefully fixed, e.g. with "earthing clips", which completely surround the cooler windings, and with the aid of which these windings are screwed into a 4 mm gap between two parallel steel strips (Messrs. Seibert & Stinnes) (cf. Fig. 160). The windings of lead

Fig. 159.
Cross-section through a cooling
element.
a: Pipe strap;
b: cooler winding;
c: brass tube;
d: glass tube;
e: fixing plate.

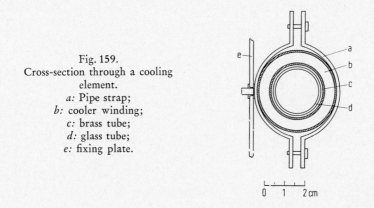

tubing are first soldered onto 6 cm long brass cylinders with a diameter corresponding to that of the tube containing the charge. (Fig. 159). This is not difficult if the lead tubing is first slightly flattened by being passed between two adjacent rollers and the brass tubes, fitted with stoppers, are dipped together with the lead windings into soldering tin. The heaters (electric ring heaters, cf. Fig. 104) are then fitted between the cooling elements. The best procedure is not to mount each heater individually onto an eternite insulating sheet, but to fix them all together on a glass tube pushed through the cooling cylinder. In this case the boat or tube containing the charge does not come into direct contact with the metal, but this has no adverse effect on the accurate formation of the molten zone.

The heaters are made by bending two strips of copper sheet 2.5 cm wide into cylinders, and inserting between these three similarly shaped strips of mica. The middle mica strip carries the heater windings, which are made of fine resistance wire. Each heating ring has a power consumption of 30 watts. The heating temperature at 220 V is higher than 320° C. Lower temperatures are obtained with the aid of a variable voltage transformer. The heaters are connected in series in groups of four to avoid high currents.

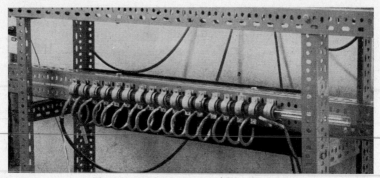

Fig. 160. 16-Stage zone-melting apparatus.

The finished zone-melting apparatus is shown in Fig. 160. The zone-melting tubes are again drawn through the coolers and heaters at a speed of between 1 mm/h and 1 cm/h by a synchronous electric motor (Messrs. AEG; 1 revolution/24 h). It is not

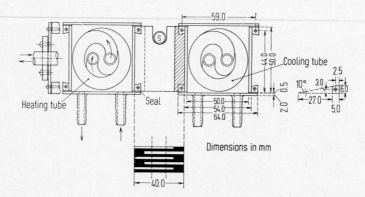

Fig. 161. Cross-section of the plate zone-melting apparatus. Heating lamella shown between hot and cold containers. The boat S lies in the lamella. Insulating lamella shaded.

necessary to provide a continuously variable speed control; it is in fact sufficient to fit pulleys of various diameters on the motor shaft.

The apparatus illustrated in Figs. 158 and 160 permits the zone melting of 10 to 200 g of material, the latter with a tube of the maximum length and ²/₃ full, depending on the length of the tube and the level of the charge. However, since even compounds with low thermal conductivity can still be melted through the entire cross-section in tubes 5 cm in diameter, this design can also be used in apparatus for the zone melting of larger quantities. A better method is to pass several tubes simultaneously through zone melting units arranged above and alongside one another. Only one motor is then required for transport, and the cooling brine (if water cannot be used) can also be drawn from a single reservoir. It is also possible to coordinate the heating, in which case the latter is preferably carried out with the aid of heated metal plates connected via a common heat container. Several holes with diameters only slightly larger than that of the tube containing the charge are bored in these plates.

Fig. 161 shows a zone-melting apparatus in which the heating and cooling are carried out with brass plates of the same shape. The heating and cooling plates are 1 mm thick and rectangular in shape, with a dovetailed recess on one side. To ensure that the boat is heated and cooled as uniformly as possible, slots are cut in the plates in such a way that, when the lamellas are placed together, the slots form a channel 1.5 cm deep and with a semicircular bottom (see Figs. 161 and 162). This apparatus is constructed on the same principles as the micro-apparatus described earlier (see p. 115): rectangular hot and cold containers fitted with copper tubes are laid parallel to each other. The lamellar extensions movably connected to the containers are interleaved with one another in such a way that cooling plates alternate with heating plates (see Figs. 161 and 162). The cooling and heating plates must naturally be insulated from one another and from the hot and cold containers; adequate insulation is usually provided by air.

To assemble the apparatus, the two metal boxes are placed alongside one another and connected by 10 insulating lamellas. Cooling lamellas are inserted between the dovetails and insulated from the heat container by the same number of screens. A number of insulating

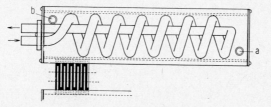

Fig. 162. Heat container with heating coil in the plate apparatus. The insulating material between the cooling and heating lamellas is shown in black.
a: Inlet; *b:* outlet.

lamellas are then added, followed by the heating lamellas, again with screening pieces to prevent radiation of heat. Each lamella increases the length of the molten zone by about 1 mm, if this is the thickness of the brass plate. The glass tube containing the charge is drawn by an electric motor, and slides slowly in the channel provided for this purpose. If open boats are used, they may be covered with suitable microscope slides to prevent the entry of dirt.

The cooling is carried out by passing methanol, cooled in a thermostat, through the cold container. For very low temperatures, it is better to pass Frigen through the internal copper coil; fine adjustment of the temperature is effected with the aid of a methanol bath which is heated with an immersion heater in a by-pass container inserted before the coil. Heating is carried out in a similar manner: hot oil is passed either directly through the container or through the internal copper coil, in which case oil is used as the heat-transfer agent.

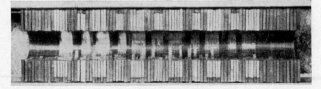

Fig. 163. Arrangement of the cooling, heating and insulating lamellas (top view). Together they form a channel to accommodate the glass boat.

Two extensions can be made to the apparatus. Provision can be made for operation with three boats simultaneously, by drilling two holes in the lamellas below the first slot. Even more holes can be provided in the case of larger plates. However, the extra ingots cannot then be observed directly; in this case the boat which slides in the channel must be used as a guide.

The other possible extension is to add an extra set of heating or cooling plates to a free wall of the container (see Fig. 161), so that each container carries two sets of heating or cooling lamellas.

These considerations are important when large quantities of substance are to be zone-melted at the same time, since experience gained so far has shown that the diameter of the tube cannot be increased indefinitely without the risk of obtaining irregular and uncontrollable phase boundaries. After a certain critical diameter has been reached, it is necessary to divide a thick tube into a number of thinner tubes.

6.3.2.1   *Apparatus for the Zone Melting of a Circular Charge*

The resolution of mixtures of substances which are difficult to separate requires a large number of zone passes, and when a straight ingot is used, the boat must always be returned to its starting position at the correct moment. In this case it is simpler to use a circular charge, since this avoids the need to reverse the direction of travel. Moreover, even with a large number of structural units, the entire apparatus is still compact, and can therefore be easily protected against atmospheric moisture and oxygen [60].

Fig. 164. Ring zone-melting apparatus. The apparatus is placed in the bottom part of a desiccator. The boat lies in a ring-shaped channel in the four cooling segments. The four heating wires are inserted into slits between the segments.

The most important part of a ring apparatus for small charges is the annular cooling and heating unit which is shown in Fig. 164.

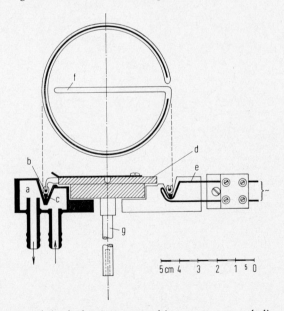

Fig. 165. Cross-section through the ring zone-melting apparatus, excluding motor, and top view of the ring-shaped container.
a: Cooler; *b:* channel; *c:* wedge; *d:* disk; *e:* heater; *f:* engagement piece; *g:* motor shaft.

The four coolers, which are separated by slots, are rigidly fixed and have separate inlets and outlets for the cooling liquid. The heaters are situated in the slots, and the circular glass boat containing the charge is joined to an engaging piece which slides it slowly over the heaters and coolers. The disk in the center is in effect a rotating platform with two mutually perpendicular grooves to accommodate the engaging piece of the boat. The disk is driven by the motor, which is situated underneath, and which makes one revolution in 24 or 48 hours. The heaters are introduced into the

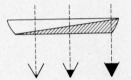

Fig. 166.
Distribution of material in a boat-shaped
container;
above: side view; below: cross-sections.

heating slots from the outside; these are simple wire loops adjustably secured by screws to the supports provided for this purpose around the apparatus, with a porcelain insulator and a brass screw holder.

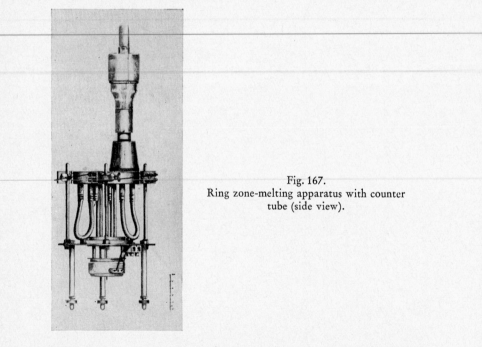

Fig. 167.
Ring zone-melting apparatus with counter
tube (side view).

A wedge-shaped channel is provided in the cooling segments (cf. Fig. 165) to accommodate a wedge-shaped boat. If it is desired to use the more readily produced round boats, the bottom of the channel is rounded off with suitable wedges.

The wedge-shaped boat permits the zone melting of fairly large as well as very small charges with a constant ingot length and zone length, i. e. with a constant L/l ratio. Moreover, the displaced material has room to build up vertically, so that the distribution of material after several zone passes should be as shown in Fig. 166. The containers are always left open at the top to permit the removal of samples during the zone melting.

If radioactively labeled compounds are used, a thin metal cover, e. g. a sheet of aluminum, can be placed over the boat to avoid contamination of the apparatus and the counter tube. The progress of zone melting can be checked continuously if the counter tube is fitted over a cool segment. For the zone melting of highly radioactive substances, the apparatus is surrounded by lead tiles. Even in this case, a thin screen of sheet lead usually is sufficient; this is placed around a dessicator filled with an inert gas, in which the whole apparatus is housed, even for normal working, to avoid oxidation and exclude atmospheric moisture when low cooling temperatures are used (see Fig. 167).

Thermostatically Heated Circular Zone-Melting Apparatus

To obtain an apparatus [61] for the zone melting of ice with the smallest possible space requirement, a new circular apparatus was built, based on the prefabricated principle described earlier. The most important objectives in its design were:

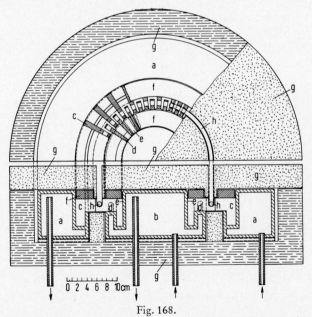

Fig. 168.
Top view and cross-section of the thermostatically heated ring zone-melting apparatus.
a: Cold container; *b:* heat container; *c:* cooling lamellas; *d:* heating lamellas; *e:* insulating lamellas; *f:* connecting ring; *g:* insulation; *h:* boat.

(1) reproducible conditions, (2) adaptable cooling and heating systems, (3) economical and continuous operation, and (4) a wide range of applications.

Experience has shown that continuous operation can be achieved at moderate expense by the use of the ring method. This gives a compact zone-melting apparatus which can be easily housed to protect it against atmospheric moisture, and which can be screened when radioactively labeled compounds are to be used [132].

Reproducible conditions are obtained if brass plates suitably shaped to give intimate contact with the heat and cold containers are used for heating and cooling. The cooling and heating liquids therefore wash around the cooling and heating plates (Fig. 168) in the channels of the cold and heat containers. To ensure that all the plates are actually at the same temperature, they are also linked together by a heavy brass connecting ring. This gives a closed cooling or heating ring from which only part of the plates project; those projecting outwards are for heating and those projecting inwards for cooling. The projecting parts of the plates are slotted to accommodate the boat; thus when the apparatus is assembled, a channel is formed by the cooling and heating elements, separated from one another by air or by insulating lamellas.

In this channel lies the ring-shaped glass boat (see Fig. 169) or a container consisting of a silicone rubber tube. The circular boat shown in the illustration is filled with spermaceti. The light parts are where the substance was molten and has solidified in the polycrystalline form; the intervening transparent regions are partly monocrystalline. The boat is moved by an engaging piece which is pivoted in the center and slides in the channel. The whole apparatus is surrounded by insulating material (wood, glass wool, and crushed fireclay).

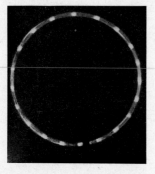

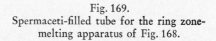

Fig. 169.
Spermaceti-filled tube for the ring zone-
melting apparatus of Fig. 168.

6.4 Apparatus for the Zone Melting of Frozen Liquids

The zone melting of substances which are liquid at room temperature can also be carried out, by freezing and allowing them to melt again. All processes involved are exactly as in the zone melting of solids, except that the cooling must be much more intense. Liquid mixtures (e.g. solutions) can even be resolved simply by freezing, if this is controlled and if the liquid remaining over the "ice" is constantly stirred. So it is possible to concentrate dilute solutions.

A suitable apparatus can be improvised quite cheaply. The only materials are a test tube, a container with a jacket through which cooling brine is passed, and

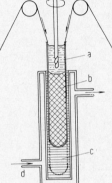

Fig. 170.
Simple apparatus for normal freezing.
a: Solution; *b:* solid; *c:* glycol; *d:* inlet for
cooling brine.

a stirrer (Fig. 170). The test tube is connected to the hour arbor of an alarm clock by two threads, and as the threads unwind from the arbor or from a pulley attached to it, the test tube sinks under the force of gravity into a heat-exchange liquid, e.g.

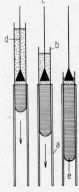

Fig. 171.
Growth of a crystalline rod from a solution, where the
height of the interface is constant, with stirrer above
interface.
a: Cooling tube; *b:* tube for material; *c:* stirrer;
d: solution; *e:* crystallizate.

glycol. Consequently the ice ingot grows upwards (at a rate of 5 cm/h). The position of the phase boundary is constant, and a stirrer is mounted slightly above the interface (see Fig. 171).

If very dilute solutions, and possibly non-aqueous extracts, are to be concentrated under mild conditions, it is better to use a reliable apparatus such as that shown in Fig. 172 [16, 133]. The cooling is effected with the aid of various cooling mixtures in a Dewar flask. The heat is exchanged by interchangeable metal tubes, which also act

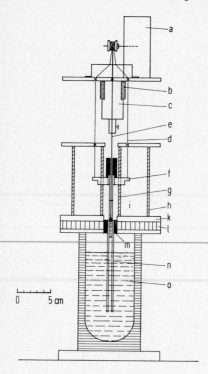

0   5 cm

Fig. 172.
Longitudinal section through the freezing apparatus [133].
a: Alarm clock with interchangeable pulley on its minute arbor, for the supporting thread; *b:* clamp for stirrer motor; *c:* stirrer motor with adaptor for stirrer; *d:* three supporting threads connecting the pulley and the disk *f* via a cross-piece; *e:* stirrer, the height of which is adjustable with the aid of the stirrer motor adaptor; *f:* disk with rubber seal to accommodate sample container, and with stirrer guide placed on top; *g:* guide rod; *h:* stabilizer; *i:* sample container; *k:* staging of the apparatus, formed by four plates of synthetic resin paper laminate, which supports the superstructure; *l:* Corblanite insulation, which is fixed to the stand together with the plates; *m:* cork stopper as central mounting for copper tube *n*, permitting easy interchange of the latter; *n:* copper tube with lower end dipping into cooling bath, giving a sharply demarcated cold zone; *o:* Dewar flask to accommodate cooling bath.

as guides for the tube containing the substance, and the diameter of which determines the volume from which the desired substances are to be isolated.

The solution which is to be concentrated is pipetted into a 1.2 ml tube, and the latter is then inserted into the rubber seal of the lowering disk (see Fig. 172).

While the stirrer and guide are being fitted, the top of the copper tube is covered with a piece of cardboard to provide a safe support for the tube containing the substance.

The level of the phase boundary depends on the temperature of the cooling bath, the rate of stirring, and the rate at which the tube is lowered. Consequently the level of the stirrer must be so adjusted that the stirrer cannot freeze in, whilst still providing optimum mixing at the phase boundary. Thus while the substance tube is lowered by about 1 to 5 mm into the copper tube, the stirring is carried out very slowly at first, until the first crystal nucleus has formed. (This nucleus forms more readily if a drop of lubricating oil is introduced between the substance tube and the copper tube at the beginning of the experiment). When a sharp zone has formed between the solution and the crystallizate, the lowering mechanism is released and the rate of stirring is gradually brought to the desired value (cf. Fig. 173).

When the experiment is complete, the clamp is raised together with the entire lowering equipment and the substance tube. The stirrer and guide are removed and the substance tube is taken from the seal. The concentrate can the be thawed out and removed with a pipet. Alternatively, the crystallizate together with the substance tube can be cut with a glass file.

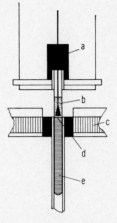

Fig. 173.
Diagrammatic representation of the formation of the interface at the cold zone.
a: Lowering device, with stirrer and container for sample; *b:* solution; *c:* insulation; *d:* interface; *e:* crystallizate.

The whole experimental arrangement, including the rectifier for the stirrer motor, is shown in Fig. 174.

Fig. 174.
Arrangement of apparatus for normal freezing.

Matthews and Coggeshall [134] have used a similar arrangement for normal freezing, to freeze out pure benzene from a benzene solution of impurities, some of which could no longer be detected. The concentration of the impurities in the final concentrate was 20 times higher than in the starting solution.

Whilst these authors froze the benzene by pumping an acetone — dry ice mixture through a cooler from a storage vessel, Dickinson and Eaborn [135] simply lowered a tube containing 300 ml of "pure" benzene into ice water. Acetone — dry ice mixtures were also used for lower-melting compounds.

Solid compounds can also be purified by normal freezing if the apparatus is fitted with a heater (cf. Fig. 175). Air-cooling is often adequate in the case of high-melting substances.

Benzene, as an organic liquid which freezes readily and as a good solvent, is an elegant test substance for freezing experiments. Röck [99] also used benzene to test the efficiency of the zone melting of frozen liquids in an apparatus of his own design (see Fig. 176). The benzene was placed in a deep circular slot, where it was frozen

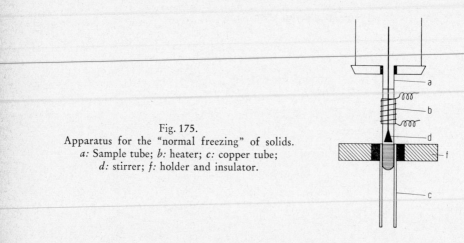

Fig. 175.
Apparatus for the "normal freezing" of solids.
a: Sample tube; *b:* heater; *c:* copper tube;
d: stirrer; *f:* holder and insulator.

in the usual manner with cooling mixtures; a narrow zone was melted from the inside by an electric heater. The heating coil moved upwards, causing the molten zone to move in the same direction through the cylinder of benzene. To remove the impurities from 100 ml of technical benzene, 10 ml were thawed out at the top and poured off.

Schildknecht and Mannl [63] designed an apparatus with an efficient cooling system so that several zones could be passed simultaneously through an ingot of ice. Liebig condensers were inadequate for this purpose, and were replaced by a large sheet of copper folded to form a long cooling channel (see Fig. 177), which could accommodate a cooling coil 22 mm thick in its outer longitudinal folds. This arrangement was capable of maintaining a temperature of $-30°$ C or below in a closed container for as long as was required, despite the presence of several heaters. Transverse slots were cut in the channel, and the heaters, which were arranged on a

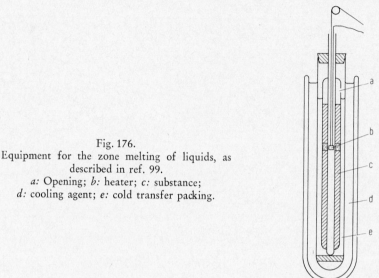

Fig. 176.
Equipment for the zone melting of liquids, as
described in ref. 99.
a: Opening; *b:* heater; *c:* substance;
d: cooling agent; *e:* cold transfer packing.

bar and could be moved in all directions, were inserted into the slots. The distance between the heaters was always the same.

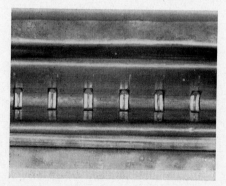

Fig. 177.
Cooling channel of the ice
zone-melting apparatus,
with heaters (top view).

Owing to the rigid arrangement of the cooling system, the heaters were made movable. In particular, they could easily be moved upwards or downwards, thus providing a means of regulating the temperature, especially when the current could not be varied. To avoid unnecessary heating of the cold space, the heaters were embedded in steatite bearers, which were sawn out of a steatite sheet before firing.

The glass boat, which is 12 to 15 cm long, is roughly half-filled with the solution to be zone-refined, and the open end is closed with a stopper. The rate of transport of the strongly cooled boat in the cooling trough is 1 to 10 mm/h. After concentration of the impurities, the boat is removed from the apparatus and cut into segments (on dry ice) with a glass cutter. Particular care must be taken in the separation of the part which solidified last, since this part usually contains the desired (or in the case of organic solvents, undesirable) components (see Fig. 178).

Fig. 178.
Accumulation of methylene blue at the end of the boat after 8 zone passes.

The purification effect cannot always be observed with the naked eye, as is the case in Fig. 178. With colorless compounds in open boats, a narrow strip of filter paper may be laid on the surface of the frozen material, heated for a short time with a hot air drier, and then removed (cf. Fig. 179). In this way a very thin surface layer is melted, and is immediately absorbed by the paper. The substances are then detected in the paper strip as in paper chromatography.

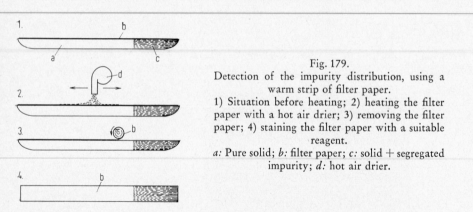

Fig. 179.
Detection of the impurity distribution, using a warm strip of filter paper.
1) Situation before heating; 2) heating the filter paper with a hot air drier; 3) removing the filter paper; 4) staining the filter paper with a suitable reagent.
a: Pure solid; *b:* filter paper; *c:* solid + segregated impurity; *d:* hot air drier.

An example of this method of detection was the technique used to follow the concentration of Salyrgan from a very dilute aqueous solution (a few µg/l). The color distribution along the paper strip on treatment with dithizone[136] clearly showed that all of the mercury complex had travelled to the end of the boat after 20 zone passes.

Since displacement of matter occurs during the zone melting of organic solvents, certain difficulties are encountered in preventing the substances from mixing again on thawing. Semi-circular steatite "hurdles" 5 mm high are therefore built into the boat. Material passes over these during the zone melting, as a result of transport of matter. They therefore provide a type of fractionation, so that after many zone

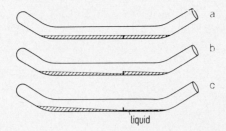

Fig. 180. (a) Before zone melting. The hurdle is 2.5 cm away from the right-hand end of the boat. (b) After 7 zone passes at 20 mm/h, the benzene has flowed over the hurdle. (c) After a further 7 zone passes, the portion to the right of the hurdle no longer solidifies (m.p.—26 to —30° C); the thiophene is highly concentrated in this portion.

passes the purified solvent is all at the beginning of the boat, whilst the part behind the hurdle remains liquid owing to the strong depression of the freezing point. It is therefore only necessary to pour this solution away.

Fig. 181. Part of an apparatus for the zone melting of frozen liquids, showing copper coolers separated by electric heaters.

Fig. 181 shows the heaters and coolers of a large apparatus for the zone melting of frozen liquids in quantities of up to 250 g[98]. The interior of the cabinet is well insulated, and can be cooled to −65° C; this temperature is maintained even when all 24 heaters are in operation. The cold is produced in 25 cooling elements by evaporation of Frigen F 22, which enters from a cooling unit with an air-cooled 2.6 HP compressor (Messrs. Göldner, Stuttgart, Type III H 300) via two valves at two separate points in the series-connected coolers. Each cooler is 1.6 cm away from the others, and is in the form of a ring (outside diameter 6 cm, inside diameter 2.4 cm, width 3 cm). Electric ring heaters 1 cm wide are situated in the spaces between the coolers. The same apparatus can also be used in conjunction with a cold thermostat with cooling brine. For very low temperatures, however, it will pay to use a gas refrigerator with a ventilator head.

With the exception of the cooling unit, the whole arrangement is housed in a trough-shaped wooden box 2.5 m long (see Fig. 182), lined with "Corblanite"

Fig. 182.
Overall view of an opened apparatus for the zone melting of frozen liquids.

(Messrs. Grünzweig & Hartmann, Ludwigshafen) insulating slabs 11 cm thick and zinc sheet, to give a wall thickness of 13 cm. The cover is hinged, and has a large window (12 × 75 cm) consisting of five panes of glass, one on top of the other, with a space between each pair. The transformer is situated outside the box.

Schildknecht and Schnell[150] solved the cooling problem by the use of Peltier elements. A microapparatus was made with a single element, and an apparatus for 10 mm tubes was made with a set of 10 elements in series together with two elements for a cooled guide rail.

SPECIAL SECTION

1. Zone Melting of Elements and Inorganic Substances

1.1 Semiconducting Elements

A semiconductor is a crystalline solid with a specific electrical conductivity somewhere between that of an insulator and that of a metal. In contrast to the case of metals, the conductivity of semiconductors increases rapidly with increasing temperature. The room temperature value for most semiconductors is between 10^4 and $10^{-1} \Omega^{-1} cm^{-1}$, and is greatly affected by minute imperfections in the crystal lattice, e.g. as a result of the occupation of lattice sites by foreign atoms. Consequently, the semiconductors used for diodes and transistors must be extremely pure. This high purity cannot, however, be attained by the normal chemical methods and it was only with the development of zone melting that it became possible to prepare large quantities of semiconductors, principally germanium and silicon, of the required purity. On the other hand, it is also necessary to blend these very pure elements again with foreign atoms at a definite concentration to give either excess conduction (n-conduction) or defect conduction (p-conduction), according to the density of the electrons or defect electrons. Zone leveling provided a suitable method of carrying out this doping.

1.1.1 Germanium

Burton [137] has published a review dealing with the impurities occurring in germanium. With the aid of electrical measurements, Pfann [138] showed that, after as few as six passes in the zone refining of germanium, only one foreign atom remained per 10^{10} germanium atoms. Mass-spectrometric studies showed that the zone-refined germanium contained less than one part in 10^7 of atomically dispersed impurities [139].

1.1.1.1 Preparation in the Pure State

The starting material for the preparation of pure germanium [140] is germanium dioxide (GeO_2) (cf. also [141]).

Germanium dioxide is dried for 20 h in a graphite boat at 200° C, and traces of chlorides are also driven off at the same time. Two full boats are then placed in a heated quartz tube, flushed with nitrogen, and reduced at 675° C for 3.5 h in a current of hydrogen (40 l/min).

The resulting germanium powder is fused at 1010° C, and the melt is allowed to solidify by normal freezing, by withdrawing the graphite boats from the heated zone at a rate of 0.6 cm/min. The temperature of the "cool zone" is still maintained at about 400° C. The germanium ingots obtained in this manner are further purified by zone melting in a graphite container with a zone speed of 0.4 cm/min. The boat must be inclined to the horizontal during this operation, since germanium contracts on melting and exhibits transport of matter during zone melting [142].

Jensen [143] has described an arrangement with which up to 1 kg of germanium can be zone-refined in a single operation, whilst Butuzov and Dobrovenskii [144] favor an apparatus in which the process is carried out either under vacuum (6×10^{-4} mm Hg) or in an inert gas. These authors report that four quartz boats can be processed simultaneously at a rate of 10 to 80 mm/h, to give four single crystals of pure germanium, 30 cm long and 10 mm thick. In the normal zone refining of germanium, however, the ingots obtained are generally polycrystalline and have a specific resistance, on the average, of 20 to 50 ohm·cm at 23° C [145]. The

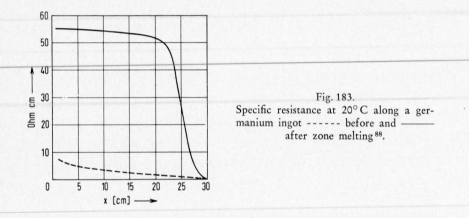

Fig. 183.
Specific resistance at 20° C along a germanium ingot ------ before and ———— after zone melting [88].

specific resistance of the starting material is between 7 and 0.3 ohm·cm (cf. Fig. 183).

Part of the contaminated end of the germanium ingot still has a better resistance characteristic (20 to 0.5 ohm·cm) than the starting material, so that further zone melting of this portion can still yield very pure germanium. The same is true of the repeated zone melting of portions with specific resistances of 0.5 to 0.05 ohm·cm.

In general, the rate of travel of the molten zone should not exceed 0.4 cm/min, even when a cooling system has been installed, as suggested by Herkart and Christian [140]. If the boat is drawn through the induction heaters more rapidly, a distinct decrease in purity is observed, even in the main part of the ingot (see Fig. 184), owing to the dependence of the effective distribution coefficient on the rate of freezing.

The purification effect at the beginning of the ingot is naturally greater after 12 zone passes than after 6 (see Fig. 185).

A German patent describes the prelimininary purification of germanium which contains sulfur, phosphorus, and selenium, i.e. elements with distribution coefficients which do not favor rapid zone refining[146]. The conditions are much more favorable in the case of the

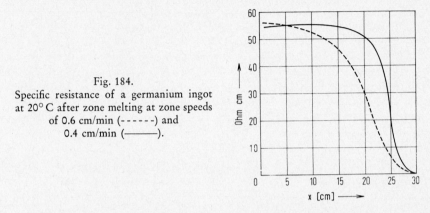

Fig. 184.
Specific resistance of a germanium ingot at 20° C after zone melting at zone speeds of 0.6 cm/min (------) and 0.4 cm/min (———).

chlorides, so that an appreciable purification can be achieved simply by normal freezing of the impure germanium tetrachloride in liquid air or solid carbon dioxide, particularly if the residual liquid is constantly stirred. The impurities with $k < 1$ accumulate in a portion of germanium tetrachloride which solidifies either right at the end or not at all, and are rejected with this portion. The substances with $k > 1$ are isolated from the first crystallizate, which

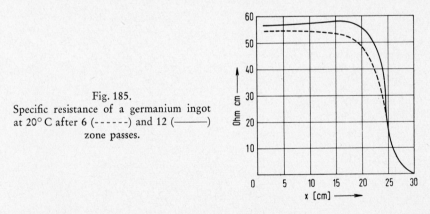

Fig. 185.
Specific resistance of a germanium ingot at 20° C after 6 (------) and 12 (———) zone passes.

should consist of about one-half of the starting material, and which is then again subjected to normal freezing. After several normal freezing passes, the germanium tetrachloride is finally oxidized as usual to germanium dioxide, and this in turn is reduced to germanium.

1.1.1.2 Doping

To produce semiconductor crystals, the very pure germanium obtained by zone melting is doped with elements of groups 3 or 5 of the periodic system. This doping can be carried out using the simple arrangement described by Pfann and Olsen [138, 147].

At the beginning of the zone leveling, a small pellet of antimony/germanium or indium/germanium alloy is placed in front of the germanium ingot (length about 30 cm), followed by an oriented crystal to serve as a nucleus. The process is carried out in a sooted quartz boat. The crystallization nucleus is not melted during the zone leveling. The mixed melt is then allowed to solidify in such a way as to give a homogeneous single crystal when the additives have been uniformly distributed. This single crystal is usually about 30 cm long and 500 g in weight. The quality of the single crystal can be improved by drawing it more slowly and by minimizing convection in the molten zone as a result of the induction current required for heating. Consequently the zone travels more slowly than in zone refining, and care is taken to ensure uniform heating, so that crystals with a dislocation frequency of 2 to 300/cm² are obtained.

Whereas in growing single crystals the temperature change at the interface is kept small, the emphasis in purification is rather on a steep temperature gradient to suppress the back-diffusion of copper, nickel, and lithium in the germanium. Copper $(D \approx 10^{-5}$ cm²/sec) diffuses particularly rapidly in germanium. The publications by Logan and Schwartz [148] and by Krömer [149], dealing with the removal of copper from solid germanium, are also of interest in this connection.

A technique suitable for doping has been described by Bennet and Sawyer [118], whilst Billig [151] has discussed the influence of the conditions of growth on the dislocations in germanium and silicon crystals. The nature of the dislocations in zone-leveled germanium has been investigated in particular detail by Pfann and Vogel [152].

Pfann and Dorsi [56] obtained single crystals of germanium saturated with lead by temperature gradient zone melting. The resulting germanium/lead solid solution still gave a lifetime of 30 μsec for the charge carrier.

Whether the single crystal is grown from the melt or obtained by the zone leveling of a pure germanium ingot which contains the additives only at the foremost tip or already distributed along the entire ingot, it is always advantageous to know the distribution coefficients of the additives. Substances with low k-values immediately give a very uniform ingot [153]; thus antimony ($k = 0.003$) is regarded as a good donor and indium ($k = 0.001$) as a very useful acceptor.

An interesting variant of Czochralski's technique [154], the so-called "floating crucible" method developed by Philips Laboratories [155], always yields homogeneously doped single crystals, irrespective of k. In this technique the crystalline rod is drawn from a small crucible filled with liquid germanium, and the germanium removed from this crucible is replaced from a larger container connected to the crucible by a capillary tube. As the germanium is replaced, the foreign additive is also replaced so that the concentration of the additive in the germanium reservoir is equal to that in the single crystal, whilst the concentration in the small crucible is $1/k$ times this value.

The k-values of the important additives for germanium are listed in Table 10; with the exception of the value for boron, all these are less than 1.

Table 10. Distribution coefficients of doping elements for the
solid/liquid equilibrium in germanium.

Additive	k	Additive	k
P	0.12	Au	3×10^{-5}
As	0.05	Ag	10^{-4}
Al	0.10	Cu	1.6×10^{-5}
Ga	0.10	Ge	1
Sb	0.003	B	20
In	10^{-3}	Zn	0.01

Since the distribution coefficients depend on the solidification conditions, it is possible to produce a sudden change in the concentration of the additive in the recrystallizing material by making a sudden change in the rate of solidification, i. e. the rate of zone travel during the zone melting. This is how the desired p-n junctions are produced, e. g. in the doping of germanium with antimony [48].

Owing to the relatively small distribution coefficient of bismuth in germanium, material doped with bismuth is very uniform [157], and has a specific resistance of about 3 ohm cm.

1.1.2 Silicon

Silicon is the starting material for the manufacture of diodes, transistors, and solar batteries. Owing to its high melting point (1412° C), it cannot be zone-refined or drawn into single crystals as easily as germanium.

The conventional method has been used with success by Hartman and Ostapkovich [158], who used a very thin-walled container made of ultrapure quartz (cf. also [159]), and minimized wetting of the vessel by the melt by painting the wall of the vessel with a fluoride mixture [137]. Boron and oxygen are however always difficult to eliminate, boron acting as an acceptor and oxygen as a donor.

To avoid the need for the high melting temperature, Pfann suggests that silicon be zone-melted with the addition of tin. This author places the silicon at the end of an ingot of tin and allows it to migrate progressively to the beginning of the ingot in the course of zone melting [56]. The impurities form a multi-component eutectic with the tin, which accumulates at the end of the ingot. Silicon purified by this method always contains a little tin.

The best method of preparing physically pure silicon is probably the floating zone method; this avoids contamination by the material of containers which are readily attacked by the molten silicon. The donors antimony and phosphorus and the acceptor aluminum are readily removed by zone melting. Kaiser et al.[160] and Akiyama and Kubo[161] report that the oxygen content is reduced to below the detection limit during this process. Boron, on the other hand, with a distribution coefficient of 0.8 is tenaciously retained by the silicon. Since a specific resistance of a few thousand ohm·cm can only be achieved with a boron content not greater than about 10^{12} atoms/cm³, Theuerer [162] oxidized the boron in the molten zone with water vapor. Owing to its insolubility in solid silicon, the resulting boric oxide is carried with the molten zone to the end of the ingot, or may even be vaporized in the meantime. Other impurities may also be vaporized during the zone melting if, as described by Bourassa [163], the operation is carried out in ultrahigh vacuum (10^{-5} mm Hg) and with a high pumping rate (ca. 10 m³/min). The working pressure thus lies below the vapor pressure of arsenic, antimony, and aluminum, so that these elements vaporize. This effect is favored by the relatively large molten area in the floating zone method. Phosphorus, which like boron is difficult to remove by other means, is also eliminated by this method.

The purification of silicon at Messrs. Merck & Co. Inc., Danville, Pa., U.S.A., described by Bourassa, begins with the preparation of silicon ingots 2.5 cm thick and 60 cm long, which are then zone-refined until the specific resistance has reached the value of 1000 ohm·cm required for the semiconductor material. As Buehler [90] reported as early as 1957, silicon can be obtained with a specific resistance of 16,000 ohm·cm, corresponding to 1 ppb of electrically active impurities, by 67 zone passes.

Dow Corning's Electronics Products Division [164] prepares single crystals of silicon by a process developed by Steward; the products are characterized by a particularly good lattice structure and by the fact that the ingots are 40 mm thick! The impurity content is again only of the order of ppb. This method was developed from techniques evolved by Westinghouse and Siemens-Schuckert.

Silicon can also be doped from the gas phase during zone melting, if no container is used. A very elegant example of this is doping with phosphorus, in which a trace of phosphine is added to the inert protective gas [142]. The phosphine then decomposes over the hot molten zone, and part of the phosphorus formed melts in the liquid silicon. The same principle can also be used in doping with arsenic and antimony, in which case arsine or antimony trichloride is added to the gas phase.

1.1.3 Germanium-Silicon Alloys

Mitrenin et al. [165] used a pressure of 3.5 t/cm² to mold powdered germanium with a specific resistance of 1 ohm·cm and acid-washed silicon into ingots measuring 9×9×95 mm, which were then sintered at 800° C. Zone melting in graphite or quartz boats gave a homogeneous solid solution of silicon in germanium containing 2.25 to 40 at-% of silicon. To obtain regions of uniform concentration, it was necessary to pass the silite heater several times over the ingot at a rate of 5 to 7 mm/h; as in zone leveling, the zone travels in alternate directions. Another method of preparing single crystals of a Si/Ge alloy by zone melting has been described in a US patent[166]. In this process the silicon is placed in a channel running through the germanium ingot. The temperature in the molten zone is about $1100°C$ for an alloy containing 95 at-% of Ge and 5 at-% of Si.

1.2 Semiconducting Compounds

In 1952, Welker[167] published his discovery that compounds of elements of groups III and V are very similar in their electrical properties to the semiconducting elements, and also exhibit semiconducting characteristics. These properties are subject to the same conditions with regard to purity as in the case of semiconducting elements. It must be noted, however, that the composition of a pure compound AB may change during zone melting, and that in theoretical considerations regarding the melt/crystal distribution equilibrium it is necessary to bear two distribution coefficients in mind. With the aid of a few general assumptions, it is possible to predict the deviations from the stoichiometric composition along the ingot as proposed by Boomgaard[168].

1.2.1 Indium Antimonide

The preparation of indium antimonide (InSb) has been repeatedly described, and this compound, with its high electron mobility, was zone-refined only a year after the invention of zone melting.

Pearson and Tanenbaum[169] have prepared indium antimonide from zone-refined elements, and have found a specific electrical resistance of 0.03 ohm · cm after zone melting of polycrystalline samples. The principal impurity was arsenic (about 0.03%). According to spectroscopic data, the concentrations of all other impurities were less than 0.005%. The composition of the compound itself was stoichiometric to within 0.2% (standard deviation); it exhibits n-conduction at room temperature, and p-conduction at $175°C$.

Electrical studies have also been carried out by Hatton and Rollin[170] between $300°K$ and $1°K$, using ingots measuring $10 \times 2 \times 2$ mm. After repeated zone refining, these authors obtained values which agreed with those reported by Pearson and Tanenbaum[169]. Measurement of the Hall effect at room temperature gave an electron mobility of 2.5×10^4 cm²/Vs. The authors also found a p-conduction at $90°K$, with a defect electron concentration of 3×10^{16} cm^{-3} and a mobility of 3×10^3 cm²/Vs.

Tanenbaum and Briggs[171] have investigated the optical properties of indium antimonide, since contradictory values had been found for the energies of the forbidden bands. Their first samples, which had a specific resistance of 10^{-4} ohm · cm, were prepared from 99.8% antimony and 99.95% indium. The transmission spectrum of sheets of indium antimonide 0.025 cm thick showed a long-wave absorption edge extending from 3.2 μ (see Fig. 186, curve a). After zone refining, particularly of the antimony and of the compound, the authors obtained a specific resistance of 7×10^{-3} ohm·cm, which is very probably the specific resistance of indium antimonide at room temperature. The absorption edge was now situated at 7.0 μ, when measured on a sheet of InSb 0.0175 cm thick (Fig. 186, curve b). It may be concluded from this that the increased transmission between 3.2 μ and 7 μ is

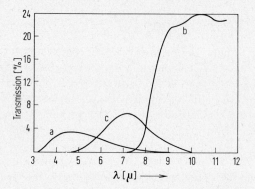

Fig. 186. Transmission spectra of indium antimonide:
a) crude;   b) zone-refined;   c) not completely zone-refined.

due to impurities (Burstein effect[172]). This is also supported by the position of curve c, which was obtained with samples which had not yet been completely zone-refined. On the

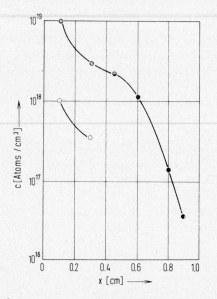

Fig. 187. Distribution of zinc •——• in an indium antimonide ingot after 5 zone passes, together with the distribution of an unknown substance ○——○ with $k > 1$, also after 5 zone passes.

basis of zone-melting investigations, the anomalous transmission is attributed to an impurity with $k < 1$, probably nickel.

Harman [173] refined indium antimonide by zone melting and then analyzed it. The compound was prepared from the elements in a Vycor glass tube, and was zone-refined in the same tube, first with long zones ($l = 1/2 L$) moving at a rate of 30 cm/h, and then with smaller zones ($l = 1/10 L$) at 1 cm/h. About 10 to 15 zones were passed along an indium antimonide ingot 20 cm long under the conditions specified last. The end containing the impurities was rejected during the zone refining. Electrical measurements showed that the whole ingot was p-conducting at the beginning of the zone melting, whilst the end which solidified last became n-conducting after a number of zones passes. Further zone passes led to extension of this region, and after the passage of 30 zones, one half of the ingot was found to be p-conducting and the other half n-conducting. Zinc was spectroscopically identified as the acceptor. During zone melting, this element migrates to the beginning of the ingot, in contrast to copper, lead, tin, and nickel.

Fig. 187 shows the concentration curves found by Harman, in one case after zone melting of indium antimonide doped with 2.6×10^{18} zinc atoms per cm^3, and in the other after zone melting of the indium antimonide to be investigated. The foreign substances migrate to the beginning of the ingot in both cases, and the rates of migration are the same. It may be accepted, simply from the similarity in the shapes of the concentration curves, that the acceptor present must be zinc.

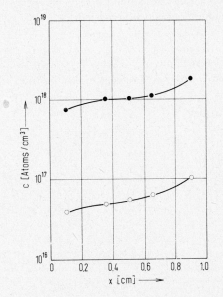

Fig. 188. Distribution of tellurium •——• and of an unknown impurity ○——○ in indium antimonide after zone melting.

Tellurium was identified as the donor by the same method. To obtain samples with uncompensated n-conduction, these were taken at a distance of about 5 cm from the p-n junction in the zone-refined ingot. Fig. 188 again shows the distribution of the unkown element in comparison with that of tellurium after zone melting of a tellurium-doped indium antimonide ingot. It can be seen that the segregation behavior of the foreign substance is very similar to that of tellurium, but not to that of sulfur or selenium (cf. Fig. 189).

It can be seen from Fig. 189 that in the zone melting of indium antimonide the rate of migration is greatest for sulfur, decreasing through selenium to tellurium. In calculations on the zone-melting behavior of substances with different distribution coefficients, Reiss[174] found the distribution coefficient of tellurium to be 0.8, that of selenium 0.5, of sulfur 0.1 and of zinc roughly 10. Kanai[175], on the other hand, found values of 1.4 and 0.52 for zinc and lead respectively. Thus after 15 to 20 zone passes, lead migrates to the end of the ingot which solidifies last, together with tin, iron, and thallium. Arsenic was found together with the zinc at the beginning of the ingot.

Besides the elements zinc, tellurium, and arsenic, mentioned above, Hulme and Mullin[176] included cadmium in their investigations on the effect of evaporation on the efficiency of purification. The results obtained by these authors did not agree with those found by Harman under the same conditions (including operation under $1/3$ atm of H_2). They obtained reproducible results by working under vacuum. However, the difference was significant: in addition to the segregation, evaporation of the acceptors zinc and cadmium from the molten indium antimonide was also observed.

To prepare pure indium antimonide by zone melting, spectroscopically pure indium and antimony were allowed to react in a vacuum, in a quartz tube 1 cm in diameter, until the compound was formed. On solidification of the indium antim-

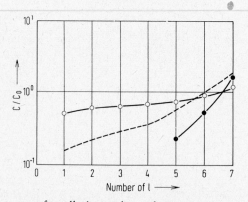

Fig. 189. Distribution curves for tellurium and an unknown impurity o———o, as well as for selenium — — — and for sulfur •———•, in indium antimonide.

onide melt, to which 20 or 40 mg of the doping element was added for doping experiments, an ingot 20 cm long was formed in the sealed tube. This ingot was then placed in a zone-melting apparatus with heating coils or with induction heating. To avoid transport of matter (see p. 74), the ingot was inclined at an angle of 5°.

An appreciable reduction of the acceptor concentration could only be achieved in an apparatus with inductive heating, whilst the apparatus with heating coils simply led to a uniform distribution of the acceptor in the ingot. This was not due, as was supposed, to less efficient mixing of the melt in the zones produced by resistance heaters, since no improvement in the results was observed at lower rates of zone travel. It was due instead to the absence of a condensate, which was deposited on the wall of the tube over the ingot in the case of induction heating. This condensate contains zinc and cadmium. The authors therefore suggested that these impurities should be removed from the original indium and antimony before zone melting, by pumping them off in high vacuum ($<10^{-5}$ mm Hg) for several hours at 700° C.

Okoniewski[178] purified indium in the same manner, by heating it for four hours at 720° C and 10^{-4} mm Hg. After cooling and removal of the condensate from the walls of the quartz distillation apparatus, the sample was further purified by distillation at 1200° C (10^{-4} mm Hg). However a publication by Adamichka and Payakova[179] shows that purification is also possible simply by zone refining. These authors obtained 99.999% pure indium by zone melting with 15 passes and a zone speed of 5 to 10 cm/h.

Vinogradova, Calavanov, and Nasledov[180] prepared very pure indium antimonide by zone melting. The zone refining was followed by measurement of the specific resistance, the concentration of impurities, and the mobility of electrons and defect electrons along the ingot. The lowest impurity concentration was about 2.5×10^{13} atoms per cm^3, and the highest carrier mobility was given as 4×10^5 cm^2/Vs at 77° K and about 10^5 cm^2/Vs at room temperature.

1.2.2   Aluminum Antimonide

Aluminum antimonide (AlSb) is also one of the semiconducting A^{III}B^V compounds described by Welker, and has the advantage of all antimonides in that it can be readily prepared, zone-refined, and doped, owing to its low vapor pressure at the melting point. Schell[181] prepared this compound from 99.99% pure aluminum and zone-refined antimony. All the impurities of the antimony, with the exception of arsenic and bismuth (k=0.2), could be removed by zone melting of chemically pure samples. The components were fused together in an alumina crucible under argon; the mixture solidified above 750° C, and was allowed to react completely at 1100° C.

The aluminum antimonide, in the form of a cylindrical rod, was placed in an alumina boat and zone-melted in a quartz tube with two circular radiators, again operating under very pure argon. Since electrical resistance heaters would have to be heated to 1200° C, i.e. the devitrification temperature of quartz glass, for the zone melting of the compound, it was better to use inductive heating via a graphite boat. The impurities introduced with the aluminum, namely copper, iron, silicon, calcium, and lead, could be removed from the compound using a zone 20 mm long and travelling at 1 to 4 mm/min. As a result of the purification, the specific resistance was increased by a factor of 500, from 0.02 to 10 ohm·cm. As was shown by the current-voltage characteristic and the sign of the thermoelectric current, the single crystals obtained by zone melting at a travel rate 0.5mm/min are p-conducting throughout. Zone leveling with Se (as Sb_2Se_3) gives an n-type semiconductor.

The preparation of aluminum antimonide has been studied in detail by Allred, Paris, and Gensel [182], who found that graphite crucibles are unsuitable, owing to the formation of free antimony and aluminum carbide, and that, of the other crucible materials available, boron nitride, silicon nitride, tantalum, magnesia, and alumina have the best properties.

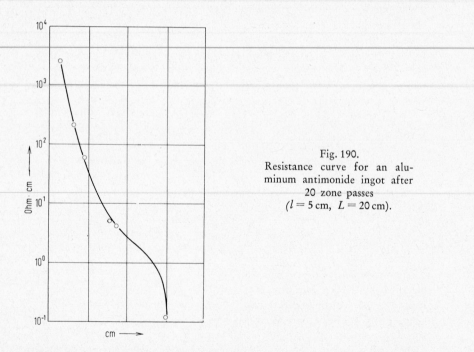

Fig. 190.
Resistance curve for an aluminum antimonide ingot after 20 zone passes
($l = 5$ cm, $L = 20$ cm).

The zone-melting arrangement is the same as that described by Schell, i.e. uniform heating of the Vycor glass protecting tube at 800° C. The apparatus is fully automatic in operation; the graphite muffle and the boat are returned to the starting position after one zone pass, with simultaneous recording of the number of zones.

Fig. 190 shows the change in the specific resistance along an aluminum antimonide ingot after purification with 20 zone passes ($l=5$ cm, $L=20$ cm). After zone melting, the specific resistance dropped from above 10^3 ohm $\cdot$ cm at the beginning of the ingot to 10^{-1} ohm $\cdot$ cm at the end. Different ingots always gave the same resistance characteristic, although the values at the beginning of the ingot varied between 10 ohm $\cdot$ cm and 10^3 ohm $\cdot$ cm. This scatter is attributed to impurities which were already present in the aluminum antimonide.

It was also thought at first that these impurities caused the unusually high resistance at the beginning of the ingot (see Fig. 190) as a result of a compensation effect; the distribution coefficients of the spectroscopically detected impurities were therefore determined by zone leveling (cf. Table 11). Since, however, all the k-values are less than unity, the impurities should have been found at the end of the ingot after zone melting. Even the transition elements vanadium and titanium have very low distribution coefficients, and accumulate at the end of the ingot. These can therefore also be ruled out as possible causes of the high resistance at the beginning of the ingot (cf. the case of iron and cobalt in germanium[183]). According to qualitative crystal growth experiments, the k-values of selenium and tellurium (which are difficult to detect by spectroscopic methods) are also less than unity, so that those donors could not be considered for the compensation of the acceptors.

Allred, Paris, and Gensel[182] grew aluminum antimonide monocrystals by the Czochralski method. It was also possible to use graphite crucibles in this case. Note,

Table 11. Distribution coefficients of the impurities occurring in aluminum antimonide, determined by the zone-alloying method (after Allred et al.[182]).

Element	k
Magnesium	0.1
Silicon	0.1
Copper	0.02—0.1
Iron	0.01—0.1
Boron	0.01—0.02
Silver	0.1
Lead	<0.01
Vanadium	<0.01
Nickel	<0.01
Manganese	<0.01
Titanium	<0.01

however, that most of the impurities come from the crucibles, and not from non-stoichiometric mixtures, since both aluminum and antimony are insoluble in aluminum antimonide.

1.2.3 Cadmium Telluride

After Jenny and Bube[184] had shown in 1954 that cadmium telluride (CdTe) can be made either n-conducting or p-conducting by doping with different elements,

Kröger and De Nobel [185] varied the cadmium/tellurium ratio. These authors obtained n-conduction with excess cadmium and p-conduction with excess tellurium; this behavior corresponds to that of the semiconducting compounds of lead, namely lead sulfide, lead selenide, and lead telluride.

The authors prepared cadmium telluride by subliming commercial electrolytic cadmium and selenium in vacuo, and allowing the elements to react in a crucible under 40 atm of nitrogen, at 500°C. After melting (at 1050°C) and cooling by blowing off the nitrogen, they obtained a polycrystalline cadmium/tellurium ingot, which was then further purified by crystallization. It was necessary to bear in mind during this operation the fact that if the cadmium/tellurium compound is melted in an open crucible without suitable precautions, elementary tellurium is liberated once more, and a large quantity of material is lost by sublimation. This can be avoided if the operation is carried out in a closed vessel under cadmium vapor at a pressure of 1 atm. A zone-melting apparatus for use with CdTe, PbS, and GaAs has been described by Boomgaard, Kröger, and Vink [127] (cf. also Fig. 154).

Single crystals of the very pure cadmium/tellurium compound were grown with particular care. The compound was placed in a sooted conical quartz container, which moved in a larger quartz tube with a speed of 1 cm/h. The larger tube exhibited a temperature gradient, and cadmium was passed in at one end. The temperature was regulated by two thermocouples.

Mochalov [186] prepared 99.995% cadmium in 70% yield, using 15 zone passes under optimum zone-melting conditions (v=5 to 30 mm/h and l=0.2 L). Further zone-refining gave a 60% yield of 99.999 to 99.9995% Cd. The remaining 40% had the same degree of purity as the starting material, and could be used again as such. Only 0.5% was lost by evaporation. An even purer zone-refined cadmium was obtained by Aleksandrow [187]. Before zone melting, this material contained 0.011% of lead, 0.006% of copper, 0.004% of zinc, 0.002% of nickel, and traces of iron. The zone-refined material was obtained as 99.99995% cadmium; 99.9998% zinc was obtained in the same manner.

1.2.4 Gallium Arsenide

Apart from Barrie et al.[188] the principal workers concerned with the preparation and the zone melting of gallium arsenide (GaAs) were Folberth and Weiss [125]. This compound was prepared by melting the components in flat, elongated crucibles, and was then allowed to solidify from one end. The boat did not burst, despite the anomalous expansion of the compound on freezing. The compound was then zone-melted in a quartz ampoule, using a tube heater in addition to the furnace used to produce the zone. The temperature in the tube was kept above the condensation or sublimation temperature of the highly volatile components, but still below the melting point of the compound. The samples of gallium arsenide obtained were characterized in the usual manner by measurement of the conductivity and of the

Hall effect between $-180°$ and $960°C$. Indium phosphide was also prepared in a similar manner.

According to Knight[189], carbon can be used as the crucible material for gallium arsenide provided that is does not come into contact with reducible oxides, such as SiO_2. Chemical analyses have shown that gallium arsenide contains less than 2.7×10^{17} atoms of carbon per cm^3 when the compound separates from the melt in contact with carbon.

Whelan and Wheatley[126], working without a crucible, have grown single crystals from zone-refined gallium arsenide, and in so doing gained a number of advantages over Gremmelmaier[190] (cf. also Richards[191]). In the first place, only a few impurities could enter, and secondly, the temperature of the molten part of the ingot could be easily controlled, so that uniform doping was achieved. Finally, the gas/liquid equilibrium could be readily established, owing to the relatively large surface area as compared with the volume of the liquid. This was important since the mono-crystals were drawn at a rate of 1 to 2 mm/min, under arsenic vapor at a pressure of 535 ± 25 mm Hg.

Izergin, Selivanova, and Melchenko[192] have prepared gallium arsenide from the elements by zone melting. They were able to maintain a certain arsenic vapor pressure by heating the components separately. High-frequency heating was employed, and the reaction was appreciably accelerated by vibration. This method is suitable for the removal of tin, antimony, bismuth, silver, iron, germanium, and nickel, all of which have distribution coefficients smaller than unity. A particularly efficient separation is achieved if the rate of zone travel is reduced to 8 mm/h.

Horner[193] obtained single crystals of gallium alone by a very interesting process, corresponding to the zone freezing of a supercooled melt.

A comprehensive review of all publications relating to the purification of gallium and many other metals, as well as the analytical chemistry of the impurities, has been published by Papp and Solymar[194]. According to this review, very pure gallium (99.9999%) can be obtained if, after an acid-alkali treatment, the metal is purified by electrolysis, followed by zone melting.

In a departure from the usual zone melting procedure, Chinese workers[195] have purified gallium in a plastic tube, which was wound round a horizontal glass tube and rotated with the latter under a long heating element. The plastic spiral revolves about its axis once every 3 hours.

1.2.5 *Magnesium Stannide*

Lawson et al.[196] prepared magnesium stannide (Mg_2Sn) in a carbon crucible, by heating a stoichiometric mixture of magnesium and tin for four hours at $850°C$. The compound was then zone-refined under argon in a closed carbon container. Large crystals were obtained by melting and slow cooling from one end of the ingot, and were studied by infrared spectroscopy between 4.2 and $294°K$ (cf. Tausend[197]).

1.3 The Purification of Metals

1.3.1 *Beryllium and Magnesium*

The zone melting of beryllium is best carried out in an inert gas, since excessive losses occur in vacuum owing to the relatively high vapor pressure at its melting point[198]. Zone refining reduces the concentration of aluminum, iron, silicon, and beryllium oxide in the pure part of the ingot[199].

Magnesium can also be purified by zone melting if it is prevented from evaporating in the molten zone[200]. Nickel is the first impurity to be removed (e.g. after 6 zone passes with v=7.5 mm/h); this is followed by copper, silicon, zinc, and lead. These elements migrate to the end of the ingot, only manganese moving to the beginning.

Schaub[216] has shown that very pure metal is obtained after 6 passes at 40 mm/h. This method gave a highly ductile metal, in contrast to the usual very brittle material, and a rod 14 mm in diameter and 14 cm long could easily be bent by hand into a circle with a diameter of 40 mm. Activation analysis showed that the concentrations of aluminum, manganese, carbon, chromium, and tantalum had been particularly effectively reduced by the zone-melting process whereas copper was not removed. Depending on the nature of the impurity, activation analysis enables the detection of 1 to 10^{-4} ppm of foreign matter.

1.3.2 *Boron and Aluminum*

Crystalline powdered boron bonded with boric oxide can be zone-melted without a container and using inductive heating (3.5 Mc/s). Greiner[201] used a slightly modified version of the apparatus described by Theuerer[162]. A mixture containing 99% of argon and 1% of hydrogen was passed through the apparatus during zone melting. The melting of boron gave a uniform cross-section along the entire length of the ingot when the molten zone moved downwards, but not when it moved upwards. Eleswhere[202], Greiner described the zone melting of boron which was bonded with phosphoric acid and then melted at about 2000°C.

Chaudron and his school[92, 203—205] have carried out a series of excellent investigations on the preparation of very pure metals by zone melting, inter alia dealing in detail with aluminum. This can be obtained as "4 nines metal" (99.99 to 99.998%), corresponding to 20 ppm of impurities, by double electrolysis. Montariol et al.[206] have succeeded in reducing the content of impurities to 8 ppm, i.e. in obtaining 99.9992% pure aluminum. The criterion used to assess the purity of the metal was its electrical resistance R_T at the temperature of liquid hydrogen (20°K) compared with that at 295°K (R_0). Thus the value of R_0/R_T was found to be 2000 after zone refining, instead of the value of 1000 initially found for 99.998% aluminum[200—211]. After determining the optimum conditions by preliminary experiments, these authors[206] obtained extremely pure aluminum by passing nine 5 cm long zones through an aluminum ingot 40 cm long at a rate of 0.5 cm/h. The contaminated end was separated from the pure part of the ingot after 3 passes, and again after 6 passes. Inductive heating with a 4kW high-frequency generator (300 kc/s) was used. The distribution curve for copper in the aluminum[212] (cf. also[213]) shown in Fig. 191 is typical of the concentration curves for the impurities after zone refining.

The contents of other impurities are given in the tables published by Albert, which show the concentrations of 40 to 50 elements in zone-refined aluminum, as obtained by neutron activation analysis [115, 214, 215]. The total concentration of impurities found by activation analysis was less than 10^{-6}.

The highly purified aluminum exhibits interesting corrosion and recrystallization behavior, which has been described by Albert et al.[207], Demmler[217], and Montariol[218, 219]. According to these authors, cold-rolled metal recrystallizes to the extent of 95% at —40°C. Below a certain limiting concentration copper and magnesium impurities have no appreciable effect on the recrystallization process, whereas above this concentration they greatly reduce the rate of growth of the new crystals. On addition of silver, on the other hand, the rate

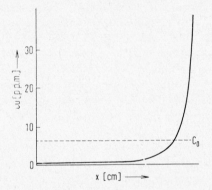

Fig. 191. Distribution of copper in an aluminium ingot after 9 zone passes[212].
——— Initial concentration.

of crystallization is reduced in accordance with the quantity of silver added[220]. According to Montariol[219], intergranular corrosion of zone-refined aluminum by hydrogen chloride proceeds more slowly than in the case of ordinary aluminum, and the corrosion resistance of the surface is also increased by zone melting, so that electrolytically polished metal maintains its surface properties for a long time in contact with hydrogen chloride.

It should be pointed out that zone refining has little effect on impurities with k-values greater than 0.2; thus, even with 9 zone passes, titanium, zirconium, and chromium cannot be removed from aluminum, since these metals all have k-values greater than unity.

Tougas[221] prepared 99.9988% aluminum from electrolytically purified 99.992% pure material, by zone melting in an induction furnace. Furthermore, according to a Chinese publication, aluminum and tin can even be zone-refined with a simple electrical resistance heater [222].

Guskov [223] has published a general review on the purification of aluminum, whilst Frois and Dimitrov [220, 224] studied the rate of recrystallization of aluminum containing traces of copper and magnesium (5 to 30 ppm). Using a boat made of alumina or pure aluminum oxide and lined with fused aluminum oxide, Braun et al. [73] purified a 99.99% aluminum ingot 44 cm long by zone melting with an induction heater. Consideration of the recrystallization times suggests that the zone refining may be considerably improved by mixing at the interface with a rotating magnetic field.

1.3.3   Tin and Lead

Starting with 99.99% tin, Tanenbaum, Goss, and Pfann [225] obtained a purity of 99.999% by zone melting with a maximum of 40 zone passes. This work was carried out in a Pyrex glass container, and lead, copper, and iron were eliminated from the ingot. Walton, Tiller, Rutter, and Winegard [226] and Kunzler and Renton [227] also succeeded in preparing 5-nines tin. Alexandrow, Werkin, and Lasarew [228] purified tin in a circular channel with a semicylindrical cross-section, and plotted diagrams showing the dependence of the zone-melting effect on the number of passes and on the rate of zone travel. In a continuation of this work, the same authors [229] introduced a preliminary purification, in which volatile compounds were eliminated prior to zone melting by heating the metal to incandescence for a long period in high vacuum. During preliminary tests, ^{65}Zn was added to the tin to facilitate examination for remaining impurities; the isotope was detected, as in work with ^{113}Sn, by activity measurements and by autoradiography [230]. It was found that efficient mixing by convection occurred in the molten zones. In the case of the Sn/0.3% Bi system "circulatory mixing" was tested in the molten zone, using an electromagnetic circulatory pump.

Reich and Montariol [231] also used radioelements to follow the behavior of impurities during the zone melting of impure tin. It was found that, after 5 zone passes, the silver content (^{110}Ag) in the first half of the ingot had fallen by a factor of more than 2500. The same authors had previously [232] succeeded in keeping the zone length constant as the zone passed along the ingot and in obtaining some definite information regarding the quantity of impurities picked up during zone melting in glass or graphite containers [233]. It was found that tin is not contaminated by Pyrex glass. The tin ingot 76 cm long was zone-refined in an atmosphere of argon (660 mm Hg) with 10 zones travelling at a rate of 5 mm/h. The material was then tested for purity by finding the ratio of its resistance at the temperature of liquid helium to that at room temperature. The ratio $\varrho_{4.2° K}/\varrho_{293° K}$ was found to be 32×10^{-6}, which is of the same order of magnitude as the value found by Kunzler [234] for zone-refined tin.

Baimokov et al. [235] passed several zones simultaneously through a horizontal tin ingot; after 50 zone passes ($l = 50$ mm, $v = 40$ mm/h), the content of lead, copper, zinc, and nickel in the first 60 to 70% of the ingot had fallen to less than 10^{-4}%. The bismuth concentration also fell to the same level, but only in the first 20% of the ingot, instead of 60 to 70%. Antimony collected at the beginning of the ingot. Baimokov and Selivanov [236] later described a zone-melting apparatus which can be used for the industrial production of 145 kg of zone-refined tin per month. The yield of pure tin with an impurity content of 2×10^{-4}% is 80 to 85%.

Ivannikov and Egorov [237] zone-refined tin in an open boat with an inclined base, so that it was possible to remove the impurities collecting at the end of the purified ingot as the purification progressed.

In 1956, Tiller and Rutter [238] published a paper on zone-refined lead alloyed with tin, silver, and gold, the main point of interest being the crystallization behavior of such alloys. The zone melting was carried out in a Vycor glass tube 1 inch in diameter, in an atmosphere of argon which had been purified at 850° C with a titanium sponge. The surface of the tube was first coated with a film of carbon by burning acetylene inside it. Adequate purification was achieved with 20 zone passes at 3 mm/min, the narrow molten zones being produced by an induction heater flanked by cooling windings.

According to Pfann and Dorsi [74], it is possible, by the use of electromagnetic agitation, not only to improve the purification effect, but also to control the effective distribution coefficient of an impurity, e. g. tin. Thus n-p-n junctions can be obtained under certain circumstances simply by changing the efficiency of agitation, i. e. in this case, by modifying the current I and the magnetic field strength H. The mathematical treatment carried out by Alexandrow et al. [230] is also of interest in this connection, as are the zone refining of lead-tin alloys containing 1% of tin and the autoradiographic recording of the distribution of ^{113}Sn in lead ingots.

In a paper published in 1959, Bolling [240] reported that the recrystallization temperature of zone-refined lead, as in the case of aluminum, continues to fall with increasing purity, and that the rate of migration of the interface is strongly affected by impurities which can be removed by zone melting [241-246].

In 1960, Alexandrov [247] published a paper on a simple method of preparing 99.99998% lead by zone melting and purification under vacuum.

1.3.4 Antimony and Bismuth

Tanenbaum, Goss, and Pfann [225, 248] were able to show that 99.8% antimony could be successfully purified with as few as 7 zone passes. The content of nickel, lead, silver, and copper immediately falls to $^1/_{10}$ of its original value; arsenic, on the other hand, must be removed by chemical means before zone melting, since its distribution coefficient is very close to 1. Mass-spectroscopic examination shows that material which has been pretreated in this way contains only about 1 ppm of arsenic and zinc after 10 zone passes.

In 1955, Schell [181] published results of the purification of antimony. This author removed most of the impurities except arsenic and bismuth by zone melting. His primary aim was to obtain a very pure single crystal of aluminum antimonide, and for this reason he fitted two after-heaters in his zone-melting apparatus; the temperature of the after-heaters was about 800° C, whilst that of the heaters proper was 1100° C.

By a suitable choice of zone-melting conditions, Trousil[249] succeeded in obtaining very pure germanium, bismuth, and antimony. Ivleva[250] prepared zone-refined antimony with maximum impurity levels of 0.00002% of Cu, 0.000006% of Ag, 0.0002% of As, 0.0006% of Rb, 0.0001% of Sn, 0.00005% of Bi, 0.0001% of In, 0.002% of Ga, 0.0004% of Fe, 0.0002% of Ni, 0.0002% of Co, 0.001% of Zn, 0.0001% of Al, 0.0005% of Si, 0.00003% of B, and 0.0002% of P.

Vigdorovich et al.[251] divided the impurities to be removed from antimony by zone melting into three groups. The first group contains elements which can be easily removed, and the second includes those which exhibit a pronounced segregation behavior, so that they attain a typical concentration distribution along the ingot in the course of zone melting. The third group contains elements which form solid solutions with antimony, and consequently migrate only slowly through the ingot. It is difficult to remove arsenic ($k = 0.64$), tin ($k = 0.3$), and bismuth ($k = 0.2$), while lead ($k = 0.06$) and germanium are rather more readily eliminated.

Wernick, Benson, and Dorsi[252] have devoted a great deal of attention to the purification of bismuth, and found that, during zone melting, iron accumulated in the part of the ingot which solidified first; this behavior has very rarely been described. Magnesium and calcium could still be detected in the adjacent part of the ingot. Silver, copper, lead, and tin could however no longer be detected by spectroscopy. The concentration of nickel in the starting material was below the limit of detection, and this metal was found in the end of the ingot only after the passage of 12 zones ($v=4.5$ cm/h). With the exeption of iron all elements mentioned above must have a distribution coefficient smaller than unity.

Sazhin and Dulkina[253] added about 10^{-4}% of zinc, antimony, copper, and silver nuclides to bismuth to examine the possibility of purifying this metal by ring zone melting. Antimony migrated to the beginning and the other three metals to the end of the circular ingot, which was interrupted at one point.

Galt et al.[254] first observed the phenomenon of cyclotron resonance[275] in bismuth; using this effect, it is possible to determine the effective mass (m_{eff}) of the electrons and defect electrons in semiconductors. The mobile charge carriers are exposed to a constant homogeneous magnetic field B, as well as an electric field with a variable frequency in the microwave range. The magnetic field compels the charge-carriers to move in a circular or helical path through which they pass with Larmor frequency $\omega_{Larmor} = (eB)/(m_{eff}c)$. When ω_{Larmor} agrees with the frequency of the electric field, absorption of the microwaves by the semiconductor reaches a maximum. This makes it possible to measure ω_{Larmor}, and, if B is known, also m_{eff}. The compounds or metals to be investigated must be extremely pure, and for this reason Dexter and Lax[255] used zone-refined antimony.

Sazhin and Dulkina[256] reduced the concentration of silver, tin, antimony, and copper in bismuth by zone melting, inter alia.

Zdanowicz[257] purified bismuth by first heating it to 600° C at 10^{-3} mm Hg for 24 hours, then zone melting with 24 zone passes at a travel rate of 20 mm/h. After only 3 passes, lead and silver could no longer be detected in 80% of the 27 cm ingot.

Nikolaenko[258] also reported a very effective purification of bismuth by distillation followed by zone melting.

1.3.5   *Yttrium, Rare Earth Metals, Titanium, and Zirconium*

An yttrium rod containing 0.052 wt.-% of oxygen and 0.65 wt.-% of fluorine was zone-melted by Carlson et al.[259] at a rate of 15 cm/h. After two passes the oxygen content remained unchanged, whereas the fluorine content had fallen to 0.002 wt.-%.

According to Huffine and Williams[260], zone refining of the rare earth metals may be of value for the removal of certain impurities.

Apart from a paper by Smith and Rutherford[261], Brace, Cochard, and Comenetz[109] also reported as early as 1955 the zone melting of titanium to remove iron. Darnell[262] confirmed that single crystals of titanium are hard to prepare, since a transition from a high-temperature β-form to a more stable low-temperature α-modification occurs at 882° C; zirconium undergoes a similar transition at 865 to 873° C.

The experimental details of the zone melting of titanium[262] are as follows: cylindrical ingot 1 cm in diameter and 15 cm long; zone length 1 cm; induction heating, frequency 4 Mc/s; rate of zone travel 6 cm/h. Darnell initially worked under vacuum, and avoided increasing surface contamination with the aid of an argon atmosphere.

The French school of Chaudron[264] zone-refined a vertical zirconium ingot in a similar manner. The starting material contained 880×10^{-6} parts of iron and 19×10^{-6} parts of nickel. Only 8×10^{-6} parts of these impurities remained after 10 passes through the induction heater.

Langeron[265] avoided contamination by oxygen, nitrogen, and carbon by working in an ultrahigh vacuum. After a preliminary degassing phase, he carried out 4 zone passes in the closed apparatus, and in this way removed practically all the metallic impurities and probably also the oxygen.

1.3.6   *Molybdenum, Tungsten, and Uranium*

According to Buehler[96], single crystals of molybdenum, tungsten, and uranium can be obtained by one zone pass under vacuum and without a container. Very pure tungsten and molybdenum can be prepared by zone melting (cf. Table 12), although the rates of evaporation of these two metals, unlike that of niobium, are relatively high at their melting points.

Table 12. Mass-spectroscopic purity of molybdenum after 3 zone passes without a container.

Impurity	Before [ppm]	After	
		Top [ppm]	End [ppm]
Tungsten	50	50	50
Nickel	5	< 0.2	< 0.2
Cobalt	10	< 0.1	< 0.1
Iron	100	1	< 0.1
Chromium	5	< 0.1	< 0.1
Aluminum	5	< 0.2	< 0.2
Phosphorus	10	< 0.2	< 0.2
Boron	0.1	< 0.1	< 0.1

In the case of molybdenum, the purification is due not to distribution of the impurities (except iron), but rather to their volatility.

The method proposed by Davis, Calverley, and Lever [84, 85, 119] of using electron bombardment to melt the zone, without a container, has also been used by Belk [266] for the purification of molybdenum. After two zone passes ($v = 3$ mm/min), the carbon content at the beginning of the ingot had fallen to $1/10$ of its initial value.

Carlson [86] also used a floating zone technique to purify tungsten rods in vacuum, the molybdenum present in the starting material evaporating off. The resulting single crystals were very pure, and were ductile at room temperature.

Schadler [267] obtained single crystals of tungsten by the same method, and used these to study the deformation behavior of zone-refined tungsten. The purity of the crystals is given in Table 13 (cf. also [268, 269]).

Shroff [270] prepared tungsten and molybdenum rods about 200 mm long and 1 to 5 mm in diameter using a 2.5 kW instrument with a tungsten electron source in high vacuum. He measured the crystallographic orientation, the electrical resistance at very low temperatures, and the hardness and ductility; solid-state mass spectrometry was successfully used to characterize the very pure metals.

Despite the high reactivity of molten uranium, Chaudron et al. [271, 272] succeeded in zone-refining this metal in the form of ingots 34 cm long and 1.2 cm in diameter, in a uranium dioxide boat under argon. The method was first tested with cobalt, to determine the optimum rate of travel, since the solvent behavior of cobalt in the solid and liquid phases towards the principal impurities, namely iron and silicon, is similar to that of uranium. The behavior of iron, silicon, nickel, copper, manganese, chromium, boron, and aluminum was investigated in further experiments; the additives could all be detected spectroscopically. The efficiency of the removal of iron from uranium after 15 zone passes is shown in Fig. 192. After 9 passes, however, a 6 cm portion permeated with iron was removed from the end of the ingot.

The carbon content at the beginning of the ingot had also fallen by 110 ppm to 10 ppm after 9 zone passes. Oxygen and nitrogen could no longer be detected after zone refining. These elements had probably evaporated out owing to their low

Table 13. Results of spectral analysis of tungsten before and after zone refining; the sign —
denotes that the given component is no longer detectable.

Impurity	Before zone refining [wt.-%]	After zone refining [wt.-%]
Calcium	0.001	—
Potassium	0.004	—
Sodium	0.002	—
Iron	0.001	—
Molybdenum	0.004	0.0001
Silicon	0.002	—
Carbon	0.007 ± 0.0002	0.002 ± 0.001
Oxygen	0.0003 ± 0.0005	0.0001

solubilities in the hot melt. Antill[273] carried out investigations on the zone melting
of uranium in which he considered ruthenium as well as carbon, oxygen, nitrogen,
and cobalt. This author worked with zone speeds varying between $1/4$ and 7.6 cm/h,

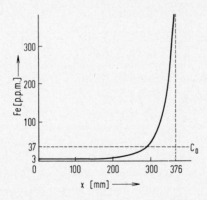

Fig. 192. Distribution of iron in uranium after 15 zone passes ($v = 0.6$ cm/h), see ref. 271.

using the floating zone method in an ingot with a diameter of $1/4$ cm. Clottes and
Mustelier[274] reported more detailed data on the stability of the floating zone in the
uranium ingot. At a critical diameter of 21 mm, the optimum zone length is 8.5 mm.
The uranium obtained by this method had a low microhardness and resistivity at
low temperatures. The recrystallization temperature was about 270° C.

According to Antill, Barnes, and Gardner[276], better purification is obtained if a
certain minimum concentration of carbon and oxygen is present. If UO_2 and UC_2
are supplied at the outset[277] by placing a thin layer of these compounds mixed with
uranium in the bottom of the beryllia container under the irradiated uranium ingot,
almost all the active material accumulates at the top of the ingot on zone melting.

Withman et al.[278] also found that fission products such as zirconium, niobium, and ruthenium can be removed from irradiated uranium by zone melting provided that complete removal is not essential. On the other hand, boron, iron, silicon, nickel, and cobalt can be eliminated from ordinary uranium.

The separation of uranium and thorium by zone melting has been studied by Garin-Bonnet et al.[279], whilst Murray's investigations[280] were more concerned with the temperature conditions during the zone melting of uranium in U_3O_8 vessels. The latter author avoided breakage of the vessel as a result of the α to β-uranium transformation by keeping the temperature of the solid uranium above the transition point (776° C).

1.3.7 Rhenium

The usefulness of zone melting without a container and with electron bombardment in the purification of metals is shown by a paper by Geach and Jones[77] describing the purification of vanadium, rhenium, molybdenum, niobium, and tantalum (cf. also[281, 282]). Homogeneous single crystals of a molybdenum-rhenium alloy with a rhenium content of 35 at.-% were also prepared. Lawley and Maddin[283] obtained rhenium monocrystals from sintered rods, again by zone melting. After 4 and 6 passes, these authors found a uniform hardness over almost the entire ingot, with an appreciable increase only at the end of the ingot.

1.3.8 Iron, Ruthenium, and Plutonium

After ascertaining the best working conditions with ^{60}Co, Talbot, Albert, and Chaudron[284] zone-melted a 34 cm long ingot of electrolytic iron in a lime boat. Nine zones 2 to 3 cm long were passed at 6 mm/h. The boat was contained in a glass tube, and argon was used as a protective gas. The results are shown in Table 14. Fischer et al.[285] found the following values for the distribution coefficients of the elements listed in the table: oxygen 0.022, carbon 0.29, sulfur 0.04 to 0.06, and phosphorus 0.17. It is interesting to note that not only was the oxygen content greatly reduced by zone melting, but the resulting iron could dissolve only a small quantity of oxygen[286]. Besnard and Talbot[326] made similar observations in the case of hydrogen.

Table 14. Content of impurities in an iron ingot before and after zone melting (after Talbot et al.[284]).

Impurity	Before [ppm]	After Top [ppm]	After End [ppm]
Oxygen	40	3	60
Carbon	40	25	25 to 66
Sulfur	15	5.4	—
Phosphorus	1 to 2	0.05	—

Both the ductility[287] and the brittleness of iron at low temperature are altered[288] by zone melting.

Hillman and Mager[289] zone refined vertical iron rods 6.8 and 10 mm in diameter, without a container; the operation was carried out in a mixture of argon and hydrogen, at a zone speed of 0.3 to 6 mm/min. The starting material was obtained by thermal decomposition of iron pentacarbonyl. The purity after zone melting

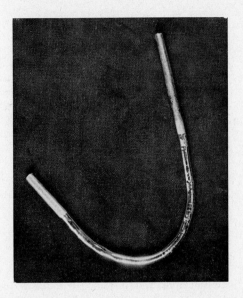

Fig. 193.
Zone-refined monocrystalline ruthenium ingot, ³/₈ inch in diameter, bent by hand through 180°[291].

could be ascertained by spectral analysis and by measurement of the coercivity. Thus after 3 zone passes, the ingot still contained 6 ppm of oxygen (initial concentration 150 ppm) and 1 to 2 ppm of nitrogen (initial concentration 60 ppm). The iron was obtained after zone melting in the form of a cylindrical single crystal 10 cm long and 10 mm in diameter.

Oliver and Schafer[290] zone-leveled pure boron with zone-refined iron by a single zone and without a container. The effective distribution coefficient of boron in iron was given as 0.16 ± 0.03.

Ruthenium monocrystals obtained by zone melting without a container, using electron bombardment, exhibited a very remarkable property in comparison with metal which had been purified by other methods: in the form of a rod with a diameter of 3/8 inch, it could be relatively easily bent by hand through an angle of 180° without fracture[291] (cf. Fig. 193). The impurities evidently affect the ductility of the metal by giving rise to lattice irregularities. However, the high ductility must be essentially a property of the single crystal, since when the monocrystalline rod is repeatedly flexed, the ductility decreases as dislocations are formed in the metal.

Rhys[291] determined the content of impurities in the ruthenium monocrystal (cf.

Table 15). According to the composition of the end of the ingot, all elements lower the melting point of ruthenium. It is also likely that most elements are evaporated off during zone melting without a container.

Table 15. Concentrations of various foreign elements in ruthenium before and after zone refining (14 passes; $v = 15$ cm/h).

Impurity	Before [wt.-%]	After	
		Top [wt.-%]	End [wt.-%]
Palladium	0.001	0.0001	0.0003
Rhodium	0.002	<0.001	<0.001
Gold	≈0.0002	<0.0001	<0.0001
Silver	<0.0001	>0.0001	>0.0001
Aluminum	traces	slight traces	traces
Cobalt	traces	—	—
Chromium	slight traces	—	—
Copper	traces	traces	traces
Iron	0.10	<0.001	0.01
Titanium	traces	slight traces	traces
Manganese	traces	—	slight traces
Nickel	0.0003	—	0.0001
Silicon	traces	traces	traces
Tungsten	slight traces	v. slight traces	traces

Bodmer, Haller, and Sulzer [292, 293] found an original application of zone leveling in the production of high-pressure fuel cells. These authors welded together a Zircaloy-2 tube and a uranium cylinder, using a narrow moving molten zone.

Tate and Anderson [294] studied the segregation behavior of impurities in plutonium by zone melting this metal in a carbide-lined tantalum container. The elements aluminum, cobalt, chromium, iron, manganese, nickel, and silicon behaved as was to be expected from the binary equilibrium diagrams.

1.3.9 Nickel, Cobalt, Copper, Silver, and Zinc

During the zone melting of molded nickel powder prepared from nickel tetra-carbonyl, the principal loss of impurities is by evaporation [295]. Morrison, Castleman, and Hees [295] have discussed various methods of detecting possible trace impurities in very pure nickel. Morral [296] reported on the zone refining of cobalt and the properties of the metal. This author obtained 99.98% cobalt by zone melting.

According to Tolmie and Robins [297], copper rods can be zone melted with a zone travel of 11 mm/h. It was observed that in this metal antimony, chromium, manganese, silicon, silver, and tin moved with the zone, while iron, cobalt, and nickel move in the opposite direction. Copper can also be advantageously zone-refined without a container, gripped between two iron rods[298-300].

Masumoto[301] has made a valuble contribution to our knowledge of the zone refining of slightly impure metals in his investigation of the zone-melting behavior of copper-tin (5.4—13.2% of tin) and copper-nickel alloys (5.8—15.5% of nickel).

On the basis of the zone-melting behavior of silver-gold and silver-copper alloys, Markali and Thoresen[302] corrected the positions of the solidus and liquidus curves in the corresponding binary equilibrium diagrams.

The large-scale preparation of lead-free zinc by zone melting was investigated in detail by examining the influence of the rate of freezing, the lead concentration, the temperature gradient, and the zone length on the separation[303]. Quartz and glass boats were used, in a horizontal position. The lead content could be reduced to rather less than half of its original value, but the energy required for this purification was 860 kcal per kg of zinc. It is believed that only 220 kcal/kg would be required if technical improvements were made.

The purification of zinc was studied[304] by mixing a zinc-cadmium-lead alloy with ultrapure zinc and zone melting the resulting material in the form of an ingot 20 cm long and with a cross-section of 2.5 cm^2. The results were contrary to theoretical expectations, since considerable diffusion anomalies intervened.

1.4   Zone Melting of Oxides and Salts

Very pure metals are frequently obtained by an indirect route, by zone-refining their compounds[305]. The elements must then be regenerated from the pure compounds without introducing further impurities. Thus Richards[306] prepared very pure gallium from zone-refined gallium trichloride. Similarly, very pure silicon was obtained from silicon tetraiodide[307], from which silicon triiodide had to be removed by zone melting.

1.4.1   Oxides

High-frequency heating cannot be used in the zone melting of substances having high resistivities, such as nickel oxide and titanium dioxide. The fact that it is nevertheless now possible to zone-refine such compounds is due to a research group at the Philips Research Laboratories, Eindhoven. As reported by Kooy and Couwenberg[309], the molten zone is produced with a carbon arc radiation furnace, the principal parts of which are two elliptical mirrors and a projector arc lamp C (Philips EL 4455). The radiation density at the focus is estimated to be about 5 W/mm^2. The furnace has the advantage of a high rate of heating, and the disadvantage that the carbon rods have a life of only $^1/_2$ to 2 h. The zone-melting process must therefore be completed during this period; consequently, it is necessary to use a zone travel of a few cm/h. Using this arrangement, it is possible to prepare single crystals of the high-melting nickel oxide and titanium oxide; mixed oxides have also been obtained, starting with mixed crystals of $MnFe_2O_4$ with other compounds having the spinel structure. The following compounds were prepared:

$Mn_{1+x} Fe_{2-x} O_4$ with $x = -0.1; 0; 0.1$ or 0.2;

$MnTi_xFe_x(II)Fe_{2-2x}(III)O_4$, with $x = 0.15; 0.30$ or 0.45;

$MnTi_{0.15} Co_{0.15} Fe_{2.7} O_4$;

$Mg_{0.45} Mn_{0.55}(II)Mn_{0.23}(III)Fe_{1.77} O_4$

Before zone melting, the powdered oxides were mixed in the desired ratios, heated, molded into a rod, and sintered. The rods themselves were 5 mm in diameter and the zones were 5 to 10 mm long. Continuous thorough mixing in the zone was ensured by rotating the solid portions above and below the zone in opposite directions at a rate of 60 to 120 rpm. This also ensured rotational symmetry of the melting and crystallizing fronts.

1.4.2 Salts

Salts can be recrystallized both from the solution and from the melt. Consequently, it is not surprising that the very first attempts by Süe, Pauly, and Nouaille[310, 311] to purify potassium by zone melting were successful. After determining the zone speed at which the distribution coefficient is closest to the equilibrium value, these authors carried out a systematic investigation of a number of mixtures containing potassium nitrate (Table 16). The impurity distributions were followed with the aid of radioactive tracers, in the usual manner. Table 16 shows the added compounds, the corresponding nuclides, the initial concentrations c_0, and the appropriate k-values.

Table 16. Purification of potassium nitrate (m.p.$=334°C$). Rate of migration 5.6 mm/h; $c_0=$quantity of impurity/quantity of KNO_3.

Additive	$NaNO_3$	$Ca(NO_3)_2$	$Sr(NO_3)_2$	$Y(NO_3)_3$	K_3PO_4	K_2SO_4
Isotope	^{22}Na	^{45}Ca	^{90}Sr	^{90}Y	^{32}P	^{35}S
c_0	10^{-3}	10^{-2}	10^{-3} to 10^{-2}	10^{-3}	10^{-3}	10^{-3}
k	0.28	0.04	0.20 0.08	0.3	0.03	0.10

Note the different k-values for the two initial concentrations 10^{-3} and 10^{-2} in the case of strontium nitrate; furthermore, the values for the Ca^{2+} cation and the PO_4^{3-} anion are surprisingly low.

Similar experiments were carried out on the purification of sodium nitrate and sodium sulfate. The latter melts at $884°C$ and was zone-melted in a platinum boat. Potassium sulfate and cesium sulfate were added as impurities. The distribution of calcium sulfate in sodium sulfate after zone melting is shown in Fig. 194. This behavior of the two sulfates can be explained with the aid of the equilibrium diagrams determined by Calgani and Mancini [312] and by Ballenca [313], according to which sodium sulfate and calcium sulfate form mixed crystals and a double salt. This

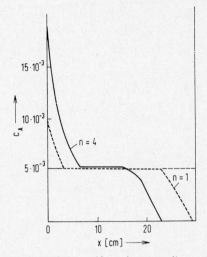

Fig. 194. Distribution of labeled calcium sulfate along a sodium sulfate ingot; n = number of zones passes; $c_0 = 5 \times 10^{-3}$ (after Süe et al.[57]).

double salt melts at 960°C, and must therefore separate out first on zone melting of the sulfate mixture (cf. Fig. 194).

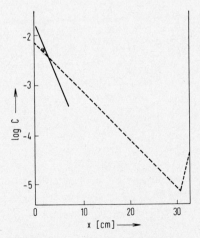

Fig. 195. Distribution of RbNO₃ ———— and of CsNO₃ ——— after zone leveling in KNO₃ with a single zone pass.

Pauly et al. zone-leveled potassium nitrate with a mixture containing 30 mg of cesium nitrate and 30 mg of rubidium nitrate, the cations of which had been activated in the Châtillon pile, by an (n, γ) process to form ^{134}Cs (β-emitter: 0.648 and 0.09 MeV) and ^{86}Rb (β-emitter: 1.822 and 0.716 MeV). Both salts were deposited at the beginning of a 30 g ingot of potassium nitrate and blended with the ingot by a single zone. The resulting distribution curve is shown in Fig. 195. This experiment formed the basis for the "zone separation" of a mixture of 1.25 g of strontium nitrate with 0.5 g of calcium nitrate. The strontium ion migrated in the opposite direction to the calcium, i.e. towards the beginning of the ingot. Mention should also be made of the zone-melting experiments carried out by Shirai and Ishibashi [314] using mixtures of ammonium nitrate with copper and calcium nitrates. The copper and calcium ions both moved with the molten zone ($v = 4.9$ mm/h).

1.4.3   *Purification of Eutectic Mixtures*

The zone-melting behavior of eutectics is to some extent like that of compounds: they crystallize from the melt without undergoing changes in composition, and only the excess components and those which do not belong to the eutectic migrate with or against the molten zone. Otherwise, eutectics and the excess components can be prepared in the pure state. Since, however, the melting point of a eutectic is always lower than of its components, eutectics can often be zone-refined at temperatures far below the melting points of the components. Experiments by Süe et al. [57] have confirmed this fact: the compounds listed in Table 17 were added to a eutectic mixture consisting of 4.7 g of lead nitrate and 5.3 g of potassium nitrate, and melting at 207°C, and the purification factors on zone melting were determined.

Table 17. Purification of lead nitrate in a eutectic melt with potassium nitrate.

$$n = 4, c_0 = 10^{-3} = \frac{\text{quantity of impurity}}{\text{quantity of potassium nitrate}}$$

Impurity	$NaNO_3$	$CsNO_3$	$Sr(NO_3)_2$	$La(NO_3)_3$
Isotope	^{22}Na	^{134}Cs	^{90}Sr	^{140}La
c at beginning of ingot	$2.5 \cdot 10^{-4}$	$2 \cdot 10^{-4}$	$7 \cdot 10^{-4}$	$9.5 \cdot 10^{-4}$
Purification factor $k_R = c_0/c_n$	4	5	1.4	1.05

2.   Zone Melting of Organic Compounds

2.1   Aromatic Hydrocarbons

2.1.1   *Naphthalene, Anthracene, Pyrene, Chrysene*

In a description of the purification of organic substances by zone melting, we should deal first with naphthalene, since this readily crystallizable low-melting

(m. p. $= 80.2°$ C) aromatic is very useful for testing zone melting equipment[61, 320]. The usual additives and the impurities present in naphthalene are given in Table 18.

Table 18. Zone melting of naphthalene.

c_0=initial concentration; c_x=concentration in the pure portion; l=length of molten zone; L = length of ingot; n = number of zone passes; v = rate of zone travel.

Additive or impurity	c_0 [%]	c_x [ppm]	Color	l [cm]	L [cm]	n	v [cm/h]	Ref.
Anthracene	—	1		—	10	2	1	129)
Anthracene	0.2	100		5	91	8	3.8	315)316)
Methyl red	traces	—	colorless	—	100	1	2.5	316)
Induline	0.03	—	colorless	5 to 12	120	—	3.8	130)
2,4-dinitro-phenylhydrazine	0.01	—	colorless	—	15	5 to 15	3	112)

The addition of colored substances may be quite useful for the demonstration of zone melting, but it cannot be used for the actual testing of an apparatus. To obtain any information regarding the efficiency of an apparatus, it is necessary to know at least the k-value, and preferably the complete melting behavior of the mixture.

Mohorcic[317] has grown very pure single crystals of naphthalene, using the principle of normal freezing rather than the moving zone method. The substance was melted in a glass tube with a heating mantle ($87°$C) and the tube containing the melt was then slowly lowered (1 mm/h) into a cooler cylinder ($61°$C). Since the temperature gradient between the solid and the liquid naphthalene and the rate of lowering were small, this method gave large crystals, 100 mm long and 60 mm in diameter.

The zone melting of naphthalene by Peaker and Robb[318] was not aimed at the purification of this compound, but at the fractionation of high polymers.

Zone-refined naphthalene was placed in a test tube 30 cm long and 2.2 cm in diameter. The top 6 cm of the naphthalene was melted, and 200 mg of polystyrene (D. C. P. J.3, Distillers Co., Ltd., Epsom, Surrey, $\bar{M}_n = 80,000$, $\bar{M}_w = 200,000$) was added. After waiting for 6 h, the molten zone was allowed to migrate to the bottom of the tube at a rate of 2.5 cm/h. Eight zone passes were sufficient to distribute the polystyrene over the entire naphthalene charge, which was then cut into 10 portions. Turbidimetric titration of the individual samples with methanol indicated a perceptible fractionation of the polystyrene.

Handley and Herington[66] purified 0.15 g samples of pyrene, anthracene, and chrysene with a semimicro zone-melting apparatus. The efficiency of the purification can be seen from the elevation of the melting point (cf. Table 19).

In an investigation on the electrical conductivity of aromatic hydrocarbons Sloan[327] used zone melting for the purification of anthracene and pyrene. The segregated impurities were then studied by gas chromatography. The anthracene was

Table 19. Zone melting of aromatic hydrocarbons
$l = 3$ cm, $v = 2.5$ cm, $L = 12$ cm; after Handley et al.[66]

Substance	Melting point of starting material [°C]	Melting point of purified compound [°C]
Anthracene	217.5—221	219.5—220
Pyrene	150 —152	152
Chrysene	248 —249.5	250 —250.5

found to contain hydroanthracene, hydroxyanthracene, methylanthracene, phen-anthrene, anthraquinone, carbazole, fluorene, and tetracene. The pyrene contained hydropyrene, hydroxypyrene, methylpyrene, anthracene, dihydroanthracene, and fluoranthrene.

2.1.2 Diphenyl

For the zone refining of diphenyl[54, 322], 38 g of "pure" colorless diphenyl flakes (m.p. 62.5 to 68.3°C) were sealed into a glass tube 37 cm long and 2.1 cm in diameter. The tube was placed vertically in hot water to liquefy the diphenyl, which was then allowed to solidify again in a horizontal position, so that the tube was about half-filled by the solid charge. After 6 zone passes at 2 mm/h it could be seen that the diphenyl was being continuously displaced towards the beginning of the tube. Furthermore, the end of the charge which solidified last was becoming increasingly discolored, whilst the first 13 cm portion was colorless and fluoresced

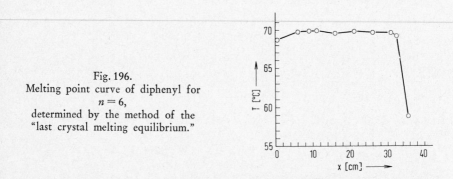

Fig. 196.
Melting point curve of diphenyl for
$n = 6$,
determined by the method of the
"last crystal melting equilibrium."

even in daylight. Some of the diphenyl had sublimed all along the tube, and had condensed on the free wall of the tube in the form of feather-like crystals. However, this did not affect the crystallization and purification of the ingot.

To check the progress of purification, the glass tube containing the diphenyl was cut into portions, and the melting point of each portion was determined and plotted against the length of the ingot (see Fig. 196). It was surprising to find that, despite the pure starting material, at the end of the charge the melting point still fell by about 10°C. After rejection of 2.5 g of the impure part and 1.5 g of sublimate,

Fig. 197.
Melting point curve of a pre-purified
sample of diphenyl
$n = 14$; $l = 2$ cm;
$L = 37.5$ cm; $v = 3$ mm/h.

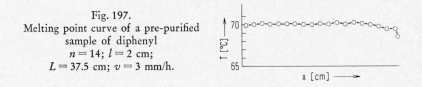

further 14 zone passes gave a melting point difference of only 2°C between the beginning and the end of the charge (see Fig. 197), and after a third run with 14 zones, it was no longer possible to observe a depression (see Fig. 198). Thus, starting with 38 g diphenyl, a total of 34 zone passes gave 27 g of very pure, almost mono-crystalline material with a slight bluish glimmer and with an odor which differed markedly from that of crude diphenyl.

Fig. 198.
Melting point curve of a 28 g ingot
of diphenyl after zone melting twice,
followed by a further 14 zone passes.
$l = 2$ cm; $L = 42$ cm; $v = 2$ mm/h.

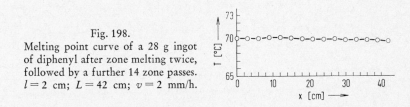

Since a readily perceptible displacement of matter had occurred during the second run, with 14 zones (see Table 20), the apparatus was tilted downwards at an angle of 2° for the last run, and a length of 8 cm at the beginning of the glass tube was left free. This wetting effect during the second run is demonstrated in Table 20 by the column giving the weight of a portion 1 cm long. The tapering portions at the beginning and the end of the charge have been disregarded.

2.1.3   Phenanthrene

Prior to zone melting[323], the sample had a melting point of 100.6°C. The melting point curve in Fig. 199 shows the result of micro-zone melting of a small sample. It can be seen that the phenanthrene contained both higher-melting and lower-melting impurities, the higher-melting material forming mixed crystals with

Table 20. Displacement of matter after $n = 14$.

Distance from beginning of charge [cm]	Length of portion [cm]	Weight of substance [g]	Weight of substance per cm [g/cm]
1.3	1.3	3.06	2.35
3.8	2.5	4.67	1.87
6.1	2.3	3.05	1.35
8.2	2.1	2.50	1.19
10.7	2.5	2.78	1.11
14.2	3.5	3.20	0.92
17.0	2.8	2.26	0.81
18.6	1.6	1.29	0.81
21.6	3.0	2.55	0.85
24.6	3.0	2.60	0.87
27.6	3.0	1.97	0.66
33.2	5.6	1.68	0.30
35.9	2.7	0.06	0.02

phenanthrene. For this reason it could be anticipated that rather long times would be required for the separation and purification.

The greater part of the sample was first zone-melted in two portions, 1 and 2, using macro-apparatus. After the passage of 25 zones through the 40 cm long ingots, the fractions melting between 100 and 102°C were combined to form a

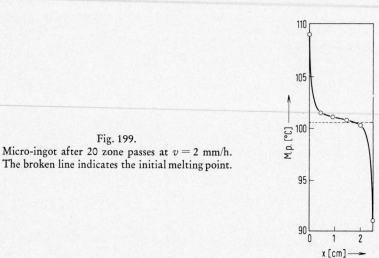

Fig. 199.
Micro-ingot after 20 zone passes at $v = 2$ mm/h.
The broken line indicates the initial melting point.

new ingot 3, as were the higher-melting (ingot 4) and lower-melting (ingot 5) fractions. In the last two cases the melting point distribution along the ingot was still very irregular, even after further zone melting.

The higher-melting impurities accumulated mainly in fractions 3 and 4; however, these still contained components which lowered the melting point. The lowest melting point, 61°C, was found in fraction 5. Further fractionation was carried out on the basis of the melting-point limits 101°C and higher, 100.5 to 101°C, and 85 to 100.5°C (fractions 6, 7, and 8). The small portions melting below 85°C were rejected.

After zone melting of these three fractions, only sample 6 still contained impurities which raised the melting point. Further impurities which lowered the melting point had been eliminated from fraction 7. These were rejected, and the remaining

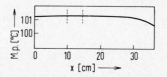

Fig. 200. Fraction 9 after 30 zone passes at $v = 2$ mm/h.
Sample taken between the broken lines.

fraction, with a melting range of 101.0 to 101.2°C, was again zone-melted to give sample 9. The result of this experiment is shown in Fig. 200.

Phenanthrene can also be used to show the analytical importance of micro-zone melting in the investigation of the separation achieved by other methods of purification [324, 325].

2.2 Substituted Aromatic Compounds

2.2.1 *Phenol and 3,4-Dimethylphenol*

Pale red commercial phenol has been zone-refined in a vertical tube in a macro-apparatus [54]. After 10 zone passes at a rate of 3 mm/h, the red impurity had collected in the last $^1/_5$ of the charge. The first $^3/_4$ of the ingot was transferred to another zone-melting tube and again purified with 10 zone passes at 3 mm/h. The resulting phenol was colorless and transparent; only the end of the ingot was slightly cloudy, and was therefore removed from the remainder.

Sørenson [328] purified technical phenol with 16 zones, 2.8 cm long and travelling at a rate of 2 cm/h, in order to determine the distribution coefficient of *p*-nitrophenol in phenol samples with melting points of 40.2°C and 40.8°C, at various rates of zone travel between 0.6 and 3.7 cm/h (cf. Table 21).

Pure 3,4-dimethylphenol is generally a reddish-white, highly crystalline substance (m. p. $= 62.3°$ C), which can be easily zone-refined [98]. For this purpose 32 g of the starting material were sealed into a glass tube 43 cm long and 21 mm in diameter, leaving 9 cm at the beginning of the tube free. After 17 zone passes ($v = 2$ mm/h;

Table 21. Distribution coefficiens of *p*-nitrophenol in phenol (m. p. 40.2 and 40.8° C).

Rate of zone travel [cm/h]	Initial concentration of *p*-nitrophenol [%]	Distribution coefficient	
		in phenol with m. p. = 40.2° C	in phenol with m. p. = 40.8° C
0.6	0.4	0.22	0.05
0.6	4.0	0.18	0.13
2.1	0.4	0.35	0.10
2.1	4.0	0.47	0.38
3.7	0.4	0.45	
3.7	4.0	0.53	

$l = 2$ to 3 cm; $L = 34$ cm) the material was found to be distributed over the entire length of the tube, in spite of the fact that the apparatus had been inclined at an angle of 2°. A further 8 passes with the apparatus horizontal gave a displacement of matter as shown in Table 22. The displacement was determined by weighing portions 3 to 11 cm long, starting at the beginning of the ingot.

Table 22. Displacement of matter in an ingot of 3,4-dimethylphenol after 23 zone passes.

Distance from beginning of ingot [cm]	Length of portion [cm]	Weight of substance [g]	Weight of substance per cm [g/cm]
2.6	2.6	4.66	1.79
7.8	5.2	9.62	1.84
12.5	4.7	5.40	1.15
17.5	5.0	2.84	0.57
23.0	5.5	4.37	0.79
26.9	3.9	2.18	0.56
31.1	4.2	0.79	0.19
42.1	11.00	2.02	0.18

Owing to the severe contamination, the wetting properties of the melt and the crystals at the end of the ingot changed so sharply that the contaminated plug broke contact with the pure material and remained separate. This effect is frequently observed (see Figs. 201 and 202).

Fig. 201. Tube 43 cm long, containing 3,4-dimethylphenol after 25 zone passes.

The 3,4-dimethylphenol, in the form of colorless, transparent crystals (see Fig. 201), with a uniformity of melting point as shown in Fig. 203, occupied about $1/3$ of the tube after zone melting.

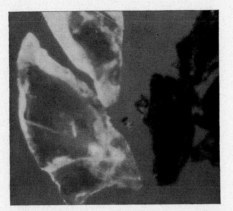

Fig. 202. Left: highly purified crystals of 3,4-dimethylphenol taken from the beginning of the ingot; right: constituents from the end of the ingot.

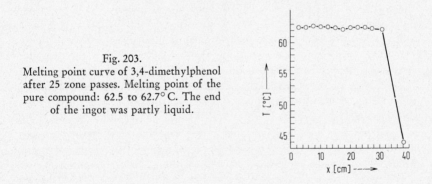

Fig. 203.
Melting point curve of 3,4-dimethylphenol after 25 zone passes. Melting point of the pure compound: 62.5 to 62.7° C. The end of the ingot was partly liquid.

2.2.2 Benzoic Acid and Acetanilide

As early as 1940, Schwab and Wichers[329] purified benzoic acid by normal freezing. They first purified only 50 g (45 to 50 ml) in a test tube with a diameter of 2 cm. Later[330], however, 500 g was purified in a larger container, 4.6 cm in diameter and 30 cm long; the tube was slowly lowered through a long circular heater (see Fig. 204), so that the melt solidified from the bottom upwards. The liquid was agitated with a current of nitrogen.

To ensure uniform lowering of the tube, the authors fixed it to a platform floating in a tank of water. The water was then allowed to flow slowly and steadily out of the tank, and as the level fell, the tube moved downwards through the heater.

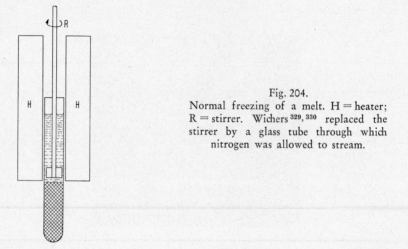

Fig. 204.
Normal freezing of a melt. H = heater;
R = stirrer. Wichers [329, 330] replaced the
stirrer by a glass tube through which
nitrogen was allowed to stream.

A purification required about 16 to 20 h, after which the residual melt was rejected. The remaining ingot was then melted and allowed to freeze again.

Benzoic acid with a purity of 99.997 mole-% was obtained in 40% yield by allowing a product with a purity of 99.91 mole-% to solidify. For larger quantities (e. g. 10 kg), the authors allowed the benzoic acid to solidify very slowly in a round-bottom flask with stirring. The remaining melt was decanted and the core of the material was melted with an immersion heater and rejected. The final products of two such operations were combined to form a new charge. The resulting product had a purity of 99.998 mole-%. This result would require eleven recrystallizations from benzene or 25 from water.

Smith and Walton, in the same laboratories, used the same method to purify acetanilide. After a single solidification they obtained a 50% yield of a product containing 99.98 mole-% of acetanilide from a starting material having a purity of 99.80 mole-%.

Handley and Herington [66] have described a method which is suitable for the zone refining of small quantities of benzoic acid. The melting point of the starting material used by these authors was 119.5 to 121.5° C, while that of the zone-refined product was 121 to 121.5° C.

2.2.3   *p-Dichlorobenzene, 4-Chloro-1,3-dinitrobenzene, 2,4-Dinitrotoluene, Nitranilines, and o-Nitrophenol*

Christian [331] showed some years ago that chlorine compounds can be satisfactorily zone-refined without decomposition. This author used *p*-dichlorobenzene, simply for demonstration purposes. This was placed in a glass tube 10 mm in diameter and melted over a length of 2.5 cm with an electric furnace. The furnace was moved forward by 1.25 cm every half hour.

Schildknecht and Hopf [101] purified 4-chloro-1,3-dinitrobenzene (Messrs. Riedel de Haen) in a multistage zone-melting apparatus (see Table 23 for experimental conditions).

Table 23. Experimental conditions for the zone melting of 4-chloro-1,3-dinitrobenzene.

l	L	n	v	Inclination of apparatus	Starting quantity
2.5 cm	40 cm	18	3.7 cm/h	0°	30 g

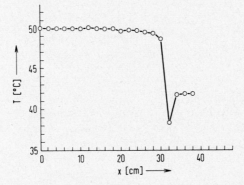

Fig. 205. Melting point curve of 4-chloro-1,3-dinitrobenzene after 18 zone passes. The end of the ingot was partly liquid, and the melting points of the solid particles in this portion were measured.

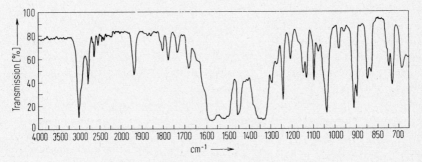

Fig. 206. Infrared spectrum of zone-melted 4-chloro-1,3-dinitrobenzene, pure portion of the ingot.

The starting material was greenish-brown, opaque, and had a melting point of 45.6 to 49.6° C. The efficiency of purification could be clearly recognized, not only from the crystal habit, and the consistency and color of the ingot, but also from the melting point curve (Fig. 205) and the infrared absorption spectrum (see Figs. 206 and 207). The latter was measured on samples taken from the beginning and the end of the ingot.

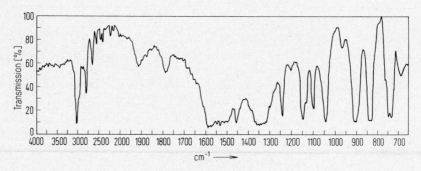

Fig. 207. Infrared spectrum of the end of the 4-chloro-1,3-dinitrobenzene ingot after 18 zones passes.

A very impure sample of 2,4-dinitrotoluene (m. p. = 57 to 65° C) containing a large quantity of occluded solvent from recrystallization was zone-refined under the conditions given in Table 24. Five zone passes were sufficient to eliminate the

Table 24. Experimental conditions for the zone melting of 2,4-dinitrotoluene.

l	L	n	v	Inclination of apparatus	Starting quantity
2.5—3 cm	39 cm	5	2 mm/h	0°	55 g

solvent. The experiment was stopped when the color along the ingot changed from pure yellow to orange. A striking feature of this experiment was the drying effect, the water present in the material separating as a pool at the end of the tube. However, the melting point curve showed that the purification was not yet satisfactory. A uniform melting point over 20 cm of the 35 cm ingot was obtained only after 14 passes (see Table 25, Fig. 208).

Table 25. Experimental conditions for the zone melting of 2,4-dinitrotoluene.

l	L	n	v	Inclination of apparatus
2 cm	35 cm	14	2 mm/h	2°

The preparation of nitranilines normally yields very impure, brownish products. After only 20 zone passes at a rate of 3 mm/h, however, crude products of this type gave orange *o*-nitraniline, deep yellow *m*-nitraniline, or yellow *p*-nitraniline at the beginning of the ingot, whilst the brown impurities had accumulated at the end of the ingot, to give a melting point in this region up to 4°C lower than that of the pure material.

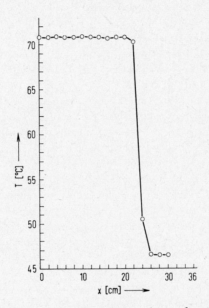

Fig. 208. Melting point curve of 2,4-dinitrotoluene after 14 zone passes.

o-Nitrophenol[321] has been zone-refined under nitrogen in a tube 19 mm in diameter. After 22 zone passes, the beginning of the ingot was removed and subjected to a further 20 passes. The fairly pure material obtained at this stage was again zone-melted, and it was found that the product was no longer autoxidizable.

2.3 Aliphatic Compounds

A petroleum fraction melting between 132 and 138°C was purified by Mair et al.[117]. After two zone passes, the melting point of the first 1/3 of a 57 cm ingot (diameter = 2 mm) was 141°C, whilst the lowest melting point was 126°C.

According to Merlin[332] and Maggi[333], cycloalkanes can be more effectively purified by zone melting than by sublimation. Ball, Helm, and Ferrin[100] have discussed the purification of petrochemicals.

2.3.1 Stearyl Alcohol and Cetyl Alcohol ($C_{16}H_{33}OH$, $C_{18}H_{37}OH$)

The starting materials were a series of carefully distilled alcohols, the melting points of which (48.5°C for $C_{16}H_{33}OH$ and 57.5°C for $C_{18}H_{37}OH$) did not agree with the literature values. The refractive indices were determined by melting the samples under the microscope and finding the temperature at which a splinter of fluorspar (n = 1.4338) became invisible in the melt[97]. The results were 65.5°C for $C_{16}H_{33}OH$, 76°C for $C_{18}H_{37}OH$, and 75.5°C for a mixture. The pure part of the zone-melted mixure gave a figure of 76°C, corresponding to stearyl alcohol, whilst the two ends of the sample exhibited marked differences. From the melting point and the refractive index it can be found whether a substance is homogeneous, or whether further purification is likely on repetition of the zone-melting process. Further information can be obtained from infrared spectra and Debye-Scherrer diagrams.

Mixtures of alcohols have also been separated by various types of micro-zone-melting apparatus[97, 102, 131]. Thus after 45 zone passes, a mixture containing 95.5% of stearyl alcohol ($C_{18}H_{37}OH$) and 4.5% of cetyl alcohol ($C_{16}H_{33}OH$) (mixed melting point = 57°C) gives a melting point of 58.5°C at the beginning of the ingot and 56.5°C at the end. However, only the higher-melting stearyl alcohol could be obtained in the pure form, and even this could not be recovered quantitatively.

A number of primary aliphatic alcohols, between nonadecanol and triacontanol, were synthesized from commercial behenic acid and stearyl alcohol by chain elongation or chain shortening[334].

The long-chain alcohols containing from 19 to 30 carbon atoms were zone-refined in the multi-stage microzone-melting apparatus described on p. 116. The purification achieved after several zone passes is shown by the melting point curves (Figs. 210 to 214). Since the process was carried out in an open boat (see Fig. 209) small particles could be removed from the ingot with a pin, so that it was unnecessary to interrupt the zone melting for sampling purposes.

Fig. 209. Small glass zone-melting boat with sample.
L = 10 mm; weight of sample 1—2 mg.

The zone refining was stopped when the melting point was uniform over the major part of the ingot.

The melting point curves of a number of alcohols (see Figs. 210 to 214) show that, in addition to the usual impurities which lower the melting point, the samples also contained substances which raise the melting point (cf. Fig. 210). Thus after melting, the two ends of the ingot must be rejected, since only the middle portion, the melting point of which is uniform, can be regarded as pure. Moreover, the

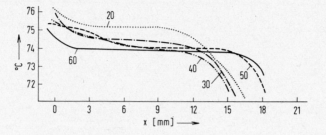

Fig. 210. Melting point curves of tricosanol.
$l = 2$ mm; $v = 2$ mm/h; after 20 (·····), 30 (—·—·—), 40 (—··—), 50 (———) and 60 (———) zone passes.

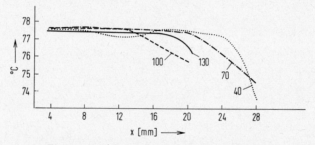

Fig. 211. Melting point curves of tetracosanol.
$l = 2$ mm; $v = 2$ mm/h; after 40 (·····), 70 (—·—), 100 (———), and 130 (———) zone passes.

ultimate state is in many cases reached only after a very large number of zone passes, e.g. 250 in the case of pentacosanol. In such cases, zone melting is naturally unsuitable for large-scale work.

It is usual to characterize organic substances by their melting points, which even make it possible to distinguish between adjacent members of a homologous series. It is a well known fact that the melting points of the fatty acids, when plotted against the number of carbon atoms, lie on two separate curves, depending on whether the number of carbon atoms is odd or even. The two curves converge with increasing chain length. Rather surprisingly, the melting points of the fatty alcohols containing 19 to 25 carbon atoms, as published by Levene and Taylor[335], all lie on a single straight line when plotted against the number of C-atoms; the values found by Jones[336] for the fatty alcohols with 28 to 35 C-atoms, on the other hand, form two curves, but these do not converge. Similarly, the melting points of the alcohols

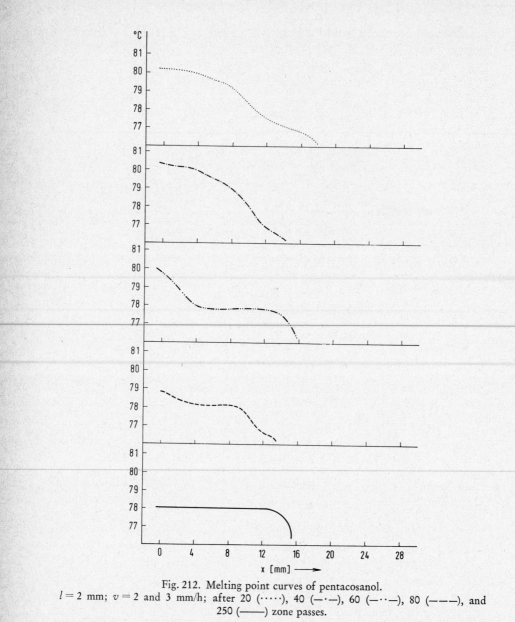

Fig. 212. Melting point curves of pentacosanol.
$l = 2$ mm; $v = 2$ and 3 mm/h; after 20 (·····), 40 (—·—), 60 (—··—), 80 (———), and 250 (——) zone passes.

mentioned above also fall on two separate, non-convergent curves; only behenyl alcohol $C_{22}H_{45}OH$ fails to fit this scheme, as shown by the circle which falls off the curve in Fig. 215. This discrepancy could be explained by the zone-melting behavior of the alcohols: the melting point of the recrystallizing behenyl alcohol remained constant at 73.5 °C, whilst the initial melting points of the others were generally too high. After zone-refining, a plot of melting points against the number of C-atoms gave two converging curves, one for alcohols with even numbers of carbon atoms and one for those with odd numbers (see Fig. 216).

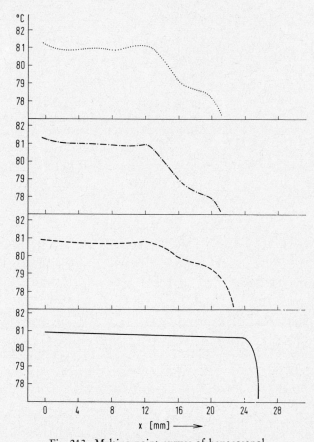

Fig. 213. Melting point curves of hexacosanol.
$l = 2$ mm; $v = 1$, 2, and 3 mm/h; after 10 (·····), 20 (—·—), 30 (———), and 80 (——) zone passes.

2.3.2 Separation of a Mixture of Stearyl Alcohol and Radioactive Cetyl Alcohol by Zone Melting

The progress of separation during zone melting can be followed automatically and continuously if one of the compounds is labeled with a radioactive tracer. This has the advantage that the state of the ingot can be examined at any time without loss of material [131]. This method will be illustrated for the case of the stearyl alcohol/ cetyl alcohol system, which forms a continuous series of mixed crystals with a melting point minimum (cf. p. 37).

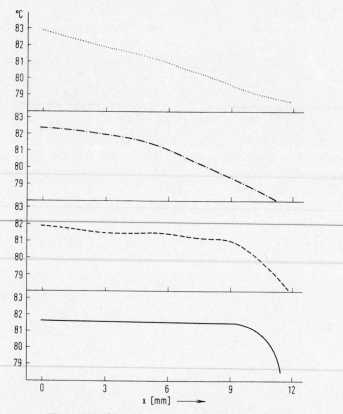

Fig. 214. Melting point curves of heptacosanol.
$l = 2$ mm; $v = 3$ mm/h; after 60 (·····), 80 (—·—), 105 (———), and 135 (——)

As in the zone refining of the fatty alcohols (see p. 182), a mixture containing about 12% of radioactive cetyl alcohol was placed in a small glass boat. After 7, 14, 21, 28, and 40 zone passes ($v = 1$ mm/h), the counting rate was recorded by slowly passing the boat under a counter tube by means of a specially constructed apparatus. The impulse rate curve can be converted to concentration units (cf. Fig. 217). It can be seen that all radioactive alcohol is gradually transported to the end of the ingot. The maximum separation was achieved after 40 zone passes.

The autorecording method provides an elegant process for following quantitatively the separation or leveling of a labeled compound. Particularly high accuracy is possible in the case of high-activity α or γ-emitters.

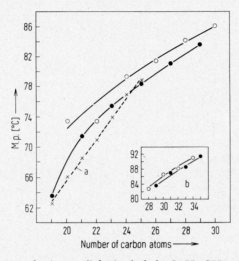

Fig. 215. Melting points of primary aliphatic alcohols, $C_{19}H_{39}OH$ to $C_{30}H_{61}OH$ according to Levene and Taylor (a) and Jones (b), together with the values found by Schildknecht and Renner[334] for recrystallized products which have not been zone-melted.

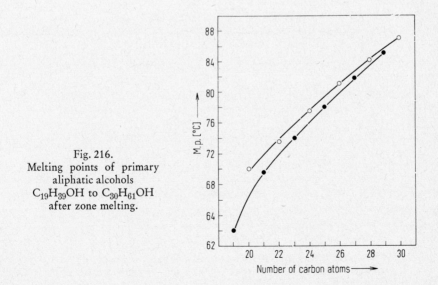

Fig. 216.
Melting points of primary aliphatic alcohols $C_{19}H_{39}OH$ to $C_{30}H_{61}OH$ after zone melting.

2.3.3   *Fractionation of a Mixture Containing 20°/o of Eicosanol and 80°/o of Hexacosanol by Zone Melting* [102]

In order to interpret or predict the zone-melting behavior of mixtures, it is necessary to know the equilibrium diagram of the system. This is particularly true

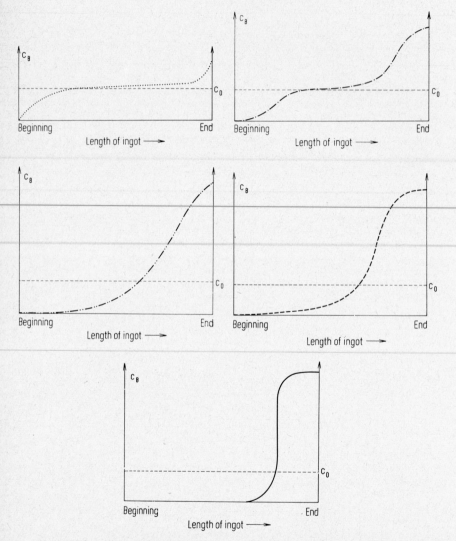

Fig. 217. Distribution of radioactive cetyl alcohol in stearyl alcohol after 7 (·····), 14 (—·—), (—··—), 28 (———), and 40 (———) zone passes.

when the components form mixed crystals, as is frequently the case with the final products of a synthesis or with natural products. The equilibrium diagram for a mixture containing 20% of eicosanol and 80% of hexacosanol is given on p. 27.

Starting with the above mixture it was possible, by fractional zone melting, to recover pure hexacosanol with a melting point of 82.3 °C. An additional purification was also observed in this case in the fact that higher melting components accumulated at the beginning of the ingot and caused a slight elevation of the melting point to 83.4 °C (cf. Fig. 218).

2.3.4   Fatty Acids

Starting with 99.5% pure samples of lauric, myristic, palmitic, and stearic acids, Schaeppi [337, 338] was able to obtain gas-chromatographically pure substances by zone melting. The tube, which had a capacity of 15 g, was cut into portions after 10 and after 20 passes.

After zone refining, pure *cis*-crotonic acid [321] was found to have a melting point of 61.2° C, while *trans*-crotonic acid melted at 95° C. Although the two isomers form mixed crystals in certain proportions, they can be easily separated by zone melting.

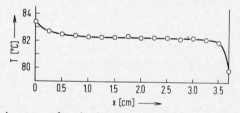

Fig. 218. Melting point curve for the hexacosanol obtained from fraction 39, after 20 zone passes at 1 mm/h and 20 zone passes at 2 mm/h [102].

2.4 Purification and Separation of Liquids

Benzene

Dickinson and Eaborn [135] purified 300 ml of "pure" benzene by normal freezing. The purification was so successful that it was no longer possible to detect impurities by gas chromatography, and the melting point had risen by 0.340° to 5.54 ± 0.01 °C. The purification was carried out by placing the liquid in a test tube 3 cm in diameter, and lowering the tube slowly (4 cm/h) into ice water; this was repeated six times. One-tenth of the initial quantity of material was rejected.

p-Bromotoluene was purified effectively by allowing it to solidify three times (rate of lowering = 1 cm/h); the melting point rose by between 15 and 25°C, so that the very pure bromotoluene melted between 26.7 and 27.2°C.

Röck[99] purified benzene by a zone-melting process described on p. 136. The purification was followed by melting point determinations using a Beckman thermometer. A heated zone was passed through frozen benzene until the melting point became constant. The mole fraction of the impurities in the starting material, namely commercial benzene, was 2×10^{-3}, whilst that for purified benzene was 8×10^{-5}.

Benzene/Thiophene and Benzene/Acetic Acid Mixtures

Schildknecht and Mannl[63] carried out a long series of experiments in which they investigated the effects of the zone speed and the number of zone passes on the separation of benzene/thiophene mixtures and the transport of matter during the zone melting of benzene.

In each case a 2 ml sample of crude benzene was frozen into a boat 11 cm long (see p. 138). After zone melting, the boat was cut into 4 equal parts which were examined for their thiophene content by spectrophotometric methods[340]. Although the individual segments were equal in length, they contained different quantities of benzene, as a result of transport of matter. The distribution of matter was uniform only after zone melting with higher rates of zone travel, e.g. 70 mm/h.

Süe, Pauly, and Nouaille[57] also started their experiments on the zone melting of liquids with benzene. These authors zone-melted an azeotropic mixture of benzene and acetic acid containing 2×10^{-2} mole of acetic acid per mole of benzene. After 10 zone passes the acetic acid content fell to 10^{-3} mole per mole of benzene.

It should also be mentioned that concentration of propionic acid in the propionic acid/water azeotrope has been reduced from 18×10^{-2} to 2×10^{-2} mole of propionic acid per mole of water after 13 zone passes.

Benzene/Toluene[91]

Even very pure benzene (e.g. Merck analytically pure grade) still contains traces of toluene, which interfere with spectroscopic investigations. It seemed likely that an effective separation could be achieved by zone melting owing to the wide difference in the melting points of benzene (5.5°C) and toluene (−95°C). In fact, small quantitites of toluene are completely removed from benzene even after a few zone passes, and the resulting benzene no longer gives the characteristic IR bands for toluene (3.4, 3.49, and 13.70 μ).

p-Xylene/*o*-Xylene and *p*-Bromotoluene/*o*-Bromotoluene[57]

The study of the separation of mixtures of isomers containing 2×10^{-2} moles of *o*-bromotoluene per mole of *p*-bromotoluene was facilitated by labeling the *o*-compound with ^{82}Br. The separation was very effective, only 2×10^{-4} mole of *o*-bromotoluene remaining per mole of the *p*-compound after 9 zone passes. The separation of *o*-xylene from an ingot of *p*-xylene was less satisfactory. The concentration of *o*-xylene fell after 6 zone passes from 10^{-1} to 5×10^{-3} mole per mole of *p*-xylene.

2.5 Concentration of Organic Compounds from Solution

2.5.1 Normal Freezing

As was described on p. 189 in the section on benzene, and explained in greater detail in the theoretical part of this book, normal freezing is a good method of concentrating traces of substances and of isolating them from greater or smaller volumes of solvent.

Matthews and Coggeshall[134] were able to detect the impurities in benzene quantitatively only after concentration by normal freezing. The benzene was placed in a glass tube 28 mm in diameter, and allowed to freeze at a rate of 5 cm/h; 65% of the impurities originally present accumulated in the end of the solid benzene ingot. This fraction (20%) was again allowed to freeze in another test tube, with an internal diameter of 22 mm, and a 1 g sample was removed for analysis. This small quantity of benzene now contained 44% of the impurities which had been present in the first concentrate. The benzene had originally contained 0.25 wt.-% of impurities, whereas the figure in the final concentrate was 5.14 wt.-%, corresponding to a 20-fold increase in concentration. It was possible in this way to find the initial concentrations of C_7 paraffins or C_8 and C_9 aromatic compounds which had not been previously detected:

0.06 wt.-% of C_7H_{16} 0.0005 wt.-% of C_8 aromatic compounds
0.001 wt.-% of C_9 aromatic compounds.

The concentration experiments carried out by Schildknecht, Rauch, and Schlegelmilch[133, 16, 341] were mainly concerned with aqueous solutions, but the following solvents, with melting points lying between $-60°$C and $-130°$C, were also investigated:

> n-octane containing 0.05%, 0.1%, and 1.0% of azobenzene
> methyl alcohol containing 0.05% of iodine
> methyl alcohol containing 0.1% of azulene
> methyl alcohol containing 0.01% and 0.005% of methylene blue
> ethyl alcohol containing 0.1% and 1.0% of chlorophyll
> ethyl alcohol containing 0.1% of azulene
> diethyl ether containing 0.05% of iodine
> diethyl ether containing 0.05% of azobenzene.

The solutes were incompletely concentrated in the case of octane, and not at all in methanol, ethanol or diethyl ether. No improvement could be achieved either by increasing the rate of stirring or by using more dilute solutions. The probable explanation for this behavior is that the solution becomes so viscous in the neighborhood of the freezing zone that adequate equilibration of concentration cannot be achieved even by vigorous stirring. Thus solvents which are viscous at room temperature, such as glycol, are totally unsuitable for this purpose, as has been demonstrated for a 0.01% solution of methylene blue in glycol.

The efficiency of concentration in methylene chloride, chloroform, and benzene, on the other hand, was extremely good. Solutions of methylene blue in methylene chloride (0.05%) and in chloroform (0.1%), of phenol in benzene (1%), and of iodine in chloroform (0.05%) were investigated at a stirring speed of 2200 rpm.

During labeling experiments with tritium oxide, it was found that loss of radioactive material could be avoided if this compound is isolated from the exchange solution by normal freezing[342]. Not only does this avoid any contamination, but it also provides a useful method of labeling very small quantities of material, since trace substances can naturally also be concentrated in tritiated water. The exchange experiments must obviously also be carried out in the container used for the freezing. After concentration, the end volume, about 25 mm^3, is pipetted off, and the substance is purified by paper chromatography. The experimental data and results for the labeling of 80 to 100 μg of resorcinol are listed in Table 26.

Table 26. Experimental conditions for the labeling of resorcinol.

No.	1	2	3
Quantity [μg]	87	98	80
Temperature [°C]	ca. 18	ca. 18	100
Time [h]	1/2	10	1
Activity [counts/min.]	377	1884	10291
Spec. activity [counts/min/mg]	4330	19190	128500

2.5.2 Ice Zone Melting

If the impurity remains dissolved in the solvent in the solid state, better results will be obtained by ice zone melting[63]. This technique is naturally also suitable for systems which can be purified by normal freezing. However, ice zone melting is more time-consuming and requires more complex apparatus than normal freezing. Since the applications of the two methods overlap, it will be necessary to decide which is the more suitable for any particular case. The decision will often depend on the apparatus available.

2.5.2.1 Concentration of Biologically Active Substances

Biologically active compounds generally occur in very dilute aqueous solutions. The usual methods of working up frequently yield even more dilute solutions, with the results that isolation of these substances becomes very difficult. Concentration by zone melting can therefore be extremely valuable in these cases.

A 0.0005% stock solution of heteroauxin which had been diluted by a factor of eight was concentrated by the passage of 7 zones to such an extent that the growth promoter, which could no longer be detected in the starting solution, could again be detected by spectrophotometry [343].

A large class of natural products whose distribution is probably wider than has hitherto been suspected are the reductones. Most of these compounds are sensitive to oxygen and heat, and are therefore particularly difficult to isolate from impure, dilute, aqueous solutions [344]. It was found that no loss of material occurred during the zone melting of a 0.25% solution of ascorbic acid. After the passage of 14 zones, 87% of the vitamin present was found in the last quarter of the glass boat. The remainder was distributed over the rest of the ice ingot, the third quarter containing 10.9%, the second 2%, and the first only 0.1% of the ascorbic acid (the concentrations were determined by Tillmans' method [345]). The concentration of ascorbic acid from a 0.025% solution was equally satisfactory. After 14 passes, 87% of the ascorbic acid was found in the last quarter of the boat. The weight distribution over the four segments was as shown in Table 27; 99.2% of the ascorbic acid introduced could be recovered intact.

Table 27. Distribution of 0.0248 mg of ascorbic acid after ice zone melting with 14 zones.

Segment I	0.0008 mg
Segment II	0.0009 mg
Segment III	0.0014 mg
Segment IV	0.0217 mg
	0.0248 mg

Phytoncides, the antibiotics found in higher plants, are liberated when plant tissues are damaged. The chemistry of these natural products is still almost completely unknown. Tokin, who discovered this class of compounds, wrote [346]: "New methods must also be found for the investigation of the chemical composition of the phytoncides, and in particular of the volatile natural phytoncides. It will presumably be necessary to work in an oxygen-free medium, paying attention to the ambient radiation, temperature, and a number of other factors". These requirements are perfectly satisfied by ice zone melting. For example, an extract of robinia obtained in the gas phase has been passed over 30 hot spots in a boat with a capacity of 2 ml. The sample was then divided into 5 fractions, and 0.1 ml of each fraction was examined spectroscopically. The phytoncide had accumulated chiefly in the last fraction. More detailed analysis showed this compound to be Δ^2-hexenal [347].

It was also possible to concentrate and isolate the phytoncides from Prunus padus by a similar method[348]. About 2 ml of extract was subjected to 30 zone passes, and was then divided into 5 fractions. The activity spectrum of the fractions is shown in Table 28. The time for the extract to take effect on house flies became shorter as the toxicity increased owing to concentration of the active compounds. The most active fractions were those which solidified last (segments IV and V).

Table 28. Activity of fractions.

Fraction	Paralysis after	Death after
I	100 sec	900 sec
II	70 sec	160 sec
III	50 sec	90 sec
IV	25 sec	35 sec
V	20 sec	35 sec

The results suggest that even the very dilute solutions encountered in field experiments can be concentrated to such an extent that a satisfactory identification of the active substances will be possible.

The extracts from the ovule of five genetically different types of oenothera were concentrated by Schildknecht and Benoni[349], using zone-melting techniques. A satisfactory assignment of the biological activity of the components of the active solution became possible only after concentration of the components by normal freezing. It also became possible to detect the chemotropically active compounds in ovule extracts from *Narcissus pseudonarcissus* after concentration in the same manner[350].

2.5.2.2 Concentration of Steam-Volatile Substances

The ice zone melting technique was used to concentrate the quinones from aqueous solutions of thymoquinone and 2,5-dimethyl-1,4-quinone, in which the initial concentrations were below the limits of spectroscopic detection and which were no longer visibly yellow. After moving over 5 hot spots for only a short time, the quinones had been concentrated to such an extent that they could again be clearly recognized in the liquid end of the ingot by the quinone coloring. After 14 zone passes through a saturated aqueous solution of thymoquinone, the latter had completely migrated to the end of the glass tube. On similar treatment of a 0.0004% solution of 2,5-dimethyl-1,4-quinone, the compound was so effectively concentrated that it could no longer be detected by spectrophotometry in the first three of the five parts into which the ingot was divided.

As an example of the steam-volatile aldehydes, let us consider vanillin. 2.5 ml of a stock solution containing 100 mg of vanillin in 100 ml of water was placed in a boat, 14 cm long, and solidified. After the passage of eight 0.5 cm long zones in a period of 17 hours, the boat was cut into eight equal parts, and the contents of the segments were titrated with N/1000 NaOH. 96.6% of the vanillin had been concentrated in the last fraction. Further experiments showed that the rate of concentration in dilute solutions increases with the degree of dilution.

2.5.2.3 Concentration of Enzymes

The behavior of these sensitive, high molecular weight substances during ice zone melting has been studied, inter alia, for catalase and arylaminacetylase. The expected concentration effect was observed in both cases when concentrated solutions were used (see Figs. 219 and 220).

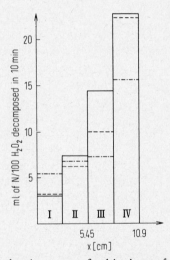

Fig. 219. Distribution of catalase in a zone-refined ice ingot after 7 (-·-·-), 14 (----), and 21 (———) zone passes. Distribution determined by Willstätter's method[351]. Loss = 15%. Initial concentration = 0.2 mg/ml.

Dilute enzyme solutions, on the other hand, could not be concentrated without large losses. For example, hexokinase in a 200 µg/ml solution (hexokinase sample from the Nutritional Biochemicals Corp., Cleveland, Ohio; 28000 K.M.V./g at 30° C) completely lost its activity even after a few zone passes. This deactivation cannot be due either to the slight heating applied during melting or to the low temperature in the zone-melting cabinet, since control solutions stored under exactly the same conditions suffered absolutely no changes. The probable reason for this effect is the repeated freezing and thawing, which may affect the enzyme either by causing cleavage of the prosthetic group, or by destruction of the helical structure of the enzyme protein[353].

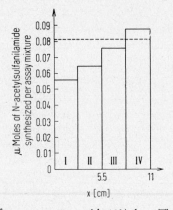

Fig. 220. Concentration of enzyme system with 13% loss. The distribution was found by determination of the acetyl coenzyme A by the method described by Lynen, Reichert, and Rueff[352]. (- - - -) Activity of starting solution.

2.5.2.4 *Concentration of Bacteria and Bacteriophages*

The successful concentration of biological substances (e. g. catalase) led to experiments with living material. This was advisable in any case, to estimate the limitations of the method for substances with much higher molecular weights.

The solution was prepared by incubating E. coli (gram-negative rods) on sloped agar for 18 h at 37° C, and the germ count was adjusted to 10^9/ml with physiological saline by determining the turbidity. The suspension, obtained by suitable dilution of the above, was frozen in the experimental tubes with acetone and dry ice. After zone melting, the charge was divided into smaller fractions in the usual manner. Preliminary tests showed that dilution with sterile tap water led to considerable losses of bacteria during zone melting. Consequently, as in freeze-drying[354], it was necessary to add a stabilizer to the bacterial suspension. 1% casein peptone solution containing 7.5% of glucose was added at first. This reduced the losses during zone melting to about 50%, and a distinct migration effect was now discernible. When the tube was divided into 7 or 8 sections 2.5 cm long, about 50% of the surviving bacteria were found in the last two fractions (=1.0 ml). Thus in passing through the frozen suspension the molten zones had carried with them a substantial proportion of the gram-negative bacteria. It is probable that the survival rate could be further increased by changing the composition of the deposition medium, the rate of zone travel, and the concentration of the suspension.

Much better results were obtained in experiments with bacteriophages (atypical coliphages, bred from sewage). Thus after the passage of 15 zones, 85% of the surviving phages were concentrated in the last two of four 0.5 ml fractions; the total loss in this was only 5%. It was possible, on average, to achieve a three to fourfold increase in concentration. Thus zone melting is probably much more suitable for the concentration of bacteriophages than the complicated methods used until now.

2.5.2.5 *Concentration of Plankton*

In order to estimate the limitations of ice zone melting when applied to low molecular weight substances in solution as well as to high molecular weight substances and living matter in suspension, the experiments were extended to plankton.

Water samples from a small basin containing aquatic plants and from a fish pond were examined, and their plankton and seston contents before and after zone melting were determined by a microscopic count [355] (cf. Table 29).

The effective limit of zone melting in its conventional form appeared to be reached at a particle size of 2 to 5 μ. Moreover, the cells were so severely deformed by the repeated freezing and thawing, i.e. by the "mechanics" of the fractional freezing, that the individual forms of plankton were often unrecognizable after only a few zone passes.

Table 29. Concentration of plankton.

Number of zone passes	Count per ml of original sample		Count per ml of "concentrated sample"	
	Total seston	Plankton	Total seston	Plankton
14	15 000	3600	poorest fraction	
			18 000	680
			middle fraction	
			20 000	800
			greatest concentration	
			26 000	320
7	25 000	1200	poorest fraction	
			13 000	1200
			middle fraction	
			25 000	600
			greatest concentration	
			26 000	500

2.5.2.6 *Concentration of Heavy Water*

Attempts have also been made to concentrate heavy water by zone melting [91]. Since the melting points of D_2O and H_2O differ by $3.8°$ C [356, 357], a separation ought to be possible. In fact, heavy water is known to segregate in glaciers, since the lower-melting H_2O melts away faster. Eucken and Schäfer [356] not only contributed to the explanation of this natural phenomenon, but also reported numerical values for the H_2O/D_2O equilibrium diagram. The calculated values give a distribution coefficient $k = 1.005$ for 81.64% D_2O and $k = 1.012$ for 42.57% D_2O. These unfavorable k-values, which lead to an increase in the concentration of D_2O on freezing out from H_2O, agree with Weston's theoretical considerations [358] and the experimental results obtained by Posey and Smith [359]. However, the results obtained by Süe et al.[57] are particularly interesting; these authors concentrated 0.98% heavy water to 0.995% with 14 zone passes, and 1.96% heavy water to 2.07% with 40 passes. Smith and Thomas [360] found that the experimentally observed change in concentration on zone melting of an H_2O/D_2O mixture containing about 43 mole-% of D_2O was different than that expected from theory. A distinct increase in the D_2O content was found at the beginning of the ingot.

2.5.2.7 *Zone Refining of Compounds in the Form of the Cryohydrate*

Salts with melting points so high that they readily volatilize or decompose on melting can be purified by zone melting of the cryohydrate, as described by Süe et al.[57]. Since the cryohydrate is a eutectic it behaves as a homogeneous compound during zone melting, and has a melting point far below that of the salt. Naturally, it is essential that the other component of the eutectic, which is added to the substances to be purified before zone melting, can easily be removed afterwards without risk of contamination. An ideal second component is water, with which many salts form cryohydrates.

REFERENCES

1 Bittel, A., Chemie-Ing.-Techn. *31*, 365 (1959)
2 Pfann, W. G., Trans. Amer. Inst. Mining metallurg. Engr. *194*, 747 (1952)
3 Kapitza, P., Proc. Roy. Soc. [London] Ser. A *119*, 358 (1928)
4 Andrade, da C. E. N., and Roscoe, R., Proc. physic. Soc. *49*, 152 (1937)
5 Findlay, A.: Die Phasenregel und ihre Anwendungen. Weinheim: Verlag Chemie 1958
6 Roozeboom, H. W. B., Z. physik. Chem. *10*, 145 (1892)
7 Kofler, L. and Kofler, A.: Thermo-Mikro-Methoden zur Kennzeichnung organischer Stoffe und Stoffgemische. Weinheim: Verlag Chemie 1954
8 Hansen, M.: Constitution of Binary Alloys; 2nd Edit. New York, Toronto, London: McGraw-Hill Book Comp., Inc. 1958
9 Rheinhold, H., and Kircheisen, M., J. prakt. Chem. *113*, 203, 351 (1926)
10 Rössler, S., Dissertation, Univ. Erlangen-Nürnberg 1961
11 Hopf, U., Dissertation, Univ. Erlangen-Nürnberg 1961
12 Vetter, H., Dissertation, Univ. Erlangen 1960
13 Vetter, H., and Schildknecht, H., Symposium "Zonenschmelzen und Kolonnen-kristallisieren", Kernforschungszentrum Karlsruhe 1963
14 Mazee, W. M.: Thermal Analysis of Normal Alkanes; in: Purity Control by Thermal Analysis, Ed.: W. M. Smit. Amsterdam, London, New York, Princeton: Elsevier Publishing Company 1957. p. 97
15 Brill, R., Angew. Chem. *71*, 430 (1959)
16 Schildknecht, H., and Schlegelmilch, F., Chemie-Ing.-Techn. *35*, 637 (1963)
17 Keess, W., Diploma Thesis, Univ. Erlangen 1959
18 Burton, J. A., Prim, R. C., and Slichter, W. P., J. chem. Physics *21*, 1987 (1953)
19 Meyer, G., Ann. Physik *61*, 225 (1897)
20 Paschke, M., and Hauptmann, A., Arch. Eisenhüttenw. *9*, 305 (1935)
21 Throvert, J., Ann. chim. phys., Series 7, *26*, 410 (1902)
22 Gordon, A. R., J. chem. Physics *5*, 522 (1937)
23 Miller, C. C., Proc. Roy. Soc. [London] A *106*, 724 (1924)
24 Trevoy, D. J., and Drickamer, H. G., J. chem. Physics *17*, 1117 (1949)
25 Lorenz, R.: Raumerfüllung und Ionenbeweglichkeit, Leipzig: L. Voß 1922, p. 207
26 Bridgers, H. E., and Kolb, E. D., J. chem. Physics *25*, 648 (1956)
27 Burton, J. A., and Slichter, W. P.: Transistor Technology, Vol. I. Princeton: van Nostrand Co., Inc. 1958; Chapter 5
28 Netter, H.: Theoretische Biochemie. Berlin, Göttingen, Heidelberg: Springer 1959, p. 312
29 Heywang, W., and Henker, H., Z. Elektrochem., Ber. Bunsenges. physik. Chem. *58*, 302 (1954)
30 Thurmond, C. D., and Struthers, J. D., J. physic. Chem. *57*, 833 (1953)
31 Stöhr, H., and Klemm, W., Z. anorg. allg. Chem. *241*, 305 (1939)
32 Stöhr, H., and Klemm, W., Z. anorg. Chem. *244*, 205 (1940)
33 Klemm, W., Klemm, L., Hohmann, E., et al., Z. anorg. Chem. *256*, 239 (1948)
34 Greiner, E. S., J. Metals *4*, 1044 (1952)
35 Taylor-Lyman: Metals Handbook. Cleveland/Ohio: Amer. Soc. for Metals 1958. p. 1140

[36] Teal, G. K., and Little, J. B., Physic. Rev. *78*, 647 (1950)

[37] Teal, G. K., and Buehler, E., Physic. Rev. *87*, 190 (1952)

[38] Pfann, W. G.: Zone Melting. New York, London: John Wiley & Sons Inc., Chapman & Hall Ltd. 1958

[39] Gulliver, G. H.: Metallic Alloys (Appendix). London: Chas. Griffin and Company 1922

[40] Scheuer, E., Z. Metallkunde *23*, 237 (1931)

[41] Hayes, A., and Chipman, J., Trans. Amer. Inst. Mining metallurg. Engr. *135*, 85 (1939)

[42] McFee, R. H., J. chem. Physics *15*, 859 (1947)

[43] "Hamming's method" in W. G. Pfann: Zone Melting, p. 35; cf.[56]

[44] Tiller, W. A., Jackson, K., Rutter, J. W., and Chalmers, B., Acta metallurg. *1*, 428 (1953)

[45] Braun, J., and Marshall, S., Brit. J. appl. Physics *8*, 157 (1957)

[46] Lord, N. W., Trans. Amer. Inst. Mining metallurg. Engr. *197*, 1531 (1953)

[47] Burris, L. jr., Stockman, C. H., and Dillon, J. G., J. Metals *7*, 1017 (1955)

[48] Hall, R. N., Physic. Rev., Series 2, *88*, 139 (1952)

[49] Hall, R. N., J. physic. Chem. *57*, 836 (1953)

[50] Burton, J, A., Kolb, E. D., Slichter, W. P., and Struthers, J. D., J. chem. Physics *21*, 1991 (1953)

[51] Matz, G., Chemie-Ing.-Techn. *36*, 381 (1964)

[52] Broda, E.: Radioaktive Isotope in der Biochemie. Wien: Franz Deuticke 1958

[53] Eldib, I. A., Ind. Eng. Chem., Process Design Develop. *1*, 2 (1962)

[54] Schildknecht, H., and Hopf, U., unpublished work

[55] Chem. Engng. News *39*, No. 28, p. 38 (1961)

[56] Pfann, W. G.: Zone Melting. New York, London: John Wiley & Sons Inc., Chapman & Hall Ltd. 1958

[57] Süe, P., Pauly, J., and Nouaille, A., Bull. Soc. chim. France, Series 5, 1958, p. 593

[58] Weitkamp, A. W., Smiljanic, A. M., and Rotman, S., J. Amer. chem. Soc. *69*, 1936 (1947)

[59] Holmann, R. T., Experientia [Basel] *14*, 121 (1958)

[60] Schildknecht, H., Z. Naturforsch. *12 b*, 23 (1957)

[61] Schildknecht, H., Habilitation Thesis, Univ. Erlangen 1958

[62] Goodman, C. H. L., Research *7*, 168 (1954)

[63] Schildknecht, H. and Mannl, A., Angew. Chem. *69*, 635 (1957)

[64] Jost, W.: Diffusion. Darmstadt: Steinkopff 1957

[65] Bohl, T. and Christy, R. W., J. sci. Instruments *36*, 98 (1959)

[66] Handley, R. and Herington, E. F. G., Chem. Industries *1956*, p. 304

[67] Handley, R. and Herington, E. F. G., Chem. Industries *1957*, p. 1184

[68] Weisberg, L. R. and Gunther-Mohr, G. R., Rev. sci. Instruments *26*, 896 (1956); cf. a. Nicollian, F. H., Gunther-Mohr, G. R., and Weisberg, L. R., IBM J. Res. Dev. *1*, 349 (1957)

[69] Tuddenham, W. M., J. Metals *9*, 346 (1957)

[70] Daniels, F. and Duffie, A., Edts.: Solar Energy Research. Madison, Wis.: U. of Wisconsin Press 1955

[71] Mullin, J. B. and Hulme, K. F., J. Electronics and Control *4*, 170 (1958)

[72] Pfann, W. G., J. Metals *7*, 961 (1955); US Patent 2 813 048; cf. C. A. *52*, 5900 a (1958)

[73] Braun, I., Frank, F. C., Marshall, S., and Meyrick, G., Philos. Mag., Series 8, *3*, 208 (1958)

[74] Pfann, W. G. and Dorsi, D., Rev. sci. Instruments *28*, 720 (1957)

[75] Burch, R. D., US Atomic Energy Comm. NAA-SR-1688, 16 (1956); cf. C. A. *51*, 7199 f (1957)

[76] Burch, R. D. and Young, C. T., US Atomic Energy Comm. NAA-SR-1735, 23 (1957); cf. C. A. *51*, 11106 c (1957)

[77] Geach, G. A. and Jones, F. O., J. less-common Metals *1*, 56 (1959)

[78] Cabane, G., J. nuclear Energy *6*, 269 (1958)

[79] Gerthsen, P., Z. angew. Physik *15*, 301 (1963)
[80] Geach, G. A. and Summers-Smith, D., Metallurgia [Manchester] *42*, 153 (1950)
[81] England, P. G. and Jones, H. N., J. sci. Instruments *35*, 66 (1957)
[82] Rocco, W. A. and Sears, G. W., Rev. sci. Instruments *27*, 1 (1956)
[83] Keck, P. H. and Golay, M. J. E., Physic. Rev. *89*, 1297 (1953)
[84] Davis, M., Calverley, A., and Lever, R. F., J. appl. Physics *27*, 195 (1956)
[85] Calverley, A., Davis, M., and Lever, R. F., J. sci. Instruments *34*, 142 (1957)
[86] Carlson, R. G., J. electrochem. Soc. *106*, 49 (1959)
[87] Allenden, D., J. sci. Instruments *36*, 66 (1959)
[88] Olsen, K. M., in: Transistor Technology, Volume 1. Princeton, N. J.: van Norstrand Co., Inc. 1958.
[89] Kretzman, R.: Handbuch der Industriellen Elektronik. Berlin-Borsigwalde: Verlag für Radio-Foto-Kinotechnik GmbH 1954. p. 269
[90] Buehler, E., Rev. Sci. Instruments *28*, 452 (1957)
[91] Schildknecht, H., unpublished work
[92] Chaudron, G., Symposium "Zonenschmelzen und Kolonnenkristallisieren", Kernforschungszentrum Karlsruhe 1963
[93] Hericy, Le J., Colloques internationaux du centre national de la recherche scientifique, XC. Nouvelles propriétés physiques et chemiques des métaux de très haute pureté. Centre National de la Recherche Scientifique, Paris 1960. p. 221
[94] Matare, H. F., US-Patent 2 897 329 (1959)
[95] Wernick, J. H., Dorsi, D., and Byrnes, J. J., J. electrochem. Soc. *106*, 246 (1959)
[96] Buehler, E., Trans. Amer. Inst. Mining metallurg. Engr. *212*, 694 (1958)
[97] Hesse, G. and Schildknecht, H., Angew. Chem. *68*, 641 (1956)
[98] Schildknecht, H. and Hopf, U., Chemie-Ing.-Techn. *33*, 352 (1961)
[99] Röck, H., Naturwissenschaften *43*, 81 (1956)
[100] Ball, J. S., Helm, R. V., and Ferrin, C. R., Petroleum Engr. *30*, C 36 (1958)
[101] Schildknecht, H., Z. analyt. Chem. *181*, 254 (1961)
[102] Schildknecht, H. and Vetter, H., Angew. Chem. *71*, 723 (1959)
[103] Heywang, W. and Ziegler, G., Z. Naturforsch. *9a*, 561 (1954)
[104] Heywang, W., Z. Naturforsch. *11a*, 238 (1956)
[105] Pfann, W. G., Benson, K. E., and Hagelbarger, D. W., J. appl. Physics *30*, 454 (1959)
[106] Emeis, R., Z. Naturforsch. *9a*, 67 (1954)
[107] Wroughton, O. M., Okress, E. C., Brace, P. H., Comenetz, G., and Kelly, J. C. R., J. electrochem. Soc. *99*, 205 (1952)
[108] Pfann, W. G. and Hagelbarger, D. W., J. appl. Physics *27*, 12 (1956)
[109] Brace, P. H., Cochardt, A. W. and Comenetz, G., Rev. sci. Instruments *26*, 303 (1955)
[110] Schildknecht, H. and Schübel, U., unpublished work
[111] Schildknecht, H., Chimia [Zürich] *17*, 145 (1963)
[112] Ronald, A. P., Analytic. Chem. *31*, 964 (1959)
[113] Research Specialties Co., Analytic. Chem., Vol. 3, No. 6, p. 73 A (1958)
[114] Maire, J. C. and Moritz, J., Symposium "Zonenschmelzen und Kolonnenkristallisieren", Karlsruhe 1963
[115] Revel, G. and Albert, P., Symposium "Zonenschmelzen und Kolonnenkristallisieren", Kernforschungszentrum Karlsruhe 1963
[116] Neuhaus, A., Chemie-Ing.-Techn. *28*, 155 (1956)
[117] Mair, B. C., Eberly, P. E., Krouskop, N. C., and Rossini, F. D., Analytic. Chem. *30*, 393 (1958)
[118] Bennet, D. C. and Sawyer, B., Bell System techn. J. *35*, 637 (1956)
[119] Calverley, A., Davis, M., and Lever, R. F., S. E. R. L. Technical Journal *6*, 56 (1956)
[120] Theuerer, H. C., J. Metals *8*, 1316 (1956)

[121] Keck, P. H. and Horn, Van W., Physic. Rev. *91*, 512 (1953)

[122] Keck, P. H., Horn, Van W., Soled, J., and MacDonald, A., Rev. sci. Instruments *25*, 331 (1954)

[123] cf. Tanenbaum, M., in: Hannay, N. B.: Semiconductors. New York: Reinhold Publishing Corporation 1959. p. 118

[124] Sheckler, A. C. and Jillson, D. C., Semiconductor Symposium of the Institute of Metals Division, AIMMPE, 25—27 February 1957, New Orleans, La.

[125] Folberth, O. G. and Weiss, H., Z. Naturforsch. *10a*, 615 (1955)

[126] Whelan, J. M. and Wheatly, G. H., Bull. Amer. physic. Soc., Series II, *2*, 120 (1957)

[127] Boomgaard, Van den J., Kröger, F. A., and Vink, H. J., J. Electronics and Control *1*, 212 (1955)

[128] Birbeck, F. E. and Calverley, A., J. sci. Instruments *36*, 460 (1959)

[129] Wolf, H. C. and Deutsch, H. P., Naturwissenschaften *41*, 425 (1954)

[130] Herington, E. F. G., Handley, R., and Cook, A. J., Chem. and Ind. *1956*, p. 292

[131] Schildknecht, H., Renner, G., and Keess, W., Fette, Seifen, Anstrichmittel *64*, 493 (1962)

[132] Schlegelmilch, F. and Schildknecht, H., Symposium "Zonenschmelzen und Kolonnenkristallisieren", Kernforschungszentrum Karlsruhe 1963

[133] Schildknecht, H., Rauch, G., and Schlegelmilch, F., Chemiker-Ztg. *83*, 549 (1959)

[134] Matthews, J. S. and Coggeshall, D., Analytic. Chem. *31*, 1124 (1959)

[135] Dickinson, J. D. and Eaborn, C., Chem. and Ind. *1956*, p. 959

[136] Iwantscheff, G.: Das Dithizon und seine Anwendung in der Mikro- und Spurenanalyse. Weinheim: Verlag Chemie 1958

[137] Burton, J. A., Physica *20*, 846 (1954)

[138] Pfann, W. G. and Olsen, K. M., Physic. Rev. *89*, 322 (1953)

[139] Hannay, N. B. and Ahearn, A. J., Analytic. Chem. *26*, 1056 (1954)

[140] Herkart, P. G. and Christian, H. M., Transistors I, RCA Laboratories, Princeton, N. J., 1956, p. 59

[141] Hühn, C. F., Telefunken-Ztg., *31* (1958)

[142] Goorisen, J., Philips' techn. Rdsch. *21*, 185 (1960)

[143] Jensen, R. V., US-Patent 2 789 039 (1957); cf. C. A. *51*, 9234 g (1957)

[144] Butuzov, V. P. and Dobrovenskii, V. V., Rost Kristallov, Akad. Nauk SSSR, Inst. Krist., Doklady Soveshchaniya 1956, p. 320;
Growth of Crystals, Rept. 1 st Conf., Moscow 1956, 252 (published 1958, Engl. Transl.); cf. C. A. *53*, 10 854 f (1959)

[145] Trousil, Z., Czechoslov. J. Physics *6*, 91 (1956); cf. C. A. *50*, 10 449d (1956)

[146] German-Patent 1 022 803 (1958); cf. C. A. *54*, 14 083 g (1960)

[147] Pfann, W. G. and Olsen, K. M., Bell Lab. Rec. *33*, 201 (1955)

[148] Logan, R. A. and Schwartz, M., Phys. Rev. *96*, 46 (1954)

[149] Krömer, H., Transistors I, RCA Laboratories, Princeton, N. J., 1956, p. 132

[150] Schildknecht, H. and Schnell, J., Symposium "Zonenschmelzen und Kolonnenkristallisieren", Kernforschungszentrum Karlsruhe 1963

[151] Billig, E., Proc. Roy. Soc. [London] A *235*, 37 (1956)

[152] Pfann, W. G. and Vogel, F. L., Acta metallurg. [New York] *5*, 377 (1957)

[153] Petrov, D. A. and Kalachev, B. A., Zhur. Fiz. Khim. *30*, 2340 (1956)); cf. C. A. *51*, 10 226 d (1957)

[154] Czochralski, J. Z. physik. Chem. *92*, 219 (1917)

[155] Goorisen, J. and Karstensen, F., Z. Metallkunde *50*, 46 (1959)

[156] Schildknecht, H. and Vetter, H., Angew. Chem. *73*, 240 (1961)

[157] Christian, S. M., US-Patent 2 820 185 (1958); cf. C. A. *52*, 9789 h (1958)

[158] Hartman, D. K. and Ostapkovich, P. L., Metal Progr. *70*, 100 (1956)

[159] Taft, E. A. and Horn, F. H., J. electrochem. Soc. *105*, 81 (1958)

[160] Kaiser, W., Keck, P. H., and Lange, C. F., Physic. Rev. *101*, 1264 (1956)

[161] Akiyama, K. and Kubo, S., Natl. Tech. Rept. *6*, 1 (1960); cf. C. A. *54*, 19 388 b (1960)

[162] Theuerer, H. C., Trans. Amer. Inst. Mining metallurg. Engr. *206*, 1316 (1956)

[163] Bourassa, F., Semiconductor Products. April 1961, p. 37

[164] Chem. Engng. News *41*, No. 5, p. 50 (1963)

[165] Mitrenin, B. P., Troshin, N. E., Tsomaya, K. P., Vlasenko, V. A., and Gubanov, Y. D., Voprosy Met. i Fiz. Poluprovodnikov (Moscow; Akad. Nauk U. S. S. R.) Sbornik 1957, p. 59. Referat. Zhur., Met. 1958, Abstr. No. 2762; cf. C. A. *53*, 15 907 e (1959); Voprosy Met. i Fiz. Poluprovodnikov, Akad. Nauk, S. S. S. R. Trudy 2-go (Vtorogo), Soveshaniya, Moscow 1956, p. 59 (published 1957); cf. C. A. *55*, 6331 i (1961)

[166] US Patent 2 829 994 (1958); cf. C. A. *52*, 12 573 c (1958)

[167] Welker, H., Z. Naturforsch. *7a*, 744 (1952)

[168] Boomgard, Van den J., Philips Res. Rep. *11*, 27 (1956)

[169] Pearson, G. L. and Tanenbaum, M., Physic. Rev. *90*, 153 (1953)

[170] Hatton, J. and Rollin, B. V., Proc. Phys. Soc. *67 A*, 385 (1954)

[171] Tanenbaum, M. and Briggs, H. B., Physic. Rev. *91*, 1561 (1953)

[172] Burstein, E., Physic. Rev. *93*, 632 (1954)

[173] Harman, T. C., J. electrochem. Soc. *183*, 128 (1956)

[174] Reiss, H., Trans. Amer. Inst. Mining metallurg. Engr. *200*, 1053 (1954)

[175] Kanai, Y., Ôyo Butsuri *26*, 586 (1957); cf. C. A. *52*, 7787 c (1958)

[176] Hulme, K. F. and Mullin, J. B., J. Electronics and Control *3*, 160 (1957)

[178] Okoniewski, S., Biul. Wojskowej, Akad. Tech. *7*, 3 (1958); cf. C. A. *53*, 2993 c (1959)

[179] Adamiczka, J. and Pajakowa, J., Rudy i Metale Niezelazne *1*, 3 (1956); cf. C. A. *53*, 1017 d (1959)

[180] Vinogradova, K. I., Galavanov, V. V., and Nasledov, D. N., Soviet Phys.-Tech. Phys. *2*, 1832 (1957); cf. C. A. *52*, 17 974 g (1958)

[181] Schell, H. A., Z. Metallkunde *46*, 58 (1955)

[182] Allred, W. P., Paris, B., and Gensel, M., J. electrochem. Soc. *105*, 93 (1958)

[183] Tyler, W. W., Woodbury, H. H., and Newman, R., Phys. Rev. *94*, 1419 (1954)

[184] Jenny, D. A. and Bube, R. H., Physic. Rev. *96*, 1190 (1954)

[185] Kröger, F. A. and Nobel, De D., J. Electronics and Control *1*, 190 (1955)

[186] Mochalow, A. M., Trudy Altaisk. Gorno Met. Nauch.-Issledovatel. Inst., Akad. Nauk Kazakh. S. S. R. *9*, 233 (1960); cf. C. A. *55*, 20 850 h (1961)

[187] Alexandrow, B. N. and Werkin, B. J., Fiz. Metal. i Metalloved., Akad. Nauk S. S. S. R. *11*, 588 (1961); cf. C. A. *55*, 16 332 h (1961); cf. also Alexandrow, B. N., ibid. *9*, 362 (1960); cf. C. A. *54*, 17 187 h (1960)

[188] Barrie, R., Cunnell, F. A., Edmond, J. T., and Ross, I. M., Physica *20*, 1087 (1954)

[189] Knight, J. R., Nature [London] *190*, 1001 (1961)

[190] Gremmelmaier, R., Z. Naturforsch. *11a*, 511 (1956)

[191] Richards, J. L., J. appl. Physics *31*, 600 (1960)

[192] Izergin, A. P., Selivanova, V. A., and Melchenko, E. N., Izvestiya Vysshikh Uchebn. Zavedeniy Fizika 1962, p. 105; cf. C. A. *58*, 13 481 e (1963)

[193] Horner, P., Nature [London] *191*, 58 (1961)

[194] Papp, E. and Solymar, K., Acta chim. Acad. Sci. hung. *24*, 451 (1960)

[195] Chih Siu, Wu Li Hsüeh Pao, *15*, 387 (1959); cf. C. A. *54*, 9664 b (1960)

[196] Lawson, W. D., Nielsen, S., Putley, E. H., and Roberts, V., J. Electronics and Control *1*, 203 (1955)

[197] Tausend, A., Leitz-Mitt. Wiss. u. Techn. *2*, 106 (1962)

[198] Basche, M. and Schetky, L. M., US. Dept. Com., Office Tech. Serv., PB Rept. 161 877, p. 48 (1960); cf. C. A. *55*, 19 668 c (1961)

199 Mitchell, W. R., Mullendore, J. A., and Maloof, S. R., Trans. Amer. Inst. Mining metallurg. Engr. *221*, 824 (1961)

200 Yue, A. S. and Clark, J. B., Trans. Amer. Inst. Mining metallurg. Engr. *212*, 881 (1958)

201 Greiner, E. S., J. appl. Physics. *30*, 598 (1959)

202 Greiner, E. S., Boron Synthesis, Structure, Properties. Proc. Conf. Asbury Park, N. J. 1959, 105 (published 1960); cf. C. A. *55*, 6328 i (1961)

203 Chaudron, G., Nature [London] *174*, 923 (1954)

204 Chaudron, G.: Über die Eigenschaften hochreiner Metalle, die durch physikalische Verfahren, wie Zonenschmelzen, erhalten werden. XVII. International Congress for Pure and Applied Chemistry, Essen (Germany)

205 Chaudron, G., Colloques internationaux du centre national de la recherche scientifique, XC. Nouvelles propriétés physiques et chemiques des métaux de très haute pureté. Centre National de la Recherche Scientifique, Paris 1960.

206 Montariol, F., Reich, R., Albert, P., and Chaudron, G., C. R. hebd. Séances Acad. Sci. *238*, 815 (1954)

207 Albert, P., Montariol, F., Reich, R., and Chaudron, G., Proc. Radioisotope Conference 1954, Butterworths, Vol. II, p. 75

208 Caron, M., Albert, P., and Chaudron, G., C. R. hebd. Séances Acad. Sci. *238*, 686 (1954)

209 Chaudron, G., Bull. Soc. chim. France, Series 5, 1954, p. 419

210 Albert, P., Dissertation, Paris 1955

211 Montariol, F., Dissertation, Paris 1955

212 Montariol, F., Chim. et Ind. *75*, 57 (1956)

213 US Patent 2 912 321 (1959); cf. C. A. *54*, 31 46 h (1960)

214 Albert, P. and Hericy, Le J., C. R. hebd. Séances Acad. Sci. 242, 1612 (1956)

215 Albert, P., Pure and appl. Chem. *1*, 111 (1960)

216 Schaub, B., Symposium "Zonenschmelzen und Kolonnenkristallisieren", Kernforschungs-zentrum Karlsruhe 1963

217 Demmler, A. W. jr., Trans. Amer. Inst. Mining. metallurg. Engr. *206*, 958 (1956)

218 Montariol, F., C. R. hebd. Séances Acad. Sci. *244*, 2163 (1957)

219 Montariol, F., Publ. sci. techn. Ministère Air *344*, 70 (1958); cf. C. A. *53*, 5071 b (1959)

220 Frois, C., Symposium "Zonenschmelzen und Kolonnenkristallisieren", Kernforschungs-zentrum Karlsruhe 1963

221 Tougas, R., Ingénieur (Montréal) *43*, 12 (1957)

222 Chen, N.-K. and Liu, M.-C., Chin Shu Hsüeh Pao *2*, 163 (1957); cf. C. A. *53*, 5066 b (1959)

223 Guskov, V. M., Byull. Tsvetnoi Met. 1957, No. 8, p. 73

224 Frois, C. and Dimitrov, O., C. R. hebd. Séances. Acad. Sci. *251*, 2344 (1960)

225 Tanenbaum, M., Goss, A. J., and Pfann, W. G., Trans. Amer. Inst. Mining metallurg. Engr. *200*, 762 (1954)

226 Walton, D., Tiller, W. A., Rutter, J. W., and Winegard, W. C., J. Metals 7, 1023 (1955)

227 Kunzler, J. E. and Renton, C. A., Bull. Amer. physic. Soc. Series II *2*, 137 (1957)

228 Alexandrow, B. N., Werkin, B. I., and Lasarew, B. G., Fiz. Metal. i Metaloved., Akad. Nauk S.S.S.R., Ural Filial *2*, 93 (1956); cf. C. A. *50*, 16 606 f (1956)

229 Alexandrow, B. N., Werkin, B. I., and Lasarew, B. G., Fiz. Metal. i Metaloved., Akad. Nauk S.S.S.R., Ural Filial *2*, 100 (1956); cf. C. A. *50*, 16 606 g (1956)

230 Alexandrow, B. N., Werkin, B. I., Lifschitz, J. M., and Stepanowa, G. J., Fiz. Metal. i Metaloved., Akad. Nauk S.S.S.R., Ural Filial *2*, 105 (1956); cf. C. A. *50*, 16 604 f (1956)

231 Reich, R. and Montariol, F., C. R. hebd. Séances Acad. Sci. *252*, 122 (1961)

232 Reich, R. and Montariol, F., C. R. hebd. Séances Acad. Sci. *251*, 2941 (1960)

233 Reich, R. and Montariol, F., C. R. hebd. Séances Acad. Sci. *251*, 2350 (1960)

234 Kunzler, J. E. and Renton, C. A., Physic. Rev. *108*, 1397 (1957)

[235] Baimakov, A. Y., Verner, B. F., Larikova, M. G., and Dmitrieva, N. K., Tsvetnye Metally 29, 51 (1956); cf. C. A. 51, 10 333 a (1957)

[236] Baimakov, A. Y. and Selivanov, J. M., Tsvetny Metally 32, 32 (1959); cf. C. A. 53, 14 874 i (1959)

[237] USSR-Patent 118 981 (1959); cf. C. A. 53, 21 568 g (1959)

[238] Tiller, W. A. and Rutter, J. W., Canad. J. Physics 34, 96 (1956)

[240] Bolling, G. F., Nature [London] 184 Ass. Number, 718 (1959)

[241] Bolling, G. F. and Winegard, W. C., Acta metallurg. [New York] 6, 283, 288 (1958)

[242] Aust, K. T. and Rutter, J. W., Trans. Amer. Inst. Mining metallurg. Engr. 215, 119 (1959)

[243] Holmes, E. L. and Winegard, W. C., Canad. J. Physics 37, 496 (1959)

[244] Rutter, J. W. and Thomas, K., Trans. Amer. Inst. Mining metallurg. Engr. 218, 682 (1960)

[245] Walton, D., Tiller, W. A., Rutter, J. W., and Winegard, W. C., J. Metals 7, 1023 (1955)

[246] Rutter, J. W. and Aust, K. T., Trans. Amer. Inst. Mining metallurg. Engr. 218, 682 (1960)

[247] Alexandrow, B. N., Fiz. Metal. i Metaloved., Akad. Nauk. S.S.S.R. 9, 53 (1960); cf. C. A. 54, 15 164 g (1960)

[248] Tanenbaum, M., Goss, A. J., and Pfann, W. G., J. Metals. 6, 762 (1956)

[249] Trousil, Z., Chemie (Praha) 9, 633 (1957); cf. C. A. 52, 10 657 h (1958)

[250] Ivleva, V. S., Chistye Metal i Poluprovodn., Trudy 1-oi (Pervoi) Mezhvuz. Konf., Moscow 1957, 223 (published 1959); cf. C. A. 55, 1348 h (1961)

[251] Vigdorovich, V. N., Ivleva, V. S., and Krol, L. Y., Izvest. Akad. Nauk. S.S.S.R., Otdel. Tekh. Nauk, Met. i Toplivo 1960, No. 1, 44; cf. C. A. 55, 5282 b (1961)

[252] Wernick, J. H., Benson, K. E., and Dorsi, D., J. Metals 9, 996 (1957)

[253] Sazhin, N. P. and Dulkina, P. Y. in: Int. Conf. on the Peaceful Uses of Atomic Energy, Vol. 9, United Nations, New York 1956, p. 265

[254] Galt, J. K., Yager, W. A., Merritt, F. R., Cetlin, B. B., and Dail, H. W. jr., Physic. Rev. 100, 748 (1955)

[255] Dexter, R. N. and Lax, B., Physic. Rev. 100, 1216 (1955)

[256] Sazhin, N. P. and Dulkina, R. A., Issledovan. v Oblasti Geol., Khim. i Met., (Moscow: Izdatel. Akad. Nauk S.S.S.R.), Sbornik 1955, p. 132; cf. C. A. 54, 7476 a (1960)

[257] Zdanowicz, W., Zeszyty Nauk. Politech. Wroclaw Nr. 25; Chem. Nr. 5, 25 (1958); cf. C. A. 53, 5072 d (1959)

[258] Nikolaenko, G. N., Chistye Metal i Poluprovod., Trudy 1-oi (Pervoi) Mezhvuz Konf., Moscow 1957, 212 (published 1959); cf. C. A. 55, 1349 a (1961)

[259] Carlson, O. N., Haefling, J. A., Schmidt, F. A., and Spedding, F. H., J. electrochem. Soc. 107, 540 (1960)

[260] Huffine, C. L. and Williams, J. M., US At. Energy Comm., AECU-4426, p. 32 (1959); cf. C. A. 55, 20 831 b (1961)

[261] Smith, R. L. and Rutherford, J. R., J. Metals 9, 478 (1957)

[262] Darnell, F. J., Trans. Amer. Inst. Mining metallurg. Engr. 212, 356 (1958)

[263] Kneip, G. D. jr. and Betterton, J. O. jr., J. electrochem. Soc. 103, 684 (1956)

[264] Langeron, J. P., Lehr, P., Albert, P., and Chaudron, G., C. R. hebd. Séances Acad. Sci. 248, 35 (1959)

[265] Langeron, J. P., Symposium "Zonenschmelzen und Kolonnenkristallisieren", Kernforschungszentrum Karlsruhe 1963

[266] Belk, J. A., J. less-common Metals 1, 50 (1959)

[267] Schadler, H. W., Trans. Amer. Inst. Mining metallurg. Engr. 218, 649 (1960)

[268] Witzke, W. R., Trans. Vacuum Met. Conf. 3 New York (1959). New York: University Press 1960. p. 140 et seq.

[269] Probst, H. B., Trans. Amer. Inst. Mining metallurg. Engr. *221*, 741 (1961)

[270] Shroff, A. M., Symposium "Zonenschmelzen und Kolonnenkristallisieren", Kernforschungszentrum Karlsruhe 1963

[271] Albert, P., Dimitrov, O., Hericy, Le J., and Chaudron, G., C. R. hebd. Séances Acad. Sci. *244*, 965 (1957)

[272] Albert, P., Nouveau Traité de Chimie Minérale, Tome XV, 1en fascicule, Paris: Masson et Cie. 1960. p. 212

[273] Antill, J. E., Nuclear Power *2*, 155 (1956)

[274] Clottes, G. and Mustelier, J. P., Symposium "Zonenschmelzen und Kolonnenkristallisieren", Kernforschungszentrum Karlsruhe 1963

[275] Schottky, W.: Halbleiterprobleme II. Braunschweig: Vieweg 1955, p. 53

[276] Antill, J. E., Barnes, E., and Gardner, M., Atomic Energy Research Estab. (Gt. Brit.) M/R *1985*, 10 (1956); cf. C. A. *51*, 170 g (1957)

[277] Brit. Patent 792 347 (1958); cf. C. A. *52*, 16 942 a (1958)

[278] Whitman, C. J., Compton, V., and Holden, R. B., J. electrochem. Soc. *104*, 240 (1957)

[279] Garin-Bonnet, A., Faraggi, H., Erler, J., and Petit, J. F., Mém. sci. Rev. Métallurgi *56*, 14 (1959); cf. C. A. *53*, 19 766 d (1959)

[280] Brit. Patent 815 074 (1959); cf. C. A. *53*, 19 825 h (1959)

[281] Miller, G. L., Plansee (Proc.), 3. Seminar, Reutte (Tirol) 1958, p. 303 (published 1959); cf. C. A. *54*, 8515 g (1960)

[282] Leadbetter, M. J. and Argent, B. B., J. less-common Metals *3*, 19 (1961)

[283] Lawley, A. and Maddin, R., Acta metallurg. [New York] *8*, 896 (1960)

[284] Talbot, J., Albert, P., and Chaudron, G., C. R. hebd. Séances Acad. Sci. *244*, 1577 (1957)

[285] Fischer, W. A., Spitzer, H., and Hishinuma, M., Arch. Eisenhüttenwes. *31*, 365 (1960)

[286] Sifferlen, R., C. R. hebd. Séances Acad. Sci. *244*, 1192 (1957)

[287] Smith, R. L. and Rutherford, J. L., Trans. Amer. Inst. Mining metallurg. Engr., Petrol. Engr. *1956*, p. 115

[288] Besnard, S., Ann. Chimie, Series 13, *6*, 245 (1961)

[289] Hillmann, H. and Mager, A., Z. Metallkunde *51*, 663 (1960)

[290] Oliver, B. F. and Shafer, A. J. Trans. Amer. Inst. Mining metallurg. Engr. *218*, 194 (1960)

[291] Rhys, D. W., J. less-common Metals *1*, 269 (1959)

[292] Bodmer, E., Haller, De P., and Sulzer, P., Nuclear Engng. *4*, 5 (1959)

[293] Bodmer, E., Haller, De P., and Sulzer, P., Proc. second U. N. int. Conf. peaceful Uses atomic Energy, Geneva, 1958, *6*, 379; cf. C. A. *54*, 2116 i (1960)

[294] Tate, R. E. and Anderson, R. W., Extract. Phys. Met. Plutonium and Alloys, Symposium, San Francisco, Calif. 1959, p. 231 f. (published 1960)

[295] Morrison, G. W., Castleman, L. S., and Hees, G. W., US Dept. Com., Office Tech. Serv., PB Rept. *144. 972*, 41 (1959); cf. C. A. *55*, 18 498 c (1961)

[296] Morral, F. R., J. Metals *10*, 662 (1958)

[297] Tolmie, E. D. and Robins, D. A., J. Inst. Metals *85*, 171 (1957)

[298] Hericy, Le J., C. R. hebd. Séances Acad. Sci. *251*, 1385 (1960)

[299] Hericy, Le J., C. R. hebd. Séances Acad. Sci. *251*, 1509 (1960)

[300] Hericy, Le J., Bourelier, F. and Montuelle, J., C. R. hebd. Séances Acad. Sci. *251*, 1779 (1960)

[301] Masumoto, K., Nippon Kinzoku Gakkai-Si [J. Japan Inst. Metals] *19*, 174 (1955); cf. C. A. *53*, 17 851 i (1959)

[302] Markali, J. and Thoresen, P., Acta chem. scand. *15*, 31 (1961)

[303] Scacciati, G. and Gondi, P., Metallurgia ital. *49*, 774 (1957)

[304] Baralis, G. and Fabbrovich, L., Metallurgia ital. *52*, 63 (1960)

[305] Nassler, J. Chemie (Praha) *9*, 785 (1957); cf. C. A. *52*, 9829 h (1958)
[306] Richards, J. L., Nature [London] *177*, 182 (1956)
[307] Chem. Engng. News *34*, 5007 (1956)
[308] USSR-Patent 118 813 (1959); cf. C. A. *53*, 22 788 d (1959)
[309] Kooy, C. and Couwenberg, H. J. M., Philips' techn. Rdsch. *23*, 143 (1961)
[310] Süe, P., Pauly, J., and Nouaille, A., C. R. hebd. Séances Acad. Sci. *244*, 1212 (1957)
[311] Pauly, J. and Süe, P., C. R. hebd. Séances Acad. Sci. *244*, 1505 (1957)
[312] Calcagni, G. and Mancini, G., Atti Accad. naz. Lincei, Series 5, *19*, 422 (1910)
[313] Ballenca, V., Periodico Mineralog. *13*, 21 (1942)
[314] Shirai, T. and Ishibashi, T., Sci. Pap. Coll. gen. Educat. Univ. Tokyo *8*, 139 (1958)
[315] Herington, E. F. G., Research *7*, 465 (1954)
[316] Handley, R., Industrial Chemist *31*, 535 (1955)
[317] Mohorcic, G., Bull. Sci. Conseil Acad., Yugoslav *1*, 43 (1953)
[318] Peaker, F. W. and Robb, J. C., Nature [London] *182*, 1591 (1958)
[319] Melville, H. W. and Stead, B. D., J. Polymer Sci. *16*, 505 (1955)
[320] Schildknecht, H. and Hopf, U., Z. analyt. Chem. *193*, 401 (1963)
[321] Schildknecht, H., Symposium "Zonenschmelzen und Kolonnenkristallisieren", Kern-forschungszentrum Karlsruhe 1963
[322] Schildknecht, H. and Maas, K., Wärme *69*, 121 (1963)
[323] Schildknecht, H. and Vetter, H., unpublished work
[324] Schildknecht, H., Maas, K., and Kraus, W., Chemie-Ing.-Techn. *34*, 697 (1962)
[325] Maas, K. and Schildknecht, H., Symposium "Zonenschmelzen und Kolonnenkristalli-sieren", Kernforschungszentrum Karlsruhe 1963
[326] Besnard, S. and Talbot, J., C. R. hebd. Séances Acad. Sci. *244*, 1193 (1957)
[327] Sloan, G. H., Symposium "Zonenschmelzen und Kolonnenkristallisieren", Kernfor-schungszentrum Karlsruhe 1963
[328] Sørensen, P., Kem. Maanedsbl. nord. Handelsbl. kem. Ind. 1959, No. 4, p. 29
[329] Schwab, F. W. and Wichers, E., J. Res. nat. Bur. Standards *25*, 747 (1940)
[330] Schwab, F. W. and Wichers, E., J. Res. nat. Bur. Standards *32*, 253 (1944)
[331] Christian, J. D., J, chem. Educat. *33*, 32 (1956)
[332] Merlin, H., Diploma Thesis ETH Zürich 1957
[333] Maggi, A., Diploma Thesis ETH Zürich 1957; Helv. chim. Acta *41*, 338 (1958)
[334] Schildknecht, H. and Renner, G., Fette, Seifen, Anstrichmittel *66*, 176 (1964)
[335] Levene, P. A. and Taylor, F. A., J. biol. Chemistry *59*, 905 (1924)
[336] Jones, R. G., J. Amer. chem. Soc. *69*, 2353 (1947)
[337] Schaeppi, W. H., Symposium "Zonenschmelzen und Kolonnenkristallisieren", Kern-forschungszentrum Karlsruhe 1963
[338] Schaeppi, W. H., Chimia [Zürich] *16*, 291 (1962)
[340] Kolsek, J., Perpar, M., and Rauschl, A., Z. analyt. Chem. *149*, 320 (1956)
[341] Schildknecht, H., Séparation immédiate et chromatographique. Publications G. A. M. S., Paris 1961, p. 37
[342] Schildknecht, H. and Schlegelmilch, F., Radioisotopes in the Physical Sciences and Industry, Vol. III. Int. Atomic Energy Agency, Vienna 1962, p. 73
[343] Stowe, B. B. and Thimann, K. V., Arch. Biochem. Biophysics *51*, 499 (1954)
[344] Hesse, G., Banerjee, B., and Schildknecht, H., Experientia [Basel] *13*, 13 (1957)
[345] Euler, von H. and Eistert, B.: Chemie und Biochemie der Reduktone und Reduktonate. Stuttgart: Ferdinand Enke 1957, p. 8
[346] Tokin, B. P.: Phytoncide. Berlin: VEB Verlag Volk und Gesundheit 1956
[347] Schildknecht, H. and Rauch, G., Z. Naturforsch. *16 b*, 422 (1961)
[348] Schildknecht, H. and Rauch, G., Z. Naturforsch. *16 b*, 301 (1961)
[349] Schildknecht, H. and Benoni, H., Z. Naturforsch. *18 b*, 45 (1963)

350 Schildknecht, H. and Benoni, H., Z. Naturforsch. *18 b*, 656 (1963)

351 Willstätter, R.: Untersuchungen über Enzyme, Vol. 1. Berlin: Springer 1928, p. 385

352 Lynen, F., Reichert, E., and Rueff, L., Liebigs Ann. Chem. *574*, 1 (1951)

353 Bersin, T.: Kurzes Lehrbuch der Enzymologie. 4th Edit., Leipzig: Akademische Verlags-gesellschaft Geest u. Portig K. G. 1954, p. 13

354 Neumann, K., Chemie-Ing.-Techn. *29*, 267 (1957)

355 Glenk, H. O., S.-B. physik.-med. Soz. Erlangen *77*, 58 (1954)

356 Eucken, A. and Schäfer, K., Nachr. Ges. Wiss. Göttingen. Mathemat.-Physikal. Klasse, Fachgruppe III (NF) *1*, 109 (1935)

357 Eucken, A. and Schäfer, K., Z. anorg. allg. Chem. *225*, 319 (1935)

358 Weston, R. E. jr., Geochim. cosmochim. Acta *8*, 281 (1955)

359 Posey, J. C. and Smith, H. A., J. Amer. chem. Soc. *79*, 555 (1957)

360 Smith, H. A. and Thomas, C. O., J. physic. Chem. *63*, 445 (1959).

AUTHOR INDEX

The numbers refer to the pages where the publications are cited.

SUBJECT INDEX